John D Vautier

History of the 88th Pennsylvania Volunteers in the War for the

Union

1861-1865

John D Vautier

History of the 88th Pennsylvania Volunteers in the War for the Union
1861-1865

ISBN/EAN: 9783744704625

Printed in Europe, USA, Canada, Australia, Japan

Cover: Foto ©ninafisch / pixelio.de

More available books at **www.hansebooks.com**

HISTORY

OF THE

88TH PENNSYLVANIA VOLUNTEERS

IN THE

WAR FOR THE UNION,

1861-1865.

BY

JOHN D. VAUTIER,

Co. I, 88TH REGIMENT P. V.

O

Our country's flag, flag of the free,
We pledge our loyal hearts to thee.

✠

PHILADELPHIA:

PRINTED BY J. B. LIPPINCOTT COMPANY.

1894.

PREFACE.

THIS book is a record of the services of the soldiers of the 88th Regiment Pennsylvania Volunteer Infantry in the War for the Union. It is briefly told in army vernacular; and while the historian is conscious of many imperfections, he has tried to indite a true and impartial narrative, and asks his comrades to skip the blemishes and look for excellences, if happily any can be found.

He tenderly dedicates the work to his living comrades and to the sacred memories of those who have laid down the armor and joined the vast army in the eternal encampment beyond the silent river.

The author is under obligations to Adjutant Cyrus S. Detre for the regiment's General Order Book from October 7, 1861, to May 11, 1863, and for the Morning Reports until January 17, 1864.

From these books the official record has been gathered, elaborated from the historian's daily diary, covering more than three years of the time; from the diary of Captain Charles McKnight, embracing the last campaigns; and from information culled from many sources. He has been especially aided by Comrades Samuel G. Boone, John Witmoyer, Secretary James G. Clark, John M. Wallace, Colonel McLean, Mr. John A. McKnight, James Hague, President Louis Wagner, and other kind comrades.

It is through the assistance furnished by these generous comrades that the publication of this book is rendered possible.

3

CONTENTS.

CHAPTER XXVII.

CHAPTER XXVIII.

CHAPTER XXIX.

LIST OF ILLUSTRATIONS.

LIST OF ILLUSTRATIONS.

HISTORY

88TH PENNSYLVANIA VOLUNTEERS.

CHAPTER I.

ORGANIZATION AND ENCAMPMENT.

THIS is not a history of the war, and it is not proper that the opening acts in that great drama should be here described ; these have all been told elsewhere, and have passed into the history of the country.

This regiment was created in compliance with the call of the President of the United States for 500,000 troops, issued May 3, 1861, and is only one of many like organizations formed in response to this and subsequent calls for men to become soldiers to fight for the preservation of the Union.

It is not asserted that the regiment was superior to other similar organizations, nor is it claimed that all the credit is due it for service in which many regiments participated, but the work is a plain narrative of the faithful service of men who, to the best of their ability and as directed, tried to serve their country and defend its flag from dishonor and disunion.

Under this call the regiment was raised in the following manner : Major George P. McLean, while serving with the 22d Pennsylvania Regiment in the three months' service, was authorized by Secretary of War Cameron, in the following order, to recruit a regiment for the war.

11

COL. GEO. P. McLEAN, Phila., Penn'a:

SIR,—The regiment which you offer is accepted for three years or during the war, provided you have it ready for marching orders in thirty days.

This acceptance is with the distinct understanding, that the Department will revoke the commissions of all officers who may be found incompetent for the proper discharge of their duties. You will promptly advise Adjutant-General Thomas the date at which your men will be ready for mustering, and he will detail an officer for that purpose, who will be instructed to muster by company.

By order of the Secretary of War.

(Sigd) JAMES LESLEY, JR.,
Chief Clerk War Department.

SEAL
WAR DEPT.
WASH.,
D. C.

Preparations were at once made to form the battalion, the following constituting part of the field and staff:

Colonel, George P. McLean, of Philadelphia, a prominent officer with much military experience before the war, and major of the 22d Regiment in the three months' service; Lieutenant-Colonel, Joseph A. McLean, of Reading, a brother of the colonel (he had served as adjutant of the 14th Regiment under the first call); Major, George W. Gile, of Philadelphia, late first lieutenant in the 22d Regiment; Benezet F. Foust, a promising young lawyer, as Adjutant; Rev. Charles W. Clothier, a Baptist minister, as Chaplain; and Daniel D. Jones as Quartermaster. These officers, together with Surgeons John H. Seltzer and George H. Mitchell, completed the commissioned field.

The time of the three months' troops expiring in July and August, made good recruiting for the new regiment, which, in honor of the Secretary of War, was called the Cameron Light Guard.

Company A, from Reading, was the first company ready, and was mustered into the United States service, as full-fledged volunteers, on August 23. 1861. Companies B and H, also from Reading; Company C, from Manayunk, Conshohocken, and vicinity; and Company D, from Philadelphia, quickly followed. Companies F, I, and K, from Philadelphia, followed early in September. Companies E and G were organized as distinct companies after the regiment left the city.

It was the original intention to have fifteen companies, and enough recruits were enrolled and positions expected by different persons to fill almost all the official places in a regiment comprising fifteen companies; but a general order, issued by the War Department to all colonels then recruiting, informed them that but ten companies would be allowed each regiment, consequently some dissatisfaction was caused by this change in the program.

To make an impartial selection of the necessary commissioned officers for the ten accepted companies, Colonel McLean empowered the line officers to appoint from their number a committee to make the choice, which was done. This completed the organization with the following

ROSTER.

Colonel, GEORGE P. McLEAN.
Lieutenant-Colonel, JOSEPH A. McLEAN.
Major, GEORGE W. GILE.
Adjutant, BENEZET F. FOUST.
Quartermaster, DANIEL D. JONES.
Surgeons, DR. JOHN H. SELTZER and DR. GEORGE H. MITCHELL.
Chaplain, CHARLES W. CLOTHIER.
Band-Leader, E. ERMENTROUT.

COMPANY OFFICERS.

A.—Captain, Geo. W. Knabb; Lieutenants, Frederick R. Fritz, Albert H. Seyfert.
B.—Captain, Henry A. Myers; Lieutenants, Edmund A. Mass, George B. Rhoads.
C.—Captain, John J. Belsterling; Lieutenants, J. Sarazin Steeple, Harry Hudson.
D.—Captain, Geo. W. Fairlamb; Lieutenants, Louis Wagner, Wm. H. Fairlamb.
E.—Captain, Chris. S. Carmack; Lieutenants, Wm. H. Shearman, Jas. S. Johnston.
F.—Captain, Theo. W. Dunham; Lieutenants, J. Parker Martin, Wm. L. Street.
G.—Captain, John S. Dull; Lieutenants, Henry Korn, Walter S. Wingate.
H.—Captain, David Griffith; Lieutenants, George W. Rapp, Frank B. Shalters.
I.—Captain, J. Reeside White; Lieutenants, Jacob S. Stretch, Wm. J. Harkisheimer.
K.—Captain, Wm. F. Powell; Lieutenants, Syl. S. Bookhammer, Ed. V. Patterson.
Sergeant-Major, John J. Levi; Commissary Sergeant, Jacob S. Kram.

With the selection of these officers the organization of the regiment was completed, but there were many who had entered the ranks fully expecting commissions, having recruited men with that object in view.

The excellent band of twenty pieces that Leader Ermentrout

brought from Reading was the pride of the regiment and contributed very much to the enjoyment of the soldiers. The members were regularly sworn into the service on August 30, 1861, having agreed to accept the compensation allowed musicians; but being skilled performers, they were promised a salary equal to that of a second lieutenant, the difference being raised by a monthly contribution from the commissioned officers of the regiment.

Upon the arrival of the Reading companies they were bountifully entertained by the colonel and then taken to camp, and so hospitably had they been received that they were of the opinion that soldiering was not such a bad thing after all. This idea was further strengthened when they were marched to the chosen camp site, a beautiful plot of greensward, overshadowed by stately trees, situated on the sloping banks of the Schuylkill, a few hundred yards below the mouth of Wissahickon Creek. Here the tents that had been borrowed from the Green Street Methodist Episcopal Church were pitched, and preparations made to feed and shelter the embryo soldiers as they came to Camp Stokley, called so in honor of the mayor of the city, Hon. William S. Stokley. Soon the tents furnished by Uncle Sam were received, and recruiting was so brisk that by the 24th of September between 500 and 600 men were in camp, in charge of Major Gile, who employed his time in initiating the boys into the mysteries of battalion drill. While the major was resting, the company officers took it up, and continued the program with company drill; and when they had exhausted their knowledge of tactics the squads were given in charge of the non-commissioned officers (mostly three months' veterans), who, in turn, thrilled the new soldiers with sanguinary stories of the terrible battle of Falling Waters, and instructed them in the facings and other sublime evolutions of squad drill. Now it was "Left foot, right foot," which the giddy novices soon termed "Hay foot, straw foot;" then "Now step off with your left foot, all together," until the recruits were sick of the whole business, and protested that they did not come to tramp, but to fight. All motions of this sort were promptly overruled by the officers, and the green soldiers looked with awe upon their superiors, and wondered if they should ever attain the proficiency in the military art and the experience on the battle field possessed by these wonder-

HON. WILLIAM S. STOKLEY,
Of Philadelphia.

HON. FRED. L. LAUER,
Of Reading.

FRIENDS OF OUR REGIMENT.

ful campaigners. But at any rate the boys enjoyed the novelty of the new life, enlivened by the merry shouts and queer antics of the "Squeedunks," "Wide Awakes," and other nondescript squads, and mingled pleasantly with friends and visitors who thronged the camp, appreciating the "picnic" as much as the soldiers did.

The survivors of that romantic camp will long remember those balmy days and mellow nights so happily spent with friend and comrade, and how in the city a lad topped with a fatigue cap was welcome to a free ride and the choicest seat in the cars, the greatest deference and attention being shown to any so brave as to volunteer in defence of the national government. The Reading contingent were especially conspicuous by reason of flaring tricolored neckties of generous size, which had been presented to them by their fair admirers of that loyal town.

The ladies of the Union Methodist Episcopal Church, Fourth Street below Arch, were particularly active in aiding to equip the soldiers for active service, and made many donations of useful articles, which kindness was fully appreciated by the men.

At this period of the war no bounties or other pecuniary inducements were offered ; in fact, it may be reasonably questioned if many of the men knew exactly how much pay a soldier was entitled to. No selfish considerations of greed or gain actuated these men ; they would have volunteered if there had been no pay. They left their homes and business solely because their country was in danger and called for their assistance.

Colonel McLean formally assumed command of the camp on the 3d of October, celebrating the event by giving the regiment an extra measure of battalion drill. The colonel and lieutenant-colonel were brothers, and to distinguish them the men invariably spoke of them as Colonel George and Colonel Joe, terms which we will use occasionally in the present work.

Some of the younger members appeared to think battalion drill something of a frolic, laughing and joking as commands were given and evolutions performed, until the watchful eyes of Colonel Joe noticing the unbecoming hilarity, he approached the roisterers and in a few appropriate words kindly rebuked them for their trifling conduct, explaining to them the necessity of every man diligently applying himself to the movements and so becoming a proficient soldier. Every soldier within hearing felt the force of this rebuke, and respected the lieutenant colonel for the timely words spoken. But the happy times in this delightful camp could not end the war, and when the colonel received orders on October 4 to report at once with his regiment at Washington, the men were delighted with the prospect of active service. Accordingly the stragglers were gathered and preparations made to leave camp on Saturday, October 5, 1861. The regiment had no guns, and the men did not relish the idea of going to the front without suitable equipment; but there was no help for it, the orders being imperative.

This breaking camp was the first important military act we had been ordered to execute, and Colonel McLean determined to do the thing up brown, the following orders being strictly observed :

At the first tap of the bass drum, all preparations for striking tents were completed ; when tap number two sounded, the pins were drawn ; and when the third "bang" boomed over the camp, ker-wallop ! down came every tent as if struck by lightning, revealing as by magic a mass of busy soldiers yelling with delight as they performed this striking act. The regiment then fell in and headed for the seat of war *via* Ridge Avenue, the first companies being snugly packed in the horse cars ; but the supply of cars falling short, the rear companies enjoyed the luxury of an elegant march along the Ridge, in the blinding dust and under the scorching sun, until the advance companies were overtaken as they quietly rested at the dépôt.

With the magnificent band on the lead playing martial music, the march was resumed, platoon front; the regiment passed down the Ridge to Broad Street, to Green, to Fourth, to Noble, to Sixth, passing by the colonel's house on Sixth Street, below Callowhill; to Walnut, where a halt was made while Colonel McLean went into court before Judge Ludlow to answer a summons concerning a minor who had enlisted in the regiment and then ran away.

The case being amicably settled, the drums beat the march along Walnut to Third, to Chestnut, to Second, to Walnut again, thence to Third, and down Third to Washington Avenue, and thence to the Soldiers' Refreshment Saloon at the wharf. Here the tired, hungry, and dusty soldiers washed the dirt and sweat from their faces, and then put away a good substantial supper, without money and without price, the last square meal many of these pilgrims got for many a day. But all the boys heartily wished the blessings of God on the noble men and women of the Union and Cooper Shop Refreshment Saloons who so promptly and generously ministered to the wants of the soldiers passing through Philadelphia. A volunteer dressed in Union blue was sure of a warm welcome from these loyal people, and no Union soldier ever passed through the city, while the war continued, neglected or hungry.

Supper being finished, the regiment marched to the dépôt at Broad Street and Washington Avenue to take the cars for the capital. Here a large number of friends had gathered to see the boys off, to bid them God-speed, and to tell them to " Come home again soon."

> We sent them forth to fight for the flag
> Their fathers before them bore.
> Though the hot tear-drops started,
> This was our parting trust :
> " God bless you, boys ! We'll welcome you home
> When rebels are in the dust."

About nine o'clock the train rolled out of the dépôt, and the Cameron Light Guard were off to the war, followed by the earnest prayers of the many dear ones who, though they knew it not, had seen many of their braves for the last time on earth.

2

CHAPTER II.

BALTIMORE was reached about three o'clock in the morning, the sleepy soldiers being awakened and marched to the Washington Dépôt, where they lay until daylight, when breakfast was served by some gentlemen, who carried to the soldiers buckets full of hot coffee and huge baskets filled with bread and meat, all of which were freely given until the men could eat no more. In the afternoon, while waiting for the train, the regiment was paraded and presented with a United States flag.

Finally the cars were again boarded, and at dusk the great ribs of the dome of the Capitol, with the uncompleted Washington Monument in the background, came in view as the train steamed into the capital city. Here the regiment was taken into a long frame building called the Soldiers' Rest and rested for the night.

In the morning the weary men arose from their uncomfortable positions on the bare floor and fell in for breakfast, which was spread on long tables of rough boards, and consisted of a tin cup of black coffee, a hunk of bread, and a liberal piece of boiled pork, dripping with fat. There was no sugar, butter, cream, knives, forks, or other "fixins" generally found on a family table, and as the boys surveyed their breakfast, it was amusing to note the intense and unconcealed disgust exhibited at such a feed. Unaccustomed to such provender at home, they vehemently protested against being treated as hogs, and were only mollified, not satisfied, when the kind-hearted colonel assured them that it "would be all right when we got in camp and had our own cooks." With this explanation, the men partook of the spread, but rested their expectations of better times on the company cooks, hopes that were not realized in all cases.

It may be proper to remark here that these gentlemen got bravely over their dainty tastes ere long, and many times hungered for just such rations as they had so contemptuously refused that morning at the Rest.

During the morning the regiment proceeded to a pleasant common known as Kendall Green, situated about a mile from the Capitol building, and, pitching tents, called it Camp Moore, in honor of Hon. Henry D. Moore, of Philadelphia.

Not having received guns, the sentries guarded the camp armed with clubs, making a ludicrous and very unsoldierlike appearance patrolling their beats equipped in this primitive fashion. To no one was this more distasteful than to Colonel George, and the officers all being armed with swords and pistols, he requested them to guard the encampment the first night, to which they willingly complied.

Accordingly, in the evening the officers, resplendent in new uniforms with shining buttons and keen swords, assembled at the guard-house and took their stations to act as guards for the night. All went on smoothly until a terrific storm of wind and rain burst upon the camp, drenching the titled sentinels to the skin; but they bravely faced the pelting rain and wallowed in the darkness through the mire and water until daylight (at least it is reported that some of them did), when they beat a speedy retreat to their tents, a sorry set of bedraggled and disgusted shoulder-straps who had done enough of this kind of guard duty to fully satisfy them while they remained in the service. Sentry duty was ever after cheerfully left to the private soldier.

The regiment remained in this camp until October 12, 1861, when the exciting news was promulgated that we were going to the front right away, and everybody was happy when tents were struck and, boarding a steamboat, the regiment proceeded to Alexandria, down the Potomac, seven miles from Washington.

Alexandria was soon reached, and in the evening the regiment, debarking, marched out King Street and encamped on the lots near the Episcopal Church where General Washington used to worship.

Alexandria at this time was an old-fashioned city of several thousand inhabitants, most of whom were rank secessionists with decided aristocratic and old English tendencies, the very streets resounding with such royal names as King, Prince, Princess, Queen, Duke, St.

Asaph, Royal, and more of the same character, indicating the antiquity of the town as well as the Tory sentiment which prompted such names. There were many points of interest in this antiquated city, but the centre of attraction was the Marshall House, where Ellsworth met his untimely death, used subsequently as the quarters of Company K. The slave-pen was also an object of especial interest to Northerners, who viewed with horror the manacles and chains used to bind unruly negroes, the block from which they were sold, and the posts, cells, etc., where they were confined. Company C was afterwards quartered at the pen, and the soldiers took especial delight in showing and explaining to visitors the various implements which the slave-dealer had left in his flight.

On October 15 the men received muskets, a species of ancient weapon difficult to classify, and which was probably as dangerous to the man behind the gun as to the one before it ; however, they were better than none, so the boys received them gladly.

On the 18th the companies broke camp and, moving into the town, relieved the 5th New Jersey Regiment and proceeded to police the city, patrolling the streets and posting sentries on nearly every corner. The companies were quartered in different large buildings, the city being divided into districts; the soldiers settled down to the monotony of guard duty, varied in the afternoons by a parade and battalion drill by Colonel McLean.

On October 25, 1861, Private James Y. Grace, of Company D, died of lung-disease, the first soldier in the regiment to give his life for his country. On this date the regiment numbered 831 men, of whom 755 were present with their respective companies.

On the 30th, Gosline's famous regiment of Philadelphia zouaves passed through the city and was given a cordial reception by the men of the 88th. About this time the number assigned to the regiment was received, and it henceforth ceased to be called and reported as the Cameron Light Guards, being now known as the 88th Pennsylvania Volunteer Infantry.

On November 15 the command escorted to the wharf the sailors who had been stationed at Fort Ellsworth, and on the 28th a like compliment was extended to the 36th and 53d Pennsylvania and 4th Rhode Island Regiments, passing through the city. During the night of the 29th some of the companies were sent out on the railroad as far as Springfield, on some sort of a reconnoissance, but what it amounted to, other than to give the men a most uncomfortable soaking in the rain, has never been known.

A very important and pleasing affair occurred on January 4, 1862, being the presentation of an elegant silk flag to the regiment on behalf of the State of Pennsylvania. The command paraded before the colonel's quarters, Hon. William D. Kelley, of Pennsylvania, delivering the flag to the safe-keeping of the regiment in an eloquent speech, and Colonel McLean, on receiving it, feelingly pledged the honor of the regiment that it would be returned with honor to the governor. Addresses were also made by Hon. Galusha A. Grow, Colonel Hays, Mayor McKenzie, Colonel Joe, and others, but probably the best-received speech was made by General Heintzelman. Much against his will, he was elbowed to the front and said, "I can't make a speech, boys; but when there's a fight about, why, count me in." Immense applause greeted this pungent oration, and the grim and grizzled old soldier fell back blushing like a schoolgirl.

On the 10th of January the man-of-war Pensacola, which had been anchored in the Potomac, sailed down the river, successfully passing the rebel batteries blockading the river below Mount Vernon. The Johnnies gave the tars a hot reception as they passed by, the sound of the enemy's guns being heard at Alexandria, the first echo of real war the regiment had heard. A few days after, the brig Perry followed the Pensacola down the river and, except a few scars from the Southern cannon, arrived in good order at Fortress Monroe.

The welcome face of the most popular officer in the service, the paymaster, appeared on the 18th, and gladdened the hearts and fattened the purses of the boys with two months' pay, some of it in gold, the ration for a high private being thirteen dollars per month and roast beef—if he could get it.

About the last of the month, Captain Carmack, Lieutenant Wagner, Sergeants Beath, Richards, and Donohue, and Corporal Lorenzo Wilson were detailed on recruiting service. During the latter part of January the 8th Illinois Cavalry, a fine body of rugged-looking sol-

diers, was quartered in the town, and, intermingling with the men
of the 88th, many warm ties of friendship were formed between the
two regiments.

Just about this time an incident occurred, in which the men of
both organizations participated, which at one time threatened a
tragic ending. As before mentioned, many of the Alexandrians
were disloyal to the government, claiming that their allegiance was
due to the Southern Confederacy, and exhibiting their sympathies
for the forbidden cause whenever they could conveniently do so.
Many of these people worshipped at St. Paul's Episcopal Church,
where the minister in his prayers omitted the President of the
United States, substituting instead the President of the Confederate
States, and for this treasonable conduct he was arrested and taken
before the provost marshal. This action incited his sympathizers to
indulge in much vehement and disloyal talk, which provoked the
soldiers to retaliate by nailing Union flags on the houses of some of
the leading secessionists and intimating to them that it would be
exceedingly unwise to remove the flags.

On February 10 the office of the *Alexandria Gazette*, an intensely
Southern newspaper, was destroyed by fire, together with two adjoin-
ing buildings, the fire being checked by the efforts of the soldiers
present, who, manning the dilapidated fire apparatus, prevented a
conflagration that might have destroyed the city.

A day or two after a crowd of soldiers gathered in front of St.
Paul's Church, presumably to raise the national flag on the peak,
when some nervous sentinel sent word to the quarters of Company I
that a riot was imminent, and the company coming down on the
double-quick to the scene of the supposed disturbance added to the
noise and confusion, drawing all the idlers in town to the locality.
Captain White ordered the crowd to disperse, and, they showing no
disposition to comply, formed his men to clear the street at the
point of the bayonet.

Affairs were assuming a serious aspect, it needing but a spark to
cause a serious explosion, when some gifted genius made a happy
and telling shot by yelling at the top of his voice, "Three cheers
for the three eights!" a combination of the regimental numbers of
the 8th Illinois and 88th Pennsylvania. This was responded to with

a will, putting the soldiers in good humor, and Major Gile, appearing at this time, ordered the men to their quarters, thus avoiding further difficulty.

But the men were dissatisfied with the duty in Alexandria, and Colonel McLean requested orders for active service. The colonel, in the absence of General Montgomery, had been acting as military governor of Alexandria in addition to his duties as garrison officer, and, finding the duties very distasteful, asked the Secretary of War to send the regiment to the front.

At length the welcome orders came for a part of the regiment to move, and on February 18, Companies A, C, D, E, and I, bidding farewell to the Alexandrians, reported, not to the front, but to General Barry at Washington, leaving Companies B, F, H, and K at Alexandria under command of Major Gile.

CHAPTER III.

UPON reporting to General Barry, Colonel McLean was ordered across the Eastern Branch and directed to find a suitable camp ground near Fort Stanton; so the battalion, 450 strong, trudged through the mud beneath a most disagreeable winter rain until the prospective camp ground was reached.

The men at once tried to make themselves comfortable, but the surroundings, at the best, were very discouraging, as but little of the camp equipage had arrived and everything was saturated with rain. Some of the companies took possession of some log houses on the place and crawled in out of the wet; but Captain Belsterling, with wisdom born of experience, instructed his command how to pitch their tents, and breaking off the branches of the pine and other evergreen trees, shook the water off and, using them for feathers, soon had the best quarters on the ground. The next day, the weather clearing, a nice camp was located near Oxen Run, and the time was pleasantly spent in drilling and in guarding Forts Baker, Davis, Goodhope, Ricketts, Greble, Stanton, Snyder, and two uncompleted earthworks that could not afford an official name.

The armaments of the forts and the details from the battalion were: Fort Baker, seven smooth 24-pounders, not mounted; Davis, six, same calibre; Good Hope, four 32-pounders, mounted; Ricketts, four, same calibre; Greble, thirteen 32-pounders and two Parrotts; Carroll, some 32-pounders and two Parrotts; Stanton, sixteen 32-pounders; and Snyder, six 32-pounders,—all mounted except those mentioned in Baker and Davis. The details were: from Company A, eighteen men; C, eighteen men; D, seven men; E, twelve men; I, eighteen men; but the details generally numbered 100 men. When the boys mounted the parapets of these immense fortifications, bristling with the big barkers, they felt that a great responsibility rested upon them in the defence of the capital, and tremblingly assumed the task ; but upon becoming familiar with the surroundings they felt equal to the job, and only wanted a few brigades of Johnny Rebs to come along and be knocked sky-high by these big guns, yawning and rusting for something to do. No Johnnies came, though, the only shootable things appearing being crows and rabbits, and as the first flew too high and the latter ran too fast, the embryo artillerymen had nothing to practise on ; but a couple of nights' guard duty in the rain and mud, without any kind of shelter, chilled to the bone and as miserable and wretched as it was possible to be, took the romance out of the business of taking care of these forts.

When not on duty, the remainder of the men were industriously kept on drill until April 15, when the colonel was ordered to report at once to General Duryea at Cloud's Mills. In the mean time Major Gile's battalion had been on duty at Alexandria until early in April, when it was ordered to picket the line of the Orange and Alexandria Railroad, which duty it faithfully performed until ordered to report at Cloud's Mills simultaneously with the other wing of the regiment.

COPY OF ORDERS.

SPECIAL ORDER, 43.

The 88th Regiment, upon being relieved by the 99th Pa. Vols., will proceed to Manassas by way of Alexandria, and guard the R. R. from Lancaster Station to Catlett's, head-quarters at Manassas. Col. McLean will report to Maj. Gen. McDowell on taking post, and will previously report to Brig.-Gen. Wadsworth for verbal instructions. Those companies of the 88th at Alexandria have been ordered to Manassas.

April 14, 1862.   By order
                                   BRIG.-GEN. DOUBLEDAY.

To COL. MCLEAN.

It is my intention that your regiment should be reunited and report to Brig.-Gen. Duryea at Cloud's Mills. He is moving out now. The order to report to Genl. McDowell is countermanded.

April 16, 1862.   J. S. WADSWORTH,
                                              Brig. Gen.

Passing through Alexandria, Colonel McLean's battalion proceeded a mile or two out the railroad and encamped. On the 17th of April, Major Gile arrived with the other companies and the regiment was reunited.

The ground assigned for the camp was a horrible place, very aptly called by some Camp Dead Horse, because of the many rotten carcasses of those animals lying around, tainting the air with the most sickening and poisonous stench. Tents were willingly struck at this miserable place on the 19th, when the regiment reported to General Duryea at Cloud's Mills, being assigned to the right of his brigade; the 107th Pennsylvania, an exceedingly fine body of men, on the left.

General Duryea, being a strict disciplinarian, desired to ascertain the proficiency of the regiment in the movements of the battalion, and requested the colonel, on the following day, to exercise the regiment for two hours under his personal observation. Accordingly, at the appointed time the regiment was drilled by the colonel in all the movements of forming, deploying, ploying, changing, wheeling, and other difficult movements. At the end of the drill the general and his staff approached and, after being received by the proper salute, complimented the officers and men upon their proficiency in battalion movements and welcomed the regiment as worthy the post of honor in his brigade. This was a well-deserved compliment, the regiment now being in its prime: 848 men on the rolls, of whom 799 were present, the highest number mustered during its entire history. On April 23, Captain John S. Dull joined the regiment, and Company G, being told off, took its place in the line. The captain brought with him Lieutenants Korn and Wingate, and C. S. Marks, H. N. Blackford, John Nice, F. Ferkler, C. Poulson, G. W. Tyler, G. A. Scholl, H. Hutt, A. N. Reigert, and D. Mundell.

After a short stay at Cloud's Mills, on April 25 the regiment was ordered to picket the railroad from Bull Run to Catlett's Station, Company E being left near the bridge, the other companies posted at intervals along the road. The enemy had evacuated this position a few weeks before and gone to a more congenial place, but there were many points of interest and much abandoned and ruined war material scattered around everywhere, indicating that a large force had garrisoned this place, with every indication of a permanent occupation.

The winter-quarters of the Confederates consisted of many clusters

LIEUTENANT-COLONEL JOSEPH A. McLEAN.
(Killed at Second Bull Run.)

MAJOR DAVID A. GRIFFITH,
Lieutenant Colonel U. S. Vols.

MAJOR BENEZET F. FOUST,
Brevet Brigadier-General U. S. Vols.

ADJUTANT CYRUS S. DITEL

FIELD OFFICERS

of commodious and comfortable log houses, built like villages, and large enough to quarter a very strong force, while extensive forts and continuous lines of breastworks commanded the country in every direction. Bull Run battle-field, some five or six miles distant, was an object of especial interest, and many pilgrimages were made by the men to that sanguinary field, the points of interest being the plateau upon which were located the Henry and Robinson farms and buildings.

While guarding the road, Company B was posted at Sangster's Station, and while there learned that a party of Confederate soldiers were accustomed to make occasional nocturnal visits to their homes in the vicinity. It was resolved to make an effort to capture them, and one dark night Sergeant Boone with a select squad of volunteers undertook the job, but by some unknown signal the enemy were warned of the trap laid for them and gave Boone and his party a wide berth.

The regiment remained on this pleasant duty until the 3d of May, when, pulling up stakes, it returned to Cloud's Mills and rejoined the brigade.

While on guard duty along the railroad the members of B Company spent much of their spare time in fishing and gunning. Gray squirrels were the favorite game, their bushes being fastened to the caps, in imitation of Colonel Kane's famous "Bucktail" regiment. The company officers felt proud of the unique appearance of the men adorned with this novel head-dress, and determined to give the colonel a pleasant surprise by appearing on dress parade with the new plumage. Accordingly, at the first dress parade after returning to camp, every man in the company who appeared in line was topped off with a squirrel-tail, and the left of the regiment appeared in striking contrast with the other companies on the right. The usual formalities of dress parade were performed, but those who were stationed near the colonel noticed that his glances in the direction of Company B were neither gentle nor kind, and at the proper time he summoned the commander of the company before him and said, "Captain, you will have those things removed from the caps of your men at once, and hereafter appear in the regulation uniform only." The tails went instanter.

In camp the soldiers were puzzled to know what the next move would be, countless rumors circulating as to where we were going. The wise ones, who talked knowingly, as if their information came direct from head-quarters, reasoned that, McClellan having taken the greater part of the army to the Peninsula, the regiment would soon follow, and that Richmond would then be captured and the war brought to a speedy and successful termination, though many of the despondent ones were very downhearted at the prospect of the war being over so soon, and confidently predicted that we shouldn't get even as much as a smell of a real battle. This despondency was especially noted after the news of the Union victories at Forts Henry and Donelson, and many of the men bitterly lamented the unfortunate position of the regiment, predicting that the Confederacy would go to eternal smash before we could see a real live reb. But everything comes to them that wait, and plenty of it came to these impatient ones in good time.

On May 6 more recruits were received for G Company, among them being Daniel J. McLean, C. Wiant, and Evan S. Yerger.

CHAPTER IV.

TO FREDERICKSBURG : MAY, 1862.

HOWEVER, rumors and speculations were ended when, on May 7, the colonel received orders to report at Aquia Creek, and, striking tents, line was formed and the band, piping the inspiriting Fisher's Hornpipe, led the way to Alexandria again. Colonel Gregory's 91st Regiment was quartered there, and honored the command with an escort through the city.

In the afternoon the regiment paraded on Washington Street, where a magnificent sword was formally presented to Colonel McLean by Mayor McKenzie, in behalf of the loyal citizens of the town, the colonel receiving the gift and making a suitable reply.

On the following morning the regiment embarked on the steam-boat North America and steamed down the broad Potomac. The frowning battlements of Fort Washington, all lined with great cannon, were soon passed, and when opposite Mount Vernon the bell of the boat was slowly tolled, a custom of all the boats passing this historic plantation.

Aquia Creek was reached in due time, and upon debarking the companies marched to the hills back of the landing and, having no tents, erected brush arbors as shelters from the sun. The 56th and 90th Pennsylvania were encamped here, both regiments receiving the new-comers with open tents and hearts. On the hills were quite a village of log huts, erected by the Confederates when they occupied this point, and on the 9th a fire was kindled by some means among these cabins, which for a time threatened to burn the surface of the entire neighborhood, and which required hard work to extinguish by details from the regiments encamped near by. While the fire raged there was lively hustling on the part of the numerous rabbits, squirrels, snakes, birds, and reptiles, which fled in terror from the flames.

The men very appropriately called this place Whippoorwill Hill, from the numerous whippoorwills that nested here and sang their plaintive songs all night long; but the regiment bid good-by to these melancholy serenaders on May 11, taking up the march to the Rappahannock near the little city of Fredericksburg, names destined to become famous in the annals of the war. This was the first solid march the boys had enjoyed, but the least said about the enjoyment the better, they being burdened with enormous knapsacks, containing about everything a soldier needed and much that he didn't need, including changes of clothing, letters, relics, etc., the supply of the last named being especially abundant. While they had hoarded and prized these treasures for the past seven or eight months, they quickly found on this march that they had no need for nearly three-thirds of the contents of their "trunks," and the road from Aquia to Falmouth was strewn with enough miscellaneous articles of clothing to stock an untold number of hand-me-down shops, could their proprietors have been present to secure the spoils.

Under these loads the march proved very hard, and before the river was reached the boys were nearly played out, and eagerly questioned every native who hove in sight as to how far it was to Fredericksburg; but small comfort was derived from the replies, as one would "reckon it was nigh onto five mile," and after tramping that distance and again inquiring, the reply would in all probability be, "A right smart chance; about five or six miles, I reckon." This conflicting opinion about distances was a peculiarity of the Virginians that held good during the war. But at last the river was reached; the regiment, being minus tents, bivouacked in the fields opposite the town and again erected brush shelters, which, while protecting the men from old Sol's scorching beams, didn't turn the rain-water worth a cent.

Fredericksburg is an old town of very small size, back of which is a low range of hills, made famous by the sanguinary battles fought there later on. In the river, below the town, were the charred wrecks of several large steamboats, destroyed by the rebs to prevent them from falling into Uncle Sam's hands; they also burned the railroad bridge, but this was quickly replaced by a substantial trestle bridge, constructed by the Pioneer Corps of the Pennsylvania Reserves.

The Sunday service on the 18th was conducted by Chaplain Clothier, and after church 86,000 rounds of ball cartridges were issued, the regiment then being well supplied with both spiritual and carnal ammunition for the anticipated warfare.

By order of General Ricketts, on May 20, Quartermaster D. D. Jones was appointed brigade commissary, succeeding Lieutenant L. Frank Binder, relieved at his own request. A very large force had now assembled at this place, and the men were in another ferment of expectancy as to the next move.

General McDowell reviewed Ord's division on the 20th of May, and on the 21st the overcoats and surplus baggage were sent to Washington. Shields's division arrived on the 22d, and on the 23d, President Lincoln, accompanied by many famous civil and military people, reviewed the entire army, the divisions forming long lines, and after the President had critically inspected each battalion, the regiments broke into column, company front, and passed in review,— a magnificent spectacle, as the 40,000 soldiers, in perfect alignment, with glistening bayonets and fluttering colors, marched proudly on before the President.

After this review it was expected that the corps would join Mc-Clellan, and if this had been done, it is very probable that the doom of Richmond would have been sealed and the seat of war carried farther south. This movement was contemplated and fully intended, orders having been issued to move south on May 26; but the Confederates prevented this march, playing on the fears of the Washingtonians by sending the redoubtable Jackson on an excursion into the Shenandoah Valley with such effect that the greater part of McDowell's corps was sent to meet this irruption and trap "Old Jack," who, after smashing the combination, slipped from the Valley and moved post-haste to the rescue of Lee at Richmond. The final results of all these manœuvres have passed into history.

With this digression we will again fall in with the regiment, which still lay opposite Fredericksburg, anxiously waiting the signal for the grand march southward. The two bits of canvas called shelter tents by the powers that be, but styled dog tents by the boys, were issued on the 24th of May, and the following day the general was sounded; the men, breaking up housekeeping and packing their carpet-bags, formed line and waited several hours for the head of column to pull out, in what direction no fellow could tell. After a tiresome delay the drums rattled the "fall-in," and about three o'clock, with the head-quarters flag on the lead, the line stretched out towards the river-bank; but presently, much to the disappointment of the troops, the column turned towards the rear and headed for the Potomac, at Aquia Creek Landing.

Under the rays of a scorching sun, through clouds of stifling dust, with knapsacks and accoutrements that felt as if they weighed a ton, the men marched on the quickstep to the landing, and by the devious way taken it must have been at least fifteen miles if it was a step, though some of the boys said it seemed as if "it was nigh onto a hundred miles." The result was that many of the soldiers were completely used up and compelled to fall out by the way, though Major Gile, from his position on the left of the regiment, encouraged the men by kindly informing them that this was one of the marches they would read about.

About ten o'clock at night the vicinity of the landing was reached, and the weary soldiers, throwing themselves on the grass, quietly rested until morning, sleeping the sleep of the tired, if not of the just.

The next morning, Monday the 25th of May, the various regiments, taking boats, steamed up the broad Potomac to Washington, then back again to Alexandria, where the troops landed, and, taking the cars, reached Manassas Junction at midnight and bivouacked in the fields.

COPY OF ORDER.

HEAD-QUARTERS 2D DIV. 1ST ARMY CORPS, May 28, '62.

SPECIAL ORDER, NO. 6.

The division will march for Front Royal. Ricketts's 1st Brig. will take the advance with one of Major Tillson's Batteries. Two companies of Allen's 1st Maine Cav. will be detailed as advance guards. Hartsuff's 3d Brig., to which Matthews's and Leppien's Batteries and Allen's Cav. will be attached, will follow. Gen. Duryea's 2d Brig. will bring up the rear. Reveille will be beaten at four o'clock and the division will start at five each morning.

By command of
MAJ.-GEN. ORD.

CHAPTER V.

THE SHENANDOAH VALLEY: MAY AND JUNE, 1862.

THE division concentrated at Manassas Junction on the 27th of May, and on the afternoon of the 28th the bugles called into line and the march was on for the Shenandoah Valley, along the line of the railroad. As the long column, with martial music and fluttering colors, wound over the plain, it presented a spectacle of military pomp and splendor not often seen and in sharp and sad contrast to the sad sight presented by this same division on this same ground a few months later on.

Now, regiment after regiment, battery, and squadron promptly took position in the sinuous line of blue, while the glinting sunbeams merrily flashed and reflected in glittering rays of light on the shining surface of miles of polished steel, intermingling with the bright colors of the flags, as they were proudly carried along the marching line. There were many excellent regiments present, including the 11th, 90th, and 107th Pennsylvania; 26th, 83d (9th New York State Militia), 94th, 97th, 104th, and 105th New York; 12th and 13th Massachusetts; 1st Maine Cavalry, and many others,—in all, about 9000 strong, commanded by General Ord.

At night the division halted near Gainesville; the following morning the drums called the men up at the first blush of daylight, and after a hasty breakfast the march was resumed, the little hamlet of Haymarket being soon reached and the column halting about three o'clock P.M., after passing through Thoroughfare Gap, a gorge in the Bull Run Mountains, having made about fifteen miles.

The marching was not severe, but the men had enormous knapsacks, besides being encumbered with extra ammunition, rations, accoutrements, and a twelve-pound rifle. It was no light task to carry this burden, that must have weighed fifty or sixty pounds, but on a long march felt as if it weighed a couple of hundred, and it

8

was interesting to see the boys, when a halt was ordered, open their sacks and carefully survey the contents to see what could be most readily dispensed with. The first article to go would possibly be a woollen blanket, then an extra pair of trousers, followed by a dress-coat or other heavy clothing. At all succeeding halts a like critical inspection would be made, until almost everything was cast away, the last to go being the knapsack; all extra "duds" were dispensed with except the ammunition and rations, though many of the men ate the surplus stock of the latter to avoid carrying them in their haversacks.

Reveille sounded early on the morning of the 30th, and at six o'clock the march was resumed, the sun being very hot until the afternoon, when a cold rain drenched the men to the skin, and continued, with intermittent spells of sunshine, for nine successive days, making the marching in the mud and lying on the wet ground extremely uncomfortable and unhealthy.

During the day the column passed through the villages of White Plains and Salem, halting for the night near Oak Hill, and pitching tents in the fields near this place. After the shelters were arranged, a fine flock of sheep was discovered in a field close by, and some of the boys determined to have a ration of mutton for supper. Accordingly, the flock was corralled in a corner and a cautious advance made upon it, care being taken to select some of the choicest lambs for the prospective victims. All things were about ready for a grand grab, when the entire herd made a simultaneous and successful break for liberty, all escaping except one old ram of *ante bellum* days, the ancient wether of the flock, who, not being as spry as the younger sheep, fell a victim to the greed of the foragers. A second foray on the flock, however, proved successful in securing something more tender, and the men had an abundant supply of mutton boiled, mutton broiled, and mutton fried for supper and breakfast.

The march was begun at daybreak the next morning, and upon reaching a small place called Piedmont, the knapsacks were left and a forced march made, with Front Royal as the objective-point. Markham was passed late in the afternoon, and when Manassas Gap was reached night had settled down over the mountains, making the passage dangerous and difficult ; but the soldiers trudged wearily along over the ties in silence, soaking wet and uncomfortable, until late at night, when the column turned off into the fields and halted near Front Royal, the men being so completely exhausted that they threw themselves on the ground in the rain and slept until morning, many of them awakening to find themselves lying in pools of water.

The next day was the 1st of June, and, forming column, the division marched through Front Royal, taking position in line of battle over the Shenandoah, at the place where Colonel Kenly's force had been routed by the enemy a few days before. The line was quickly formed, colors unfurled, batteries galloped into position, and, un-limbering, the cannoneers stood by their guns waiting for the advent of the enemy ; but at this hour Jackson was no nearer than Strasburg, ten miles away, with no thought of coming to Front Royal to accommodate McDowell with a fight, but being industriously engaged in ''gitting'' up the valley, away from the forces that would soon make it very hot for him if he tarried longer in this neighborhood.

While lying here, General Shields, with his wounded hand wrapped in bandages, came along at the head of his famous division and passed through our lines on the quickstep, marching up the Luray Valley to head off the Confederates at Harrisonburg. The men heartily cheered the gray old soldier and his brave troops, but after they passed by the men quietly settled down to rest as best they could in the rain and mud. Having neither blankets nor tents, the soldiers suffered very much, and, to make matters worse, the rations fell short, but five crackers per day with a meagre supply of coffee and meat being allowed for each man, and sometimes this scanty allowance was all that was issued for two days' subsistence.

The constant rains causing a freshet in the Shenandoah, the regiment was brought over to the south bank before the bridges were washed away; but the 26th New York was not so fortunate, being left on the opposite bank to take care of itself.

The camp equipage and knapsacks arrived on the 5th, a camp being laid out in the woods near Front Royal, and while here the paymaster arrived and gave each man two months' pay. The weather

cleared off balmy and warm on the 8th, and from this time our experience in this beautiful valley, with its waving crops and pleasant
scenery, was of the most charming nature, in part compensating for
the hardships and toil the soldiers had experienced the past two
weeks.

On the 18th of June, 1862, marching orders were received, and,
striking tents, the division took the cars bound for Manassas Junction, the chase after Stonewall having proved a lamentable failure,
to say the best of it.

CHAPTER VI.

FROM MANASSAS TO CULPEPER: JUNE TO AUGUST, 1862.

THE boys did not enjoy the night ride in the freight cars much, though it was a free excursion at Uncle Sam's expense, and were glad to reach Manassas about three o'clock on the morning of June 19. At daylight the camp was located on the ground that had been occupied prior to the trip to the Valley, but in the afternoon it was moved about two miles from the Junction, and the men, presuming that they were fixed for a while, laid out a very neat encampment; but, much to the vexation of all except the moving spirit, the next morning another shift was made, this time near some rebel huts, these being occupied by the officers, while the soldiers pitched their white tents near by. Here, Captains White and Powell and Lieutenant Shearman, having resigned their commissions, left the regiment and went home. On the 21st of June the splendid band belonging to the regiment, in conformity to a general order from the War Department, also left. The boys were greatly attached to and justly proud of their band, and sorrowfully saw the good fellows composing this famous organization turn their faces towards Berks County. Before leaving they serenaded the command, performing about all the music in the book with a vim that was long remembered, the *finale* being "Home, Sweet Home;" then they packed up and marched away, followed by the huzzas of the soldiers so long as they were in sight.

General Ord having been transferred to another department, on June 23, General Ricketts assumed command of the division, General Tower being assigned to command the brigade.

On July 1 the number present with the regiment was 664, of which 615 were for duty, indicating a loss of upward of 100 men since the 24th of May, entirely caused by the exposure and hardships incident to the march to the Valley, as not a gun had been fired at a deadlier foe than a pig or a chicken. To make up this loss a detail for recruiting service was ordered, consisting of Lieutenant Mass, Lieutenant Harkisheimer, Sergeant-Major Levi, and Sergeant Nuskey, to report to the Adjutant-General's office at Washington.

While encamped here great preparations were made to celebrate in a fitting manner the "Glorious Fourth," a grand program being arranged, including speeches, fireworks, and something else that the commissary furnished, the last being mostly for the officers. The camp had been tastefully decorated with evergreens, arches, bowers, and other trimmings, presenting a beautiful and unique appearance. But man proposes and the general disposes, for early on the 4th the general sounded, and in one hour an angry and disgusted division was marching southward, scorched by the sun and smothered by the dust, instead of having a good time jollifying in camp. After an easy march, the column halted in the evening near Gainesville and rested for the night.

At day-dawn on the 5th the bugles called the men up, and after feasting on coffee, hardtack, and pork, the march was continued, passing through New Baltimore and Buckland, quiet little hamlets of a few houses each, and arriving at Warrenton late in the day. Upon approaching this pleasant town the lines were dressed and, with flying colors and rattling drums, the column marched through the main street, halting a couple of miles beyond, having marched some sixteen or seventeen miles since morning. During the march the sun was blistering hot and the clouds of thick dust stifled the men, causing many to fall out of the ranks to seek water and rest; consequently, when the halt was ordered there was but a corporal's guard present with each company. This annoyed Colonel George exceedingly, and when the stragglers came into camp they had the law laid down to them in a way they did not soon forget.

The brigade remained here until July 22, when the camp was moved to near Waterloo Bridge on the Rappahannock, the ground assigned to the 88th Regiment being a miserable plot, covered with briers, bushes, and stumps.

On July 27, George W. Boger was appointed butcher for the brigade, relieving Andrew Carter, of Company G. Here the time was passed in drills, reviews, and in preparing for the inevitable

QUARTERMASTER ALBERT C. WEBSTER.

CHAPLAIN CHARLES W. CLOTHIER.

SURGEON JOHN WINDSOR RAWLINS.

LIEUTENANT HARRY O'NEILL,
(Companies I and K.)
Quartermaster Sergeant.

JOHN F. KELLER,
Principal Musician.

conflict that every one felt would soon be on. General Pope was organizing the Army of Virginia to take an active part in the coming campaign as circumstances might direct. The advance on the Peninsula against Richmond had proved a failure, and there were good reasons for expecting that Lee would soon turn his attention to this army, and especially to General Pope. The general reviewed Ricketts's division, now in the zenith of its strength, on August 1, and complimented General Ricketts on the discipline and excellent bearing of his soldiers.

While in this camp a detail from the 88th guarded a large herd of cattle corralled in a field west of the camp. One night thirty-four head upset the fence, and in the morning, when the sentinels awoke, they had gone "over the hills and far away." The frightened guards at once went in pairs to scour the country for the lost steers, their steps quickened by fearful thoughts of terrible punishment by court-martial and the like. At day-dawn two of the scurrying guards struck the trail of the fugitives and followed it through the woods, expecting to overtake them before they had gone far; but the tracks led them mile upon mile, over the crest of the mountain and through the valley beyond, until, after a weary chase, they were discovered at last quietly resting in the yard of a farm-house, around which many people were seen, it appearing as if the cattle had been purposely driven there. The two pursuers, being entirely unarmed, were at first inclined to make a quiet retreat and get re-enforcements, but after a brief council of war on the steer question, they determined upon the recovery of the cattle before they could be driven farther away; so each one sticking a big corn-cob under his blouse to resemble a huge pistol, they boldly marched up and claimed the herd, in the mean time loudly suggesting to one another the propriety of shooting one or two recalcitrant beeves who exhibited a disposition to go every way but the right way. The confident bearing of the two blue-coats had the effect of keeping the occupants of the farm-house quiet, and, after a feeble show of resistance, they allowed the herd to be driven away, to the intense relief of the guards, who soon met an armed force coming from camp to their assistance.

Having had no breakfast, the guards were very hungry, and, stopping at a comfortable-looking farm-house, politely asked for break-

fast.   Bread and milk was all that could be obtained, and when this
had vanished, "mine host" presented his bill,—twenty-five cents
for each soldier fed.   Nathan White, of Company I, acted as treas-
urer of the squad, but all the available funds was a bogus quarter,
which he kindly gave the gentleman, telling him that the next time
he passed that way he would pay the rest.

Dr. Seltzer, the regimental surgeon, having resigned and gone
home, on July 27, Dr. David Kennedy was temporarily assigned for
duty with the regiment, by order of the brigade surgeon.

After a further stay in this pleasant place, the movement southward was begun.   On August 5 the division struck tents, and, marching through Jeffersonville, halted. near Culpeper on the afternoon of
the 6th.   The marching was not severe, but the men suffered intensely from the hot sun, the smothering dust, and the lack of good
drinking-water.   This part of Virginia is noted for a scarcity of
pure spring water, the springs and wells being few and far between,
and when a clear stream of water was reached it was quickly rendered unfit for use by the dipping in of hundreds of cups and canteens by the thirsty soldiers, who, caring only for their own personal
wants, were not careful to leave the stream clear for those who came
later on.   The official order for this march issued by General Tower
directed the brigade to move in the following order : first, 94th New
York ; second, 88th Pennsylvania ; third, 90th Pennsylvania ; fourth,
26th New York.   On the second day's march the formation was by
regiments,—thus, 88th, 90th, 26th, and 94th,—ambulances and trains
bringing up the rear.

Things now began to look interesting, and most of the boys were
inclined to think that after all we should see some very active service,
and they were not very hard to persuade, either.   Some of the officers
had been absent from their commands, but when the signs betokened
battle they quickly came back, to be with the boys if there was to be
any fighting.   Adjutant Foust returned on the 4th, Captain Wagner
and Lieutenant Wingate on the 6th, and Colonel McLean on the
7th,—all just in time for the regiment's initial battle.

CHAPTER VII.

CEDAR MOUNTAIN : AUGUST 7 TO 15, 1862.

THE regiment remained near Culpeper on the 7th, but the cavalry reporting the enemy crossing the Rapidan, fifteen miles below, Ricketts's division, on the afternoon of the 8th, was marched through the town and formed in line of battle about two miles out.

On Saturday morning, August 9, the Confederates pressed the cavalry back, and Banks's corps having just arrived, was ordered down to meet them. Banks had a splendid body of men, and as they marched by with stirring music and fluttering colors, many expressions of admiration were passed upon their soldierly bearing and appearance as hardy, robust men. Many old friends were recognized in the ranks of the 28th, 29th, 46th, 109th, and 111th Pennsylvania Regiments, and Collis's Zouaves, and many a hand was shaken and good-by spoken for the last time.

These troops struck the van of the enemy in the afternoon, and made it hot and lively for Stonewall until he got his troops well in hand ; then he turned the tables on Banks, forcing his exhausted regiments back by overwhelming numbers; it was an unequal con-test, the proportion being about seven or eight Union soldiers to twenty or twenty-five Johnnies. From our position the sound of the battle was distinctly heard, and the balls of white smoke from the bursting shells could be seen over the trees. The Confederates had a very heavy gun planted on the mountain-side, and every few minutes the loud report of this piece came rumbling·through the woods above the roar of all the other cannon engaged.

Late in the day, Ricketts's division was ordered to the rescue, and, hurrying down the road through the wounded and stragglers, soon came to the edge of the battle-field. The remnant of Banks's corps, after being terribly cut up, was stubbornly contesting the enemy's advance, but in imminent danger of being completely

swept away by the Confederates, who were pushing their compact
lines of fresh brigades in our direction. Tower's brigade formed
quickly in line, supporting Hall's and Thompson's batteries, Colonel Christian's 26th New York and the 88th on the right, the 90th
Pennsylvania, Colonel Lyle, and Colonel Root's 94th New York
being on the left. The pop and bang of the rifles sounded nearer
and nearer, while the shot and shell from the rebel cannon
dropped uncomfortably close, as they cautiously felt their way
onward; but the men stood quietly in line, waiting for them
to uncover in our front, the batteries being on a slight eminence
in the rear, with the cannoneers standing by their guns ready for
action.

The deepening shades of night were fast covering the sombre
scene with a pall of gloom and smoke, the woods mingling their
lengthening shadows in the gathering darkness, as every man waited
and watched the mountain anxiously, not knowing just where the
enemy was; but the occasional "zip" and the dull droning of a
spent ball indicated that his skirmishers were close at hand and
hunting for business.

We had not very long to wait. Suddenly in front, lightening up
the gloom of the woods, came a score of bright flashes resembling
fire-flies, followed quickly by the crack of the rifles and the sharp
"zip, zip" of the balls as they sung merrily overhead. Every man
took a firmer hold of his musket, while Colonel McLean, going
along the line, gave the command, "Steady, men; steady, now."
Scarcely had these words of caution been passed along when the
woods in front flashed with the fire of a Confederate battery, and
the shot came hissing and screaming overhead, leaving a trail of
fire through the darkness. Our batteries at once accepted the chal-
lenge and opened a quick reply, and for a half-hour the duel was
kept up, until the enemy ceased firing, when our guns also slackened
their fire and finally stopped barking altogether. This *rencontre* was
caused by the desire of General Jackson to push on to Culpeper that
night, and it was Pegram's battery, supported by Field's brigade,
that was advancing to see if the coast was clear. The Confederate
General Hill reported that Pegram's loss in men and horses was so
severe that he was soon silenced. He had two guns dismounted,

and was glad to back out and let the Yankee gunners alone, having got all the fight he wanted for one night.

Tower occupied this line until near day-dawn, when a position was taken a little in the rear and preparations were made to meet the anticipated attack; but it did not come, and when the skirmishers advanced to feel for our Southern friends, it was discovered that they had fallen back too, being in line on Cedar Mountain, which position they evacuated on the 11th, retreating across the Rapidan. The loss in the regiment was only one man, George Teed, who was wounded by a fragment of shell.

On the 11th the brigade advanced over the battle-field, and the havoc wrought by the Union batteries in this night duel could be seen. Lying all around were dead men, mangled artillery horses, broken gun-carriages, and accoutrements of war, evidently mostly belonging to Pegram's battery, which must have had a hot time trying to hold its position. Everywhere were new-made graves; all over the battle-field, by the roadside, in fence corners, and under the trees,—every place was dotted with the fresh earth turned over some soldier who had fought his last battle and whose life-blood had reddened the ground as he struggled in his agony to drag his mangled form to some place for shelter and relief. Within the Southern lines the graves were also numerous, no place being without a full complement. Where the regiments stood the men fell in rows and heaps and were buried mostly where they fought and fell. In looking at these festering and bloated bodies, a soldier could truly realize what little value was placed upon that most precious gift, human life.

So ended this premature and somewhat remarkable contest, in which General Banks with about 8000 men attempted to drive Jackson's entire corps, composed of eleven brigades, upward of 20,000 of probably the best soldiers in the Southern army, who, having assisted in the repulse of General McClellan's army before Richmond, were confident of achieving an easy victory over General Pope's scattered divisions.

The Union loss was 2400, that of the Confederates 1500. On the following day, General Pope, having concentrated his army, had within supporting distance Ricketts's division, 8000 strong; Sigel's corps, 11,000; and King's division, nearly 9000 well-disciplined troops, in addition to Banks's used-up corps, and if an advance had been promptly made, Jackson would undoubtedly have been placed in an embarrassing position. If he had remained to accept battle, the result would scarcely have been doubtful. But no aggressive movement was made, and after the enemy had retreated across the Rapidan the Federal army occupied the mountain, Tower's brigade marching down to the river on the 15th, going into camp within cannon-shot of the insurgent position. On the 14th, Assistant Surgeon Joseph H. Hayes reported for duty to the regiment.

CHAPTER VIII.

FROM THE RAPIDAN TO BULL RUN: AUGUST 16 TO 29, 1862.

THE stay of the regiment on the Rapidan was of few days and full of trouble, but camp discipline was rigidly maintained. On the 16th, Colonel McLean treated the command to battalion drill among the briers, in plain view and within cannon-shot of our friends the enemy. It is not known what they thought about the drill, but the boys in the regiment had a decided repugnance to marching through blackberry bushes, and expressed their opinions in some pungent remarks that would have been entirely out of place in a Sunday-school. Camp was changed on the 17th to near Mitchell's Station, and on the night of the 18th the army was ordered to fall back to the line of the Rappahannock.

The situation was briefly this: General Pope held the line of the Rapidan, with Sigel's corps on the right, McDowell's in the centre, Reno's division on the left, and Banks's at Culpeper,—in all, barely 40,000 troops of all arms. Across the little stream called the Rapidan River the Southern army was being rapidly concentrated to crush Pope before he could be re-enforced to any considerable extent from McClellan's army, which had been ordered by Halleck to come to Pope's assistance, thereby transferring the war from the vicinity of Richmond to this point. Cedar Mountain is about equidistant between Richmond and Washington. The railroad from the Rapidan to Culpeper runs almost due north, but, with the other main roads, turns sharply to the right after leaving the town. Owing to the trend of these roads, the Southern forces at the lower fords of the Rapidan were actually nearer to the Rappahannock railroad bridge than was the main body of the Union army. Lee's plan was to cross the lower Rapidan on the 18th of August, destroy the railroad bridge at Rappahannock Station by means of Stuart's cavalry, then break Pope's left wing, and so take the Union army in reverse and

crush it.   With his great numerical superiority at that time this movement might have succeeded ; but General Pope was quick to see his
danger, and before Lee could consummate this movement, the Union
army had fallen back behind the Rappahannock.

On the night of the 18th, after the army had quietly marched
away, Tower's brigade struck tents and, after replenishing the
numerous camp fires, silently followed the rest of the army towards
Culpeper, thus forestalling Lee's movement, which in all probability,
had the proposed march been made in time, would have been disastrous to Pope's army.

Before moving, orders were received to detail a force under command of Lieutenant Hudson, of Company C, to assist in destroying
the railroad bridge over Cedar Run.   When the detail reached the
bridge the pioneers had cut the stringers almost through, and as
Hudson was about stepping on the bridge it fell with a crash, a piece
of broken timber striking him in the body, rendering him unconscious and inflicting injuries from which he died the following day.
He was a very popular officer, being highly esteemed by every man
in the regiment, and was the first commissioned officer in the 88th
to give his life for his country.

The brigade, bringing up the rear of the army, made only a couple
of miles the entire night.   The head of column would scarcely get
started before meeting some obstruction which would cause a long
delay, and so the weary night passed and at day-dawn the brigade
had hardly reached Cedar Mountain battle-field.

At daylight the brigade was formed in line of battle near the
battle-field, expecting the enemy to cross the Rapidan immediately
upon learning of the retrograde movement ; but after waiting a
couple of hours and the Johnnies not appearing, the line of march
was resumed, and, passing through Culpeper, the brigade pulled
out for the Rappahannock.   Night came before the river was reached,
but the regiment with the brigade pushed on with scarcely a halt
over the roughest and rockiest kind of a road until late at night,
when, tired, sleepy, and hungry, we crossed the river, and soon the
entire force except the guards was sound asleep on the hard ground.
This was an exceedingly severe march, and the surviving members
of the regiment who were there will readily recall it to mind.   By

the route chosen the regiment had tramped over twenty-five miles since morning.

On the 20th, Lieutenant Hudson was buried near the river, and the regiment was drawn up in line of battle on the north bank, a detail being sent across to the south bank to dig intrenchments. Colonel Coulter was across the river with his regiment, being stationed on the red hills near the bridge, and, throwing his command out as skirmishers, kept the enemy in check, his line being in sight near the woods.

The 20th of August passed without a fight, but about ten o'clock on the morning of the 21st the enemy suddenly opened a rapid and accurate fire, directed upon the red hills, from several batteries of artillery, the position occupied by Coulter's regiment and a detail of pioneers being completely raked by the enemy's shell, which, bursting, scattered their whizzing fragments in every direction. A portion of Hartsuff's brigade, with Thompson's and Matthew's Pennsylvania batteries, passed over the river on a rough bridge which had been laid by the pioneers, and the guns opening a rapid fire upon the Confederates, soon silenced them and drove them away.

The 22d was passed in lively skirmishing and cannonading, but with no decisive result, except that a few men were wounded by the enemy's fire and many more badly scared. One straggler, while coming from the rear, observed an unfriendly solid shot making a bee-line for his head, the ball striking the ground and ricocheting as it came along; but a lively juke saved the threatened head and the cannon-ball spent itself harmlessly in the rear.

It was General Pope's intention to throw quickly a large force over the river and make a determined attack on Lee's army while it was strung out along the river from Kelly's Ford to Waterloo, but a very heavy rain spoiled the plan and made it necessary to recall the detachment on the south bank before the bridges should be swept away by the rapidly rising waters, already assuming the force of a flood. Accordingly, on the 23d the detachment was withdrawn, when the enemy at once pushed forward his artillery and infantry to occupy the vacated position. A hot fight immediately ensued, principally between the artillery, the Union guns on the north bank consisting of Hall's, Leppien's, Matthew's and Thomp-

son's batteries, while the Confederates were represented by the first
and third companies of the Washington Artillery, the Macbeth and
Dixie Artillery, and Stribling's battery, supported by Anderson's,
Evans's, and other brigades of infantry. The Union loss was not
severe, though several men in the 88th were wounded by fragments
of shells; but it is interesting to know that our opponents had anything but a nice time in trying to cross the river. Captain Boyce,
commanding the Macbeth Artillery, galloped his battery up the hill,
and reports that in less than two minutes he was compelled to retire
without being able to fire a shot, and in that short time lost seven
men and seven horses. The first battery Washington Artillery was
driven off with a loss of fourteen men and twenty-one horses.
Evans's brigade lost 111 men, the other brigades and batteries also
suffering greatly. The total loss of the enemy in this spirited affair
was between 200 and 300 men. At the termination of the contest,
on the afternoon of the 23d of August, the Union army held its
position, the enemy having been foiled in every attempt to force a
passage of the river.

   During the day a body of Confederate horsemen attempted to ford
the river, but were quickly repulsed, a well-directed shot emptying
the saddle of the leading horse. The animal, subsequently coming
across the river, was captured by Corporal Albert Williams, of Company D, and confiscated by Lieutenant Fairlamb, then acting adjutant of the regiment. The enemy finally gave up the attempt to
drive our forces away, and began a movement up the river, which
necessitated a corresponding move on the part of General Pope's
army.

   This affair at the bridge will not be called much of a fight, but it
nevertheless was a gallant attack and an obstinate and successful
defence. The five Confederate batteries engaged threw away 1182
rounds of ammunition, the amount fired by the Union cannon
(to more purpose) being probably much greater. The men of
the 88th exhibited commendable coolness and discipline under
the heavy fire to which they were subjected. While lying in the
woods many shells burst overhead, scattering with their singing
fragments the limbs of the trees and wounding several of the men ;
but the boys lay low until Colonel McLean took them along the

road, where the shells made less noise and probably did less damage.

During this fierce artillery duel a detail of volunteers from the 88th was sent to assist in working Hall's battery, the men remaining with the guns several days. In the afternoon the Pennsylvania Reserves, just from the Peninsula, marched by in a drenching storm, the rain descending in bucketfuls, making the situation anything but a picnic. At dark a detail was sent to fire the railroad bridge, and Tower's brigade, bringing up the rear, commenced a weary night march in the mud to some point up the river. Whenever a perilous point was to be guarded, Tower's brigade was chosen for the job, because the commander and command stood so high in the estimation of the general. Probably if the boys had understood it better at the time the honor might have been appreciated more than it really was. It was the unanimous opinion of the men marching in the column that the mud on these roads took first premium for stickiness and tenacity. Many of the soldiers were completely mired, having to be extricated from the mud that clung to their feet like glue, and not a few had their shoes torn off, losing them in the darkness. About two o'clock the column halted, the exhausted men sleeping soundly in the mud until daylight.

On the morning of Sunday, May 24, the march was resumed, but we had not gone far before the sound of battle was heard in the direction of Sulphur Springs, when the column about-faced and proceeded in that direction; but, assistance not being needed, turned again, and at nightfall halted on the Culpeper road, midway between Warrenton and the Rappahannock.

The 25th was passed in marching forward and backward over the hills, through the briers and stones, much to the discomfort of those of the men who had no shoes to protect their feet from the thorns and sharp boulders lying in the fields.

The 26th of August was an exceedingly hot day, but there was no rest for the weary, hungry, and bewildered troops engaged in watching the mysterious movements of the enemy, supposed to be across the river. At daybreak the bivouac was abandoned, the head of column being directed to the left; but it had not gone far when the heavy booming of artillery in the direction of Sulphur Springs

4

caused the division to turn in that direction. It appeared, however, that King's division was able to hold its own, so the column halted in the grateful shade of a thick woods, but presently turned again towards Warrenton, marching slowly and wearily on until dusk, when a halt was ordered and the tired and supperless men threw themselves on the ground and rested until morning. These conflicting and tiresome movements were as mysterious as provoking to the men, and they could not understand why they were made.

The key to the situation is found in the following explanation :

General Jackson cut loose from Lee on the morning of the 25th to get between Pope and Washington. He reached Salem at night, passed through Thoroughfare Gap on the 26th, and arrived at Bristoe Station the same afternoon, appropriating everything he could lay his hands on and burning what he could not carry. He was consequently in the rear of the Union army and broke its communications with Washington. He left Manassas Junction on the night of the 27th, concentrating near Sudley Springs, where he will be found later on, ready to tackle any Union force that should come within his reach.

The 27th of August was very hot and sultry, and the brigade lay in the fields several hours, the Union generals apparently at a loss what to do or where to go ; but in the afternoon the column made a hurried march through Warrenton, and, keeping the road until two o'clock in the morning, halted near New Baltimore. At the first streak of daylight on Thursday, the 28th, the march was resumed, but it was difficult to keep all the soldiers in the ranks, some of them being sick, large numbers utterly exhausted, and all tired and half starved ; consequently the roads were lined with stragglers, most of them very unwillingly so, but they were unable to keep their places in line, being weakened from want of food, the commissary department wagons having been lost and no rations issued since the previous Saturday.

When Haymarket was reached the knapsacks were piled in a heap and the division hurried out to Thoroughfare Gap to prevent Longstreet coming through to the help of Jackson, who with more than a dozen brigades was reported to be roaming somewhere over the country east of the mountains, with several divisions of Union

CORPORAL LEWIS W. BONNIN.

GEORGE W. BOGEE.

LIEUTENANT GEORGE W. GRANT.

JOSEPH CHAMPION CLEMENT.

HENRY READ.

troops in hot pursuit. The column reached the vicinity of the Gap in the afternoon, meeting the cavalrymen retiring before the enemy, whom they reported in possession of the defile. Skirmishers were thrown out and the enemy forced back into the gorge, when the artillery opened a brisk fire upon the Gap and surrounding heights.

The brunt of the fighting was borne by Colonel Coulter's regiment, which lost eighteen men killed and thirty-seven wounded. While Ricketts's division was forming and fighting on the eastern side of the mountain, General Lee was carefully scanning the position from the west, with Longstreet's corps rapidly arriving. Lee finally ordered a direct assault, also flanking columns to cross the heights to the right and left. However, Ricketts held the enemy in check until dark, then fell back to Haymarket, and, recovering knapsacks, the command marched to Gainesville before halting for the night, while the gray veterans of Longstreet, passing through the Gap, unknowingly bivouacked within cannon-shot of the Union division at Gainesville.

This Gap movement was a very important one, and many military writers claim that Ricketts should not have allowed Longstreet to pass through to the help of Jackson. Undoubtedly this would have been a commendable act, but Ricketts would surely have been overwhelmed on the morning of the 29th by the twelve or thirteen brigades of infantry which were with Longstreet. As it was, Ricketts took the safest course when at dark he drew back to Gainesville, resting there until daylight, while the Confederates marched through the Gap, Jones's division on the advance, and bivouacked a short distance beyond. The Union division rested near Gainesville until daybreak; then, supposing the enemy to be at Manassas Junction, marched to Greenwich in search of the main body of General Pope's army; but this movement was a mistaken one, for at that hour the bulk of the army was near the stone bridge over Bull Run, which point could easily have been reached by the Warrenton pike if the opposing commanders had offered no objection. However, the troops were ignorant of the situation at this time, and struck for the railroad near Bristoe, but finding no enemy, came to the Junction and halted to look around and get breath.

The division was in hard lines, officers and men being almost

famished, the soldiers eagerly searching among the abandoned camps
for pieces of crackers, bones, cob-corn, or anything that would satisfy
their hunger; but there wasn't a square meal in sight, and the boys
had to rest content with growls and curses loud and deep against the
quartermaster and his missing rations.

In the afternoon the sound of cannon was heard towards Bull
Run battle-field, and to that point the head of column was
directed, passing Porter's corps, which was skirmishing with the
enemy in the woods. The rebs had come in a direct line from
Gainesville, and had got here considerably before Ricketts's men
put in an appearance. The vicinity of the stone house was reached
in the evening, the command resting here till morning. Colonel
Joe was now in command, Colonel McLean having been compelled
to leave the regiment on the 25th, suffering from severe illness,
which incapacitated him from taking command for some time.

CHAPTER IX.

BULL RUN, AUGUST 30, 1862.

SATURDAY, August 30, was an extremely warm day; hot in other respects than by reason of the scorching sun to the weary soldiers who wore the blue. At the morning roll-call of the regiment scarcely 400 men answered to their names. Many had fallen out of line, some sick, others utterly played out, and of those that remained with the colors, all were so hungry, dirty, and exhausted that they were in no condition to fight a great battle. No opportunity to wash body or clothing had been given for several weeks, and when a soldier cannot keep clean, he in a large degree loses his self-respect and confidence. In line of battle by day and marching all night, minus rations, suffering intensely with thirst and from complaints induced by drinking filthy water, the men were in a pitiable condition. Many were shoeless and with their clothing in tatters, yet they clung to the regiment with a devotion and perseverance worthy of all praise; for soldiers who, under such adverse circumstances, keep their organization and, in spite of so many dispiriting events, still present a bold front to the enemy, cannot be too strongly commended.

In the morning the division was massed on the Dogan farm, near the stone house on the Sudley Springs road, but towards noon it was sent to the right, near Kearney's famous division. Its one-armed commander was carelessly leaning on a brass cannon, and as the regiment halted quite near him, the men had an excellent opportunity to see this renowned soldier. Away off, a mile or more to the front and right, a small farm-house was located, around which the enemy's skirmishers were in view, and the Union cannon were throwing an occasional shot in that direction. Presently the brigade returned to its position near the stone house, and, stacking arms, lay there until the afternoon, when news came that Lee with all his army was on the skedaddle, scooting straight to the mountains in his intense desire to escape from General Pope. A despatch to that effect was sent to Washington, and, being transmitted to the North, caused a thrill of joy in every loyal heart which was rudely dispelled a few hours later. A strong column, to be led by General McDowell, was at once formed to pursue the retreating foe, our regiment being assigned to the pursuing division, and, piling knapsacks, every preparation was speedily made by the exultant troops for a vigorous and successful chase after Lee's army.

The stock of confidence which most of the soldiers had in the means and ability of General Pope to successfully cope with Lee had been steadily diminishing during the past few days, until it was away below zero; but it now took a turn in the other direction, and must have attained a higher point than the thermometer registered, that being over a hundred in the shade. Many expressions of satisfaction were heard through the ranks, and the old saying of "having them just where we wanted them" was the favorite one used, for all trusted that our commanding general had at last outgeneralled Lee and would give him a sound thrashing before he got through with him.

The head of column soon pulled out, and at a quickstep proceeded westward on the Sudley road; but the leading brigades had scarcely gone over the hill before it was discovered that there was something wrong on the left of the Union army, and the way the column was about-faced and hurried over the Warrenton pike created a suspicion that mayhap the situation was after all not so bright as it had been represented.

The real state of affairs was that, instead of retreating to the mountains, Lee was quietly massing an immense force—fifteen brigades of infantry, two of cavalry, with numerous batteries—to strike a crushing blow on the Union left, protected by two small brigades, all unconscious of the tempest that was about to burst on them from the woods in their front. When this formidable column uncovered and advanced to the attack, the true situation of the contending forces dawned upon the minds of McDowell and Pope, and they were quick to realize their perilous position. Laying hands on all available troops, they hurried them to the threatened point, lest the Johnnies should reach the Warrenton pike and cause irreparable injury to the Union army. The 88th, with the other regiments composing Tower's brigade, left the Sudley road a short distance east of the pike and double-quicked down a slope, over a little stream of water, and up the hill on the farther side, where, being under a heavy artillery fire, the men began to drop out wounded by the pieces of shells as they burst around the column. Under a tree near the run, Captain Fessenden, of General Tower's staff, lay mortally wounded ; he had been shot while in the performance of his duty as aide.

Upon ascending the opposite hill the brigade came in view of the Confederate cannoneers and received a withering fire from several batteries of the Washington Artillery, planted in the vicinity of the Chinn house, and presently from the Macbeth and other batteries posted on the farm near by. The regiment was rushed up the hill on the double-quick, left in front, which brought Company K in advance, and upon reaching the top the companies deployed as best they could, facing the enemy's line near the house, some two or three hundred yards distant, around which were the Confederate cannon, as before mentioned.

The confusion among the troops on the hill was great ; officers and men shouting, shells tearing through and exploding, the incessant rattle of the muskets, the cries of the wounded,—all combined made up a scene that was anything but encouraging, yet every one appeared anxious to get in the proper place to do the most good. Some semblance of a line was soon formed, and the Confederate infantry being discovered at the foot of the hill, a rapid fusillade was at once opened, causing them to retreat in disorder.

About this time a section of artillery hastily galloped up, unlimbered, and went into battery directly in front ; but no sooner had the trails touched the ground than the horses ran away with the limbers—being wounded, probably—and, dashing recklessly through the ranks, disappeared, leaving the guns with only two or three rounds of ammunition. Very soon the Confederates advanced past the farm-house in many lines of battle, extending as far as could be seen ; they came on in thousands, with battle-flags well to the front and their officers urging them on, when the brigade at once opened a withering fire on them, checking their advance somewhat.

The Union cannoneers stood pluckily by their guns, and at the right time ranged their pieces and discharged them into the solid ranks of the enemy, but there being no more ammunition, the guns were useless.

All this time the cannon of the enemy were ploughing the hill with their shot, and, being so close, had excellent range, the projectiles striking with frightful precision among the ranks of blue standing shoulder to shoulder on the hill. The infantry fire was also very destructive, and came from so many directions that our men were at a loss how to return it effectively. Colonel Joe, Major Gile, and the other officers did all that officers could do to keep order and hold the position, but the yells of the combatants, the noise of the bursting shells, and the agonizing screams of the wounded and dying made the place a perfect bedlam, and it was found impossible to get the companies in order to successfully resist the Confederate brigades who were advancing, firing and yelling as they came. The officers encouraged their men to hold the position as long as possible, it being generally understood that time was required to form another line and post batteries in our rear, as this place was untenable, and the men responded bravely to their appeals, standing firmly by their colors and giving the Johnnies the best they had in the shop; but at this critical period a heavy column appeared emerging from the woods directly on the left flank of the brigade. It was at first supposed to be part of Pope's forces, but when these troops opened an enfilading fire that cut across and through our ranks, their true character was revealed. This flanking force was Jones's Confederate division, the troops in our front being Hood's division, assisted by Evans's brigade and Anderson's and Kemper's divisions. The battered battalions on the hill at once refused their left to meet this attack, seven companies of the 94th New York taking the extreme left, and in executing this movement the 88th naturally gave ground a little in front. Colonel Joe, seeing the line wavering, rallied the regiment around the colors, and about this time received a terrible wound in the thigh. Being unable to control his horse, it started to run away as the colonel fell from the saddle; but Lieutenant Rannels, of the 75th Ohio, caught the horse, and, with the assistance of some of the members of the 88th, carried the colonel back a short distance, when he was again struck and died on the field. His last words were, " I die for my country and the old flag." Many other officers of the regiment had already been disabled, among them Captain Belsterling, of Company C, killed at the head of his command. Captains Wagner and Stretch, Lieutenants Street and Patterson, Adjutant Fairlamb, with many other officers and men, were wounded. General Tower was carried off the field badly wounded, subsequently losing a leg by amputation.

There were many individual acts of personal daring and bravery exhibited by the men of the 88th Regiment as they fought singly and by squads, but where so many may justly claim recognition, it would be invidious to select one or more for especial mention ; however, the many proficient rifle-shots in the battalion had abundant opportunity to exercise their skill in this direction, and the mortality among the Confederate officers attested their success. Colonel Means, of the 17th, and Colonel Gadbury, of the 18th South Carolina Regiment, were killed directly in our front, the last-named officer just about the time the Union line was breaking.

The Federal troops, notwithstanding their desperate resistance, were being slowly but surely forced back. The men in the front rank would fire, then fall to the rear to force another cartridge down their heated and befouled rifles, but by the time they were loaded would be in the front again, the rear rank having performed the same movement. The enemy was returning this salute with interest, aided by superior numbers and a concentric fire, and the ground was thickly strewn with the dead and badly wounded, while the rear presented a woful mass of wounded soldiers and the inevitable stragglers, who, taking advantage of the confusion, were making lively tracks for the rear. But this unequal contest could not last long. The rebels were advancing in admirable order in heavy masses, brigade following brigade, the front line firing as they came, the white puffs of smoke rolling along their front in fleecy clouds sometimes obscuring their lines; but they swept on, up the hill, by the guns, and as their converging lines closed in, the Union troops scattered and retreated to the Sudley road, leaving Bald Hill in possession of the Confederates. While falling back, re-enforcements from Sigel's corps were met coming up, massed in column of division and stepping as quietly as if on parade; these men checked the foe long enough to allow the shattered remnants of Tower's brigade to rally on the Henry House hill north of the Springs road, at which place the Confederate advance was stopped. The greater part of Longstreet's men bivouacked that night on the Chinn farm, being so terribly shattered that they were in no condition to attempt more.

After rallying on the hill and along the pike, and repulsing a charge of the enemy, the Union forces, under cover of the night, with sad hearts and weary feet, marched back to Centreville. The army had been defeated, though the men felt that they had done all that good soldiers could do, and no stain of dishonor rested on their fair name for this day's sad work, but all felt mortified and sick at heart when they thought of their suffering comrades left weltering in blood on the disastrous field of battle.

The loss of Colonel Joe and Captain Belsterling and the wounding of so many efficient officers of the regiment was the beginning of a similar experience that lasted during the entire war. General Tower's wound resulted in the loss of a leg and incapacitated him from further field service during the war. He was a good officer, a strict disciplinarian, and would undoubtedly have attained high command in the service, though not very popular with the boys. But the degree of an officer's popularity with the soldiers was no gauge of his proficiency as a commanding officer; there was no more unpopular officer in the army than General McDowell, but subsequent light upon his character and motives conclusively proves that no more unselfish or patriotic general or purer gentleman wore the stars of a Union officer. All the misfortunes and disasters, short rations, hard marches, and abortive movements were blamed on McDowell. He was constantly accused of being drunk, yet the most positive proof is adduced that he had never taken a glass of liquor in his life. The peculiar bamboo hat he wore was supposed to be a signal for the enemy not to fire upon him, and more of the same stuff was firmly engrafted on the minds of the men. General McDowell is dead and beyond the range of praise or blame, but these cruel slanders were borne by him in silence, and it is due to his memory that his record be truthfully told, even at this late day.

The official report of the loss in Tower's command is given below.

The figures are in some cases not correct, as the loss in the 88th in killed was twenty-eight, instead of twelve, as given in the official tables. Some of the mortally wounded may have been simply classified among the wounded, and many of those marked missing were afterwards known to have been killed. The list of killed is corrected; but the totals are the same as in volume xii., Part 2, "Official Records of the War," as published by the United States government.

CASUALTIES IN TOWER'S BRIGADE, AUGUST 16 TO SEPTEMBER 2, 1862.

	Killed.	Wounded.	Missing.	Total.
Brigade staff	1	. .	. .	1
26th New York	26	106	37	169
94th New York	21	81	45	147
88th Pennsylvania	28	85	48	161
90th Pennsylvania	7	49	162	218
Total	83	321	292	696

HARTSUFF'S BRIGADE.

	Killed.	Wounded.	Missing.	Total.
12th Massachusetts	13	61	64	138
13th Massachusetts	20	105	65	190
9th New York State Militia	10	25	48	83
11th Pennsylvania	44	114	88	246
Total	87	305	265	657

The loss in Tower's brigade was the greatest of any brigade in the army in the battle of the 30th.

There is an old saying that misery loves company, and it may console some of these defeated soldiers to know that their opponents suffered as severely as themselves. From the official rebel reports we know how terribly they suffered, life being no consideration with their leaders when they wanted to carry a position.

Anderson's brigade reports a loss of over 800; Evan's, 734; and Hood's Texans, 638. The 17th South Carolina lost 189 out of 284 engaged; the 23d South Carolina, 152 out of 225; and the 17th Georgia, 101 out of 200 carried into action.

The 88th Regiment never recovered from the effects of this disastrous battle, and the loss sustained by it, as shown in the ghastly list of killed and crippled officers and men, very seriously impaired its efficiency in future campaigns, their absence being very keenly felt.

CHAPTER X.

A PILGRIMAGE TO BULL RUN.

IN the fall of 1885 the writer visited this region, made famous by the fierce battles fought here in 1861 and 1862. At Alexandria but little change in the appearance of the city since war times was noticed. The Marshall House has been altered into a dry-goods store and the slave-pen into dwelling-houses, but most of the old residences are precisely as they were during the war. A few miles below Alexandria a new city has been laid out, called New Alexandria, which bids fair to rival the city of "ye ancient tyme."

Most of the immense chain of forts that surrounded Alexandria and Washington have disappeared, but a few still stand in bold outline against the sky, among these being Fort Ellsworth, just outside of Alexandria, where Companies B and F, of the 88th, were stationed in 1861. This fort is in an excellent state of preservation, the parapet and embrasures for the cannon being clearly defined ; but where the ranks of the armed garrison were once dressed birds have taken possession, and sweep in peaceful troops through the places where the big black dogs of war once thrust their threatening muzzles.

A few miles from Alexandria I noticed the ruins of Cloud's Mills, and off to the right the cupola of Fairfax Seminary is still standing. Along the railroad the conductor calls Springfield, Union Mills, Bull Run,—all familiar names, bringing up a flood of memories of the days when we wore the blue and marched wearily over these dusty roads that seemed never so long to nowhere. At Bull Run the stream was muddy from a recent rain, and across the bridge, where General Taylor's Jersey brigade was overwhelmed and repulsed by Jackson's command, the country had an old-time look.

A mile or so north of the Junction are the embankments of one of Beauregard's forts, and a mile west of the Junction is another well-kept fort ; but all the rest have gone, with the gray regiments that once defended them, never to return.

The distance from the Junction to the stone house on the Warrenton pike is about six miles, over an excellent dirt road, flanked part of the way by a neat wire fence. Upon reaching the vicinity of the battle-field the topography of the country changes, and, in place of the plains near the Junction, the ground is broken and hilly, mostly covered by a heavy growth of timber.

Off to the northwest the blue outlines of the Bull Run Mountains are in view, and, looking down the distant range, the sloping of the crest indicates the location of Thoroughfare Gap, where, on the afternoon of August 28, 1862, Ricketts's division drove the skirmishers of Longstreet's advance back through the gorge.

The Warrenton and Alexandria pike runs through the centre of the battle-field, and Young's Branch, a tributary of Bull Run, crosses the road several times, and at the stone house at the intersection of the Sudley road it branches, one fork continuing along the pike past the Dogan farm, the other from the spring on the Chinn farm, south of the Bald Hill range. Straight down the pike, through Warrenton, about twenty-five miles distant, is the Rappahannock River, and, as has been before related, along the banks of this stream, as a line of defence, General Pope successfully held the Confederate army from August 20 to 25, in compliance with the request of General Halleck, on the 21st, to hold on " forty-eight hours longer and we can make you strong enough." Pope carried out his part of the contract, but how lamentably some one else failed is matter of history. He had every assurance that his communications would be effectually guarded by heavy re-enforcements from the Army of the Potomac *via* the Orange and Alexandria Railroad ; but this illusion was rudely dispelled when, on the 26th of August, the ubiquitous Jackson with his hungry legions, marching through Thoroughfare Gap, fell like a thunderbolt upon the Union stores at Manassas Junction. General Pope was loath to believe that this was more than an irruption by some of Stuart's redoubtable cavalry, and to say that he was intensely chagrined when he discovered the true state of affairs is putting it mildly ; but he at once ordered all his troops to the Junction to catch Jackson and " bag the whole crowd !" Jackson, how-

ever, was not the man to be caught in that way, and, burning what
he couldn't carry, he marched his men over Bull Run to Centreville,
and then back again to near Sudley Church, the soldiers in his ranks
feeling that they had done a big thing and were on top, while the
soldiers in Pope's army felt conscious that somebody had blundered,
and were fast losing what little confidence they had in one or two
of their generals.

Jackson planted himself near the Warrenton pike on the 27th,
and, forming his battalions in battle array, waited either the attack
of the Federals or the arrival of Lee with the rest of the army.

On the afternoon of the 28th, while Ricketts was disputing with
Longstreet at the Gap, the division of General King came marching
up the Warrenton pike, bound for Centreville, when Jackson at once
pounced upon them, expecting an easy victory over the bewildered
regiments; but these were troops unaccustomed to retreat, and
Doubleday and Gibbon, who commanded the two brigades assailed,
turned so fiercely on the five or six brigades that Jackson launched
upon them that they were glad to take their hands off and let the
Union forces go in peace.

Finally, the bagging process having proved a failure, the scattered
and wearied divisions of the Union army were concentrated in
proximity to the stone house on the 29th, and on the 30th was
fought the second battle of Bull Run, on almost the identical
ground where McDowell and Beauregard fought the first battle in
July, 1861. There was some severe fighting near Groveton on the
29th, but nothing decisive was achieved on either side, and both
armies drew off and dressed their lines for the great battle of the 30th.

Military men who are competent to judge say that Pope's true
policy would have been to fall back to the line of Bull Run and
maintain that line until the Army of the Potomac came up. Probably it was the wise thing to do; but General Pope was not the man
to run away from an enemy until he was compelled to, and he stayed
as long as he could and fought his army as best he could, though we
now see that he labored under an entirely wrong idea of the situation, and though his soldiers fought never so bravely, it was all in
vain.

We will now describe the battle, and to understand the situation

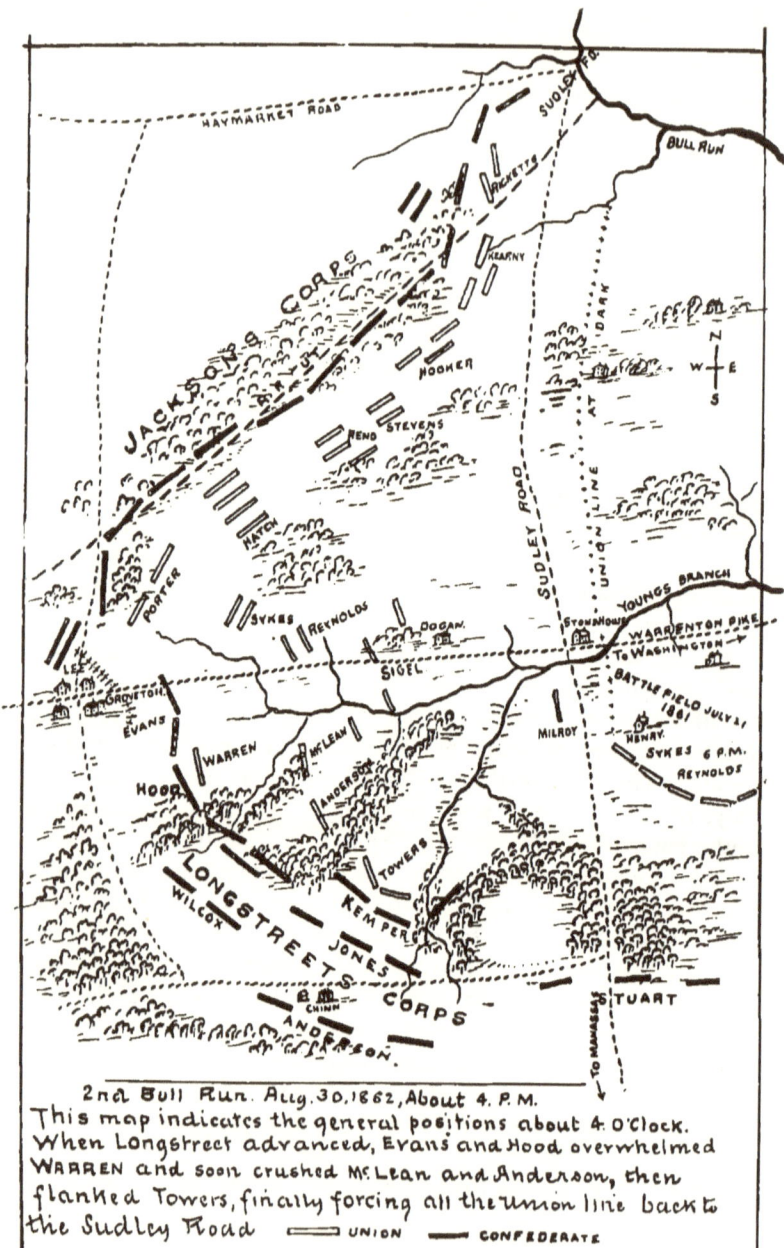

2nd Bull Run. Aug. 30, 1862, About 4. P. M.
This map indicates the general positions about 4 O'Clock.
When Longstreet advanced, Evans and Hood overwhelmed
WARREN and soon crushed Mc.Lean and Anderson, then
flanked Towers, finally forcing all the Union line back to
the Sudley Road ▭▭▭ UNION ▬▬▬ CONFEDERATE

BULL RUN, AUGUST 30, 1862.

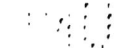

in the early afternoon of August 30 we will stand at the stone house, at the corner of the Springs road and the pike, and locate the troops of both armies. First the Confederates. About two miles straight down the pike they were formed in line of battle, Longstreet, with fifteen brigades, many batteries of artillery, and Stuart's cavalry, being posted mainly on the south side of the pike, and Jackson on the north side, along an old railroad grading, with fourteen brigades of infantry and a number of batteries, to hold the position chosen for a good defence. In round figures, Longstreet had a compact force, well in hand, of upward of 30,000 men ; Jackson's command numbered over 26,000 ; Stuart had three brigades of cavalry ; while the artillery amounted to about 4000 more, distributed among both wings of the army,—a well-seasoned army, flushed with conscious strength, composed of over 65,000 good soldiers, who believed that "Uncle Bob" and "Old Stonewall" could lead them anywhere.

We will now turn to the Union line and note the strength and location of each corps and division, standing, as before stated, at the stone house, looking down the pike towards the Confederate position. Reynolds, with the Pennsylvania Reserves, a little over 4000 strong, had been posted near Bald Hill and the Chinn farm, to our left oblique, but about three o'clock these troops were ordered to the right of the pike by the commanding general, to assist Porter's attack. This left only Warren's brigade of two regiments of zouaves and McLean's brigade of Sigel's corps on the left of the pike to withstand the shock of Longstreet's immense force when it got ready to move.

A mile or so out the pike Porter's corps was assaulting the rebel lines. Porter had, including Warren, about 8000 men in line. He was to the right of the pike, and to his right Hatch's division charged Jackson in conjunction with Porter. Then following to the right came Hooker, then Kearney, and two brigades of Ricketts's division on the extreme right. The 9th Corps was back of Hooker, and Sigel was on the Dogan farm, a half mile in rear of Porter. Tower's and Hartsuff's brigades of Ricketts's division were near the stone house on our right, but will be presently hurried to the left on Bald Hill to face Longstreet. To recapitulate the Union strength : Sigel numbered in line of battle barely 9000 men ; McDowell,

10,000; Reynolds, nearly 5000; Sturgis, 2000; Heintzelman, 8000; Porter, 8000; 9th Corps, 8000; the cavalry 2000, and artillery 3000,—in all, not 55,000 men, ill fed, weary, and falsely posted to fight a defensive battle, the advantage in everything being with the Southerners, who, understanding the situation, had a sure thing on the result.

The reason why the Union force was so badly posted to resist an attack was because General Pope conceived the idea that Lee was on the skedaddle, and he was arranging his columns for an immediate and fierce pursuit, when nothing was further from Lee's thoughts. General Reynolds knew that Lee contemplated an attack, as did also Sigel and Porter, and finally McDowell and Pope; but the storm had burst and it was too late then to get under shelter.

The battle began about three o'clock P.M., Porter, by Pope's orders, attacking along the pike, and the battle being quickly taken up by the troops on Porter's right, until it raged along the whole line; but the Union troops were repulsed, though the attack was handsomely made and gallantly sustained.

The Confederates had massed several batteries at Groveton, and when Porter's men exposed their flank in their advance, these guns gave them a terrible raking from the left, which cut through their ranks like a cyclone. No troops could stand long against such an unmerciful pelting of cannon-balls on the flank and musket-balls in front, and they were forced to fall back, after suffering an appalling loss in killed and wounded.

Seeing the Union repulse, Longstreet's eager brigades were called up and let loose on the unprotected Union left. They swept along both sides of the pike, running over Warren's red-legged soldiers and bringing square up against McLean's Ohio brigade, Koltes's brigade, Anderson's brigade of Pennsylvanians, and Hartsuff's and Tower's brigades of Ricketts's division, all having been double-quicked to the south of the pike at the time that Longstreet's graybacks uncovered and made concealment no longer necessary. These brigades presented a broken and disconnected, though stubborn, front to the enemy's advance, and delayed it long enough to enable the Pennsylvania Reserves, the regulars, and other troops to establish a line on the Henry house hill, thus effectually checking Longstreet's advance in that direction. Milroy's brigade formed along the Sudley road and held its position against repeated assaults until dark, when all the Union troops had been forced back to this point.

On the right, with Hooker and Kearney and Reno, the battle had not fared so badly; but when the left gave way the right was compelled to fall back also, prolonging the line along the Sudley road until dark, when the entire army, save the dead and badly wounded, fell back to Centreville.

There has been but little change in the appearance of the country since, and the scene of the battle was easily recognized; the stone house is still at the corner, the Henry house is on the hill, while the Chinn house and Dogan house are in plain view from the Henry house hill. Bald Hill, where Tower's and Hartsuff's brigades made their gallant and hopeless fight, is now called Battery Hill by the natives, and the wood on the left where Longstreet advanced on the flank is still there, though no treacherous foe lurks in its dark shadows.

I drove to the Chinn farm and stood where the Washington Artillery went into battery and raked the troops along Bald Hill. In the yard of the Henry house a rough monument of undressed stone was erected in war times to the memory of those who died hard by, and near Groveton is a like monument, but both were sadly in need of repairs and threatening to topple over on account of the settling of the foundations.

The losses of both armies from August 16 to September 2 are officially reported as follows:

UNION LOSS.

Army of Virginia	8,105
Army of the Potomac	4,728
9th Corps	1,523
Kanawha division	106
Total	14,462

CONFEDERATE LOSS.

Longstreet's corps	4,500
Jackson's corps	4,532
Cavalry and artillery	800
Total	9,832

In connection with the map of Bull Run, the following extract from Alfred Davenport, historian of the 5th New York, is submitted :

Your map is as near right, in my opinion, as can well be; it is impossible to place the ever-varying positions of troops in a battle in stationary attitudes like chessmen. Warren's brigade only took up a front of about a regiment; you might have made its line shorter and put the left in the woods. The 5th Texas enveloped our left; the Hampton Legion our front; the 18th Georgia overlapped our right; then came the 4th and 1st Texas. . . . We saw the whole of Reynolds's division march in front of us and over to the right, before Warren saw the necessity of advancing to take its place. I think Jackson's (Anderson's) brigade was caught on the tail end before it joined the other two north of the pike; it must have been near the pike, just south of it, and when McLean moved to Bald Ridge, it (Jackson) was in advance of and to his right. McLean says, " We could at this time see the rebels driving before them a regiment of zouaves on our front and a little to our right."

The Texas brigade was driving us, and it was they who captured Kerns's battery, supported by Jackson.

ALFRED DAVENPORT.

NEW YORK, May 11, 1894.

CHAPTER XI.

CHANTILLY TO SOUTH MOUNTAIN, AUGUST 31 TO SEPTEMBER 15, 1862.

THE night march to Centreville was a dismal one. All along the road, in the darkness and gloom, the commanders tried to collect their men, and the hoarse cries of "This way for Tower's brigade," "Fall in, 88th," resounded through the cheerless night. Colonel Christian, of the 26th New York, with the brigade flag, halted before reaching Centreville, and by daybreak the remnants of the regiments were mostly with their colors. Sunday morning, the 31st, brought a chilling rain upon friend and foe, adding greatly to the sufferings of the wounded men lying in helpless agony, with shattered bones and putrid wounds, upon the red field they had so heroically battled to win. Some were carried to hastily-equipped hospitals, but the greater part lay for days upon the damp ground, exposed to sun and rain, with no water or food ; their running wounds undressed, blown by flies and alive with maggots, they were literally rotting in their misery and helplessness.

On Sunday morning it was fully expected that Lee would follow up his victory by at once attacking our dispirited troops, a rumor being circulated that the enemy was coming up the pike in battle array, and the brigade fell into line, batteries were planted, and line of battle formed to meet the expected attack. Notwithstanding the defeat they had suffered, the soldiers appeared to revive won-derfully at the prospect of another battle, every man taking his posi-tion with alacrity and spirit, and if an attack had been made the enemy would undoubtedly have been given a warm reception. All day long many hundreds of conveyances of every description passed by slowly towards Washington, freighted with the wounded brought in from the battle-field.

On the morning of September 1 it was ascertained that the enemy

was moving to the right, consequently we were compelled to fall
back towards Fairfax. While on the retrograde heavy firing was
heard in the direction of Chantilly, and the division was double-
quicked to that place, forming line in the edge of the woods, with
a field in front and another belt of timber about 300 yards distant.
The skirmishers were popping away beyond the woods, but no enemy
appeared in our front. While standing in the rain and mud, a staff
officer rode slowly along the line and quietly exhorted the men to
make a good fight. "If we are defeated, I fear for Washington,"
he said. Under this earnest plea, and understanding the importance
of making a firm stand, the men braced up, resolving to win a victory or die where they were.

All this dreary, cheerless night the men stood or sat as best they
could in line of battle, soaked and benumbed by the chilling rain,
without shelter, minus blankets or any protection from the pitiless
storm, and probably more men were lost to the regiment from this
night's exposure than would have been from a battle. The brigade
remained in this position until the afternoon of the 2d, then moving
off, halted at dusk at Hall's Hill to rest a while from the labors of
this never-to-be-forgotten campaign.

The following table, taken from the morning reports, shows the
strength of the regiment on the dates indicated:

	Aug. 17, 1862.	Sept. 5, 1862.
Commissioned officers for duty	24	14
Non-commissioned officers for duty	95	67
Privates for duty	446	263
Total for duty	565	344
Total present	637	415

These reports show a regimental loss of 221 men, from all causes,
between the dates mentioned; of these, 175 were disabled in action,
leaving about fifty whose services were lost to the regiment by sickness and straggling, nearly all being attributable to disease. The
next two or three days were spent in trying to clean up and get in
good condition; but, as no clothing was issued, it was difficult to
improve our personal appearance except by the plentiful application
of soap and water, which was industriously applied by the men.

The camp had scarcely been formed and the guns stacked, before the hawk-eyed sutler swept down on the bivouac like a bird of prey, and such a rush by the famished soldiers would be difficult to describe; though the prices were away up, the Shylocks quickly disposed of all their goods at a tremendous profit. Everything was a dollar: canned goods, a pound of cheese, a plug of tobacco,—everything brought the "almighty dollar," and the boys esteemed it a privilege to be swindled by the sharpers.

Then came the newsboy with an immense pack of *Philadelphia Inquirers* slung over the neck of his horse, selling them for ten cents each as fast as he could whip them off his bundle. The soldiers were hungry for news; though they had been on the war-path for a month, they knew comparatively very little of what had been done, and could only form an intelligent opinion by reading the newspapers.   •

The mail messenger also put in an appearance and distributed the letters, the first mail received since the 20th of August. A very sad phase of this was the letters for comrades who had been killed in battle. These were carefully and sadly returned to the writers, with an account of the fate and possibly the last word or some token of the dead soldier.

The time given for rest and reorganization at Hall's Hill was short, for on the evening of Saturday, September 5, the general sounded "pack up," and in an hour the column headed for the river; the Army of the Potomac was again on the move. The route was through the viaduct bridge across the Potomac, through George-town to Washington, and out Seventh Street to the Maryland line. The city had gone to sleep when our part of the line passed through, and the men marched along in silence; indeed, it is doubtful if the people of Washington knew that the army was passing. All night long the march was continued, until a halt was made near Crystal Springs, and the men rested until Tuesday, the 9th, when the march was resumed until the twelve-mile stone was reached, at which place the corps again bivouacked in the beautiful fields of this fair country, that seemed flowing with milk and honey. The corn was in prime condition for roasting and the fruit-trees hung heavily laden with their ripening clusters; still, there was but little foraging done, except probably by the coffee-coolers, who had the faculty of knowing where the fattest pickings could be procured, while the faithful soldier plodded patiently in the ranks. The loyal surroundings caused a marked revolution in the feelings and expressions of the rank and file, who heartily enjoyed the warm welcome given by the patriotic people in the little towns along the route, and the sight of citizens waving Union flags would bring an outburst of lusty hurrahs from the soldiers as, with lightened step, they went marching on, singing " We'll rally round the flag, boys," or some other favorite song.

The march was resumed on September 11, the villages of Mechanicsville and Brookville being passed and camp made beyond Cooksville. The people all along the road expressed the greatest surprise at the number of men passing, saying they never thought there were that many men in the whole country.

On the 12th the column passed through Lisbon and Poplar Springs, and the next day New Market and Liberty, halting near the thrifty little city of Frederick. The Confederates had been in this region, and the citizens were more than glad to see the honest faces of Uncle Sam's boys again, and gave them a loyal reception, which was heartily responded to by the boys in the form of many hurrahs and patriotic songs as they went marching on.

On Sunday, September 14, the brigade pushed on after the enemy, but, to the disappointment of the men, the 88th was detailed with the train as a reserve. Early in the afternoon the sounds of battle beyond the mountain became very distinct, the citizens taking the keenest interest; those having horses excitedly rode to and fro, anxious for information and a sight of the conflict. These old hills had never before been stirred with the roar and rumble of opposing cannon, and it was a great day for the people. Late in the afternoon an aide came for Major Gile, with orders to report to the brigade at once, and the march was quickly resumed; passing through Middletown, we were soon swinging away to the battle, a dozen miles off.

Upon crossing the Catoctin and nearing the contested field, it became dark, and after groping around a while it was deemed advisable by Major Gile to halt and wait for morning, it being evident that the fight was over, as only an occasional flash and report could

ALFRED DUNBAR ERMENTROUT.

HENRY N. KUHN.

LIEUTENANT SAMUEL G. BOONE.

JONATHAN L. WENTZEL.

CORPORAL GEORGE W. GAYLORD.

be seen and heard. The major formed the companies in line of battle and rested, but at the first glimmering ray of light the regiment fell in, and, marching down the valley and up the hill, past a little church where the wounded not only occupied the building but lay thickly on the ground outside, soon reached the brigade, the men resting on their arms and in line of battle, occupying the contested field ; the enemy had been driven up the rough and broken side of the mountain the previous afternoon, and during the night had withdrawn his shattered battalions, leaving the field in possession of the Union army. This is one of the few contests of the war which the Confederates did not claim as a victory, their defeat being so decisive that no room was left for them to claim any sort of a triumph. As the regiment marched up the steep sides of the mountain and examined the commanding position the enemy had occupied, the difficulties the troops had encountered were fully seen, and much praise was accorded Ricketts's division for so successful an assault. Dead and wounded Confederates lay around everywhere, many yet lying where they had fought, while the buildings in the Gap and vicinity were full of the wounded and dying, abandoned to their fate.

The 88th does not claim a very active part in the battle of South Mountain ; but it was in close proximity to the field in the performance of its duty, and if not called upon it was through no fault of the regiment. However, what the boys lost here in experience was more than made up a day or two later at Antietam Creek.

On Monday, September 15, the brigade joined in the pursuit of the enemy, passing through the loyal village of Boonsborough, a mile or two west of the mountain, where the grateful and patriotic people received our soldiers as deliverers, showing by a free display of the stars and stripes and in other unmistakable ways how happy they were to see the blue-coats again. In the distance, over the trees, the smoke of the batteries which had overtaken the enemy was visible, and the rumble and roar of the cannon echoed along the mountain, causing the blood to beat faster in the veins of the soldiers in that hurrying column, as they pressed forward to the position held by the enemy, and perhaps somewhat nervously speculated upon their chances of filling a soldier's grave in the coming battle. When Keedysville was reached a halt was made, the men scatter-

ing along the roadside, resting ; while lying here a great commotion was noticed down the rear of the column, the men throwing
up their caps and cheering with a spirit which indicated that some
distinguished person was approaching. Soon a brilliant cavalcade
came trotting along,—the commander-in-chief and his numerous
escort,—and as the men recognized the general they all rose with
the most frantic demonstrations of delight, shouting " McClellan,
McClellan is coming ! hurrah for McClellan !" until they appeared
more like a crowd of boys than the staid and weary soldiers of a
few minutes before, and this noisy reception continued until the
general passed by.

Whatever may have been the merits of General McClellan as a
successful commander, there can be no question of the confidence
that the soldiers reposed in him, which found expression in the most
enthusiastic receptions whenever he rode along the lines. Probably much of this feeling could be traced to an intense desire to
have some one capable of successfully leading them against the
rebels, the failures of Pope and McDowell's disastrous campaign in
Virginia having greatly discouraged the soldiers, who, confident in
their own power, felt that there was gross mismanagement somewhere, or they would never have been defeated in that humiliating
movement ; and the presence of McClellan had a perceptible effect
in restoring that confidence so essential to success in an army of
thinking soldiers.

" Fighting Joe Hooker," as he was familiarly called (another general who occupied a big place in the soldiers' hearts), commanded the
corps, General Ricketts led the division, and Colonel Christian, of
the 26th New York, temporarily had charge of the brigade. The
88th had about 350 men present, the other regiments of the brigade
being probably a little stronger. The division rested near the creek
on the night of the 15th, and on the following afternoon advanced
to feel for the enemy on the other side.

CHAPTER XII.

ANTIETAM: SEPTEMBER 16 TO 18, 1862.

ANTIETAM CREEK was crossed on the afternoon of September 16 (Tuesday); then the brigades, breaking into column, ready to form line of battle, with skirmishers well to the front and closely supported by the artillery, moved slowly forward to find the enemy. Very soon the sharp crack of the rifles indicated that the Johnnies were on hand; then the artillery, galloping up, went into battery, shelling the woods to develop the enemy's position. The Southern troops were steadily pressed back until dusk, when our advance reached their line of battle, their cannon opening a lively fire, to which the Union cannoneers very promptly responded. The brigade was massed directly in the rear of our cannon and received the full benefit of the enemy's fire, shell bursting all around; but the men of the command behaved with admirable coolness, no flinching being anywhere noticed, though the fragments from the enemy's projectiles were cutting the air and sward in every direction.

The pall of night had fallen over the scene, hiding friend and foe, but the artillerymen on both sides did not appear to be satisfied and still kept industriously at work. Every time a piece was discharged the flash of the gun illuminated the surroundings, producing an effect similar to that of sheet-lightning; and when the other fellows sent their howling compliments back, the flash from their exploding shell fitfully lit up the ranks, and the broken particles went buzzing around in search of victims.

Presently the cannonading ceased and the brigade moved up to take position for the morning's work. The night was exceedingly dark, but all went well until the woods were reached, when the darkness became so impenetrable that it was impossible to know where to go, the men being compelled to clutch one another by the clothing or bayonet scabbard to keep together. Groping around in the

gloom and in the utmost silence, the line was advanced, expecting
every moment to get a volley from the enemy; but the position was
reached at last, very much to the relief of the soldiers, who did not
relish this stumbling around through the timber in the dark.   Then
the supperless men lay on the ground to rest until morning, though
the vigilant pickets occasionally disturbed their uneasy slumbers by
a scattering volley, mayhap to let us know that they were attending to business.   What each individual soldier's thoughts were this
eventful night, on the eve of battle, will never be known ; but there
was no trifling or jesting, a deeply solemn feeling entering the soul
of every man as he thought of the chances for entering eternity on
the morrow.

At the first blush of dawn on the 17th the order to fall in was
quickly passed along the lines, and simultaneously the battle opened
beyond the woods, a couple of hundred yards to the front.   There
was no time for breakfast or to refill canteens, not even opportunity to brush the dirt from the soiled uniforms ; but forming at once
in column of division, with the other regiments of the brigade on
the flanks, the battalion moved forward to the place assigned it.

If the brigade had been taken into Bull Run like a mob, it was
evident that that error was not to be repeated here ; but to the
anxious men in the ranks it seemed that an unnecessary amount of
drilling was performed.   The stentorian voice of Major Gile was
heard above the tumult of battle, giving the commands in quick
succession : " Forward, guide centre," then " By the right flank,"
followed by " Forward" again, the shells from the enemy's cannon
meanwhile shrieking and flying all around, striking the ground in a
wicked manner and throwing up the dirt and dust in great clouds as
high as the trees.   The hideous noise made by these projectiles as
they screamed through the air was indescribable ; it appeared to the
blue masses in that advancing host as if all the devils infernal had
been incarnated and assembled on this horrible field, with power to
make the most terrible noises that were ever heard.   At any rate, the
appalling sound caused by these missiles was enough to terrify the
heart of the bravest and cause the blood to chill in one's veins ; and
as the enemy had good range, the shells flew and fell and burst all
over the field, as some of the boys had it, in a very reckless manner.

As the shells, striking the ground, ricocheted or exploded as they struck, the hot fragments flew around in every direction, or when a fuse shell burst overhead the impinging pieces carried destruction and havoc in the ranks underneath. Many of these projectiles exploded with fatal effect, killing and wounding a number of our men before they had an opportunity to fire a shot; but the ranks closed up, not a man wavering or leaving his place without orders, and the brigade moved quietly forward, all the time subject to this horrible tempest of iron, the wounded limping painfully and slowly to the rear, but the survivors setting their faces resolutely towards the enemy. A growth of heavy timber known as the East Woods was soon reached and a brief halt ordered, the bullets meanwhile droning and zipping merrily around; but no very great damage was done, except by the artillery fire, which was still terribly effective.

About this time it was reported that the enemy was massing in our front, and as the front line was almost out of ammunition, it was decided to send us in, and Major Gile rang out, "Attention, 88th. On first division deploy column, march. Forward, guide centre. Halt. Commence firing," and the boys were in the fight. Five minutes before more than one man in that battalion would have been two hundred miles away from this unhealthy place, if wishing could have accomplished it; but now, excited by the maddening tumult of battle and encouraged by the acts and presence of comrades, all sense of personal fear fled, the surroundings making every man as brave as a Trojan, forgetful of all personal danger, and intent only upon inflicting all possible damage upon the enemy.

Directly in front and to the right of the regiment was an immense cornfield occupied by the enemy, to whom the men sent their leaden compliments as fast as they could load and fire, the graybacks doing the same favor in return. A burning barn was fiercely blazing a little to the left, while to the right heavy lines of the enemy were in sight, apparently bearing heavily on the regiments farther to the right. The Confederates in the immediate front of the regiment were mostly concealed, and it was extremely difficult to get a fair shot at them, but their fire told very severely on the ranks of the command, the men dropping like autumn leaves in a storm. During this tempest of missiles, while our regimental colors were unfurled well to

the front, a projectile from a Confederate gun came tearing and ripping through the trees, cutting off a large limb, which, falling upon
Company I, killed and disabled several men.

Though the men were in the best of spirits and felt competent to
hold the line, yet our casualties were exceedingly heavy in killed
and wounded, among the latter, Major Gile, Captain Carmack, and
Lieutenants Steeples, Wingate, Wamsley, and Quimby.   More than
one-fourth of the troops that went into action were disabled, but
the remnant stood by the colors, loading and firing as if it were
an every-day occurrence.   There appeared to be no especial commands given, every man using his own judgment and putting his
shots where they would do the most good.   After holding this position for a considerable time, word was passed along the line that the
regiments on the flanks had expended all their ammunition and it
would be necessary for the entire line to withdraw, so that other
troops could take the position ; accordingly, the order was given
to fall back, though no enemy was advancing.   Very reluctantly the
soldiers obeyed, but many lingered to get an extra shot or two after
the organization had moved back through the woods.

Upon passing to the rear, numbers of our wounded were seen and
assisted to the improvised hospitals, many of them being horribly
mutilated, among whom was Lorenzo Wilson, of Company K, whose
leg had been so badly lacerated that it appeared to be hanging by
the skin only.   In reply to an inquiry, he quietly pointed to his
dangling leg and said, "Boys, I've got it."

The regiment was rallied and reformed in the rear, and, moving
to the right, lay in reserve, supporting batteries, while other troops,
taking our place in the front, continued the battle the rest of the
day ; but Ricketts's division had been so severely handled that its
aggressive power was seriously impaired.   The regiment lay in this
position until nightfall, listening to the roar and rattle of the contest in front as the lines charged and countercharged ; sometimes
the noise would gradually recede as the Federals drove the Confederates, the hearty and manly Union huzzas rising above the din ;
but again the firing would draw alarmingly near, and the shrill rebel
yell of "Ki yi, ki yi yi" rose sharp and clear as our men were
forced back.

When the mantle of night covered this sanguinary field the firing ceased, and all was still except the pitiful cries and moans from thousands of wounded and dying men, who, writhing in dirt and blood, tortured by a consuming feverish thirst, broke the solemn stillness of the night by their plaintive cries and agonizing shrieks for aid, though the ambulance corps and medical department assiduously gleaned the fields for the ghastly harvest, tenderly caring for all that could be found.

The dull gray light of Thursday morning broke upon the exhausted armies as they lay in line of battle, each waiting for the other to take the initiative, but no forward movement was made. In the light of subsequent events it is almost certain that if the Union army had advanced on the 18th the Confederates would have been taken at great disadvantage and very likely utterly defeated, as the information afterwards gleaned from the inhabitants within their lines represented them as badly demoralized, with the roads lined with graybacks actively "dusting" towards Old Virginia again, every straggler intent only on getting out of the way of the Yanks. But no aggressive move was made, the least indication of an advance being promptly met by a sharp fire from the enemy's skirmishers, his main body meanwhile preparing for a general retreat the coming night.

To add to the discomfort, intermittent showers descended, drenching the men, who had no opportunity of erecting the little shelter tents as a partial protection from the elements. The roll was now called and the loss noted, the result indicating that there were present in line,—

Commissioned officers 7
Non-commissioned officers 38
Privates 164
                                                          ____
        Total 209

The aggregate present, including sick, details, musicians, etc., numbered 272; the aggregate present at the last report before the fight was 415, leaving a clear loss of 143; but many of these were sick and some had temporarily joined the grand army of coffee-coolers, the actual loss in the engagement being about eighteen killed and sixty wounded.

The report for September 26 aggregated 316 present, showing that the irrepressible stragglers had regained enough confidence to hunt their rations if they had no stomach to hunt the enemy, and that many worthy soldiers who had been compelled to fall out by sickness and exhaustion had so far recovered as to be able to take their places again in the ranks.

On the 18th rations were issued, the first for several days, including some green coffee, which the men roasted in their tins, crushing the berries as best they could. One group of grinders had improvised a cracker-box and a huge elongated shell for duty as a coffee-mill, and were doing a brisk business in ground coffee, when a red-edged artilleryman passing by examined the shell, and informed the astonished grinders that it was primed with a perfect percussion-cap, which needed but a slight blow to explode it. Business in that shop was suspended without further ceremony.

Details were made from the companies to bury those who had been killed in line. A shallow grave was dug and the soldier, wrapped in his blood-soaked blanket, carefully deposited therein, a piece of cracker-box or some other frail marker serving as a headboard. The following is a fair sample of many that marked these graves:

JESSE TYSON.
Co. I. 88. Regt. Penna. Vols.
Killed Sept. 17. 1862.
A brave soldier and a kind comrade.
Rest in peace.

The command waited for orders until the morning of the 19th, when it was found that the Johnnies had skipped ; then a hot pursuit began, with the result that their rear-guard was overtaken ; but they skedaddled at once without waiting for a further introduction, leaving their rations of flour and meat half cooked by the fires. The brigade encamped in the woods which they had vacated, and we were not long in discovering that our chivalrous foes had left behind them something more than their uncooked rations, in the shape of an industrious and affectionate little insect, scientifically known as the *Pediculus vestimenti;* but the boys had a much shorter name for them, though they were mostly called graybacks. During the next few days, while in this place, the men did not have much leisure time, their spare moments being occupied in renewing the battle with this diminutive enemy all along the line*ing.*

On September 23 the following detail was made for drivers and attendants to the division ambulance corps: Sergeant R. B. Clevenger, Privates Isaac Eyrich, James Doyle, John Nice, Frank Winn, Samuel Fusman, John Reed, John Myers, Daniel Beidler, Albert Reppert, and Richard W. Seidel, for temporary service.

OFFICIAL REPORT OF THE 88TH REGIMENT PENNSYLVANIA VOLUNTEERS.

September 19, 1862.

I have the honor to report that, in obedience to orders detailing the regiment as wagon guard on the 14th, we marched through Frederick and halted about two miles west of it near dark, when we received orders to join the brigade. We started on the march, passing through Middletown, and encamped on South Mountain late at night until daylight next morning (15th), when we continued our march in search of the brigade, which we reached about 10 A.M. About noon we started, passing through Boonsborough, and encamped about half a mile outside Keedysville. Late on the 16th moved forward on the left of the 90th, and laid on our arms all night in a woods. Shortly after daylight our division advanced in line of battle, our brigade supporting General Hartsuff, the 90th on our right and 94th on our left, to the end of a woods, where we relieved the 83d, and commenced firing, continuing for about two hours, when we were ordered to fall back, fill our cartridge-boxes, and draw rations. During the engagement, Maj. George W. Gile was badly wounded in the leg, and the command devolved upon Capt. Myers. Loss: killed, 10; wounded, 62; missing, 5; total, 77.

H. R. MYERS,
Capt. Commanding.

A SCATTERING VOLLEY AT ANTIETAM.

Antietam was the bloodiest one-day's fight of the war, and deserves at least a brief notice before we go marching on. More men were killed and wounded on September 17 than even in Grant's sanguinary struggles in the Wilderness on any one day. The Union loss by army corps was,—

1st Corps	2,590
2d Corps	5,138
4th Corps	9
5th Corps	109
6th Corps	439
9th Corps	2,349
12th Corps	1,746
Cavalry Corps	30
Total	12,410

The heaviest loss by regiments was,—

15th Massachusetts, 2d Corps	318
28th Pennsylvania, 12th Corps	266
9th New York, 9th Corps	235
12th Massachusetts, 1st Corps	224

It is extremely difficult to get a correct statement of the Confederate loss, but a careful examination of regimental, brigade, and division reports shows a loss of killed, wounded, and missing amounting to 13,200 from September 13 to 20; the returns being very imperfect, however, it is probable that the casualties were upward of 15,000. The Confederate regiments suffering most were,—

3d North Carolina	253
13th Georgia	217
48th North Carolina	217
13th North Carolina	190
14th North Carolina	213

The "tar-heels," as usual, were pushed to the front.

A word about the strength of the combating armies. McClellan gives his force as follows:

1st Corps	14,856
2d Corps	18,813
5th Corps	12,930
6th Corps	12,300
9th Corps	13,819
12th Corps	10,126
Cavalry Corps	4,320
Total	87,164

He omits Cochrane's brigade of the 4th Corps, which was not seriously engaged, and might as well have left out the 5th and 6th Corps also, as only two regiments of the 5th Corps, one brigade of the 6th Corps, and one regiment of the cavalry division were actively engaged, the exceptions noted sustaining nearly all the loss in those corps. The fact is that Little Mac fought about 60,000 of his men, holding the others in reserve at a time when their "influence" might have fully, finally, and forever settled the "hash" of Lee's army and with it the fate of the Confederacy. It was a tremendous game with a magnificent stake, but the Little Napoleon was afraid of his opponent's hand.

As an important opinion bearing on this subject, we quote the following extract from the admirable "History of the 106th Pennsylvania Volunteers," written by Colonel Joseph R. C. Ward, of Philadelphia :

McClellan, in his report, put his force at 87,164. Of these the 5th and 6th Corps and the Cavalry Division, all numbering 29,550, were not engaged; this would leave but 57,614 of our troops actually present for duty. From this there must be considerable reduction to arrive at those actually engaged, for Hooker, whose corps is reported as having 14,856, says he took into action but 9000; and Williams, who succeeded to the command of Mansfield's corps, which is reported as having 10,126 men, says his corps numbered but 7000.

Taking this same ratio of reduction throughout the whole army, which is but fair, as the reports show all those marked *present for duty*, and include all noncombatants, such as musicians, teamsters, hospital and ambulance details, besides the guards that were left behind to guard the knapsacks and regimental property, and we would have the following :

1st Corps	report 14,856 present for duty, but took into action only about 9,000 men.				
2d "	"	18,813	"	"	"	11,530 "
5th "	"	12,930	"	"	"	. . . "
6th "	"	12,300	"	"	"	. . . "
9th "	"	13,814	"	"	"	9,000 "
12th "	"	10,126	"	"	"	7,000 "
4th and Cavalry "	4,320	"	"	"	. . . "
	87,159				36,500

To this may be added that portion of the 6th Corps that moved into position in the afternoon, but was not actively engaged, and we will put down our number at 40,000, and we have both armies about equal in point of numbers, for Lee says "the battle was fought by less than 40,000." Now, his line was formed as a semicircle, curved outward, and as McClellan attacked his line at only one place at a time, Lee was enabled to move his forces from left to right, and some of the same troops that fought in the morning on his left were also engaged in the afternoon on his right, or acted as support to those engaged.

The Confederate estimates of their fighting force are, as usual, ridiculously small. Lee states, " This great battle was fought by less than 40,000 on our side." The irascible D. H. Hill says, " The battle was fought with less than 30,000 men. Had all our stragglers been up, McClellan's army would have been completely annihilated." General McLaws is one of the few Confederates who give intelligent figures in their reports. His division consisted of sixteen regiments and four batteries, numbering on September 14 (Manly's battery excluded) 4087 men, and lost in the subsequent actions (including Manly's), in killed, wounded, and missing, 2081. But if these figures are incorrect, McClellan's estimates, on the other hand, savor highly of bombast. He speaks of " nearly 200,000 men and 500 pieces of artillery engaged." " The enemy was undoubtedly greatly superior in number." And his detailed account of Lee's army, in which he states that it aggregated 97,445 men of all arms, shows that he constantly overrated Lee's strength, while General Pope, on the contrary, erred in the opposite direction. Pope fought blindly but manfully, and only learned the skill and strength of his adversary by bitter experience, but McClellan was always taking counsel of his fears. Pope never had even a fair chance for victory, while McClellan time and again had the prize within reach of his timid hand. All this in the light of subsequent information : we are all skilful strategists now.

A careful comparison of corps, division, brigade, and regimental reports indicates Lee's strength to have been as follows :

Longstreet	19,000
Jackson	15,000
Seventy-four batteries of artillery	7,000
Cavalry	3,000
Total	44,000

There were 185 regiments of infantry engaged, which, at 200 men to the regiment, would amount to 37,000 men. Many of the regiments went into the fight several hundred strong, as the losses prove ;

LIEUTENANT ROBERT HERRON.

CORPORAL JOHN T. WILLIAMS.

CAPTAIN JOHN J. BEISTERLING.
(Killed at Second Bull Run.)

THOMAS ALBRIGHT.

JAMES HAGUE.

others were the merest skeletons, their stragglers swarming over the country. The Union divisions that participated in the battle were almost cut to pieces, but there were many commands that had not fired a gun, and if McClellan had possessed the military intuition to gauge the condition of his opponent, he could have checkmated him in one move,—forward.

The fact is, that the Confederate army was so exhausted and broken as to be in no condition to make serious resistance on the 18th. Longstreet says on the morning of the 18th, "Our ranks were too much thinned to warrant a renewal of the conflict." A vivid picture of the demoralization in the enemy's lines on the afternoon of the 17th is given in General Garnett's words, "I found troops scattered in squads, so that it was impossible to distinguish men of different commands. I gathered as many men as I could get to follow me from among the dispersed force (which did not amount to a large number), and joined Drayton's command." General Evans reports, "About two P.M. I was ordered to rally the troops then flocking to the town. After considerable exertion, with the assistance of my entire staff, I collected about 250." General Rodes had hard work to keep his men up to their work. He says, "I found that with the exception of a few men, not more than forty in all, the brigade had completely disappeared." Colonel Bennett, commanding Anderson's brigade, speaks in the same vein: "Masses of Confederate troops in great confusion were seen; portions of Anderson's division broke beyond power of rallying after five minutes' stay." General D. H. Hill ventilates his feelings over a wider field: "The division lost 3000 out of less than 9000 engaged at Seven Pines; 4000 out of 10,000 in the battles around Richmond; but now the loss was 3241 in two battles out of less than 5000 engaged." The Confederate losses were simply awful, the men being forced to fight by their officers so long as there were any men or any fight left. The 7th South Carolina lost 140 out of 268; the 16th Mississippi, 144 out of 228; the 1st Texas, 186 out of 226; and so it goes, more or less severe, all down the ghastly list, proving that there were others deserving the name of butcher more than Grant.

It goes without saying that the whole of the defeated army was not demoralized, that the thin line that braved the Union legions would have faced the music to the end of the ball ; but what successful resistance could that ragged line have made against the 25,000 men of the 5th and 6th Corps, backed by the other corps of the Union army, if a determined advance had been made on the 18th? If we had only known then what we know now of Lee's peril ! He says of his army, '' Its efficiency is greatly paralyzed by the numerous stragglers, which evil has increased instead of diminished. A great many men belonging to this army never entered Maryland, many returned after getting there, while others who crossed the river kept aloof. On the morning after the battle of the 17th, General Evans, holding the front position, had but 120 of his brigade present, and the next brigade, Garnett's, consisted of but 100 men. The brigades of Lawton and Armistead, at Shepherdstown ford, together contained but 600 men. This is a woful condition of affairs.''

No one could with truth accuse Lee of being afraid to fight. From June 26 to September 19 he had lost in battle over 50,000 of his choicest troops, and was still facing McClellan with a chip on his shoulder, ready for a fight.

The gist of the matter is that the war could be ended only by the hardest kind of fighting, that war means blood and death and desolation, and that when the big captain took the helm he sailed over seas of blood to victory and peace. There was no other way out. The historian has had his whack at McClellan and Antietam, and the reader can have his own opinion still ; can accept the writer's views or reject them. Readers are often wrong, especially in matters pertaining to McClellan's campaigns.

CHAPTER XIII.

ANTIETAM TO FREDERICKSBURG: SEPTEMBER 19 TO DECEMBER 11, 1862.

AFTER quietly settling down in camp, many of the soldiers embraced the opportunity of visiting the battle-field and inspecting the ground over which they had fought. All over the field the bodies of the slain were scattered, friend and foe; the location of the opposing lines and the places of the many fierce charges could readily be recognized by the heaps of dead from either side. Along the pike, where the Confederates made a desperate stand, their killed lay one on top of another, while in the woods back of the Dunker Church, where the Union soldiers swept in a grand charge, the ground was strewn with the dead Federals. The bodies were swollen to an unnatural size and emitted a horrible smell, the flesh turning to a purplish black, some of them being so badly decomposed that it was impossible to move them, and they were buried where they fell. Details of Union pioneers did this work, interring the Union dead first. The bodies were wrapped in their gory blankets and deposited in long, shallow trenches, sometimes a dozen in one hole.

The dead were found in all imaginable positions and often horribly mangled. One Confederate had been killed while climbing over a fence, his body remaining in such a position that it might readily have been taken for that of a live man; another was struck while tearing a cartridge, the charge still remaining between his stiffened fingers; the head of another was taken off by a cannon-ball; while a manly-looking Union soldier apparently had no wound anywhere, but closer inspection showed that a ball had entered one ear, coming out of the other. It was simply horrible to look on these heaps and windrows of festering bodies that once contained the spirits of the best soldiers of the two armies. The cornfield near which the 88th stood was a veritable field of blood, being almost covered with gore, shreds of hair, bones, and brains, while broken guns, knapsacks, haversacks, canteens, and the usual *débris* of a battle-field were scattered in profusion everywhere. The horses also had suffered, their bloated carcasses lying all over the field, but especially where the batteries had been in action ; but the men soon sickened at these repulsive sights, few going more than once over the field.

In the mean time the camp in the woods was cleaned ; but on September 29 the regiment removed to the fields near by, about a quarter of a mile from the Potomac, where the men made themselves comfortable. An excellent spring of water was discovered in the sand on the river-bank, and the regular rations of sow-belly, salt horse, musty crackers alive with worms, and occasionally fresh meat, rice, and beans, with the usual allowance of sugar and coffee of very good quality, were issued. The men were badly off for clothing and shoes, many being in rags and almost barefoot, and consequently suffering much these cool October nights.

On October 18, Lewis Hill, one of the boy soldiers of Company G, died in camp. He had been sick for some time, and when he realized that his end was near, the great desire of his boyish heart was to see his mother before he died. Mrs. Hill was sent for and came with all possible despatch, but the means of conveyance were limited, and even a mother's piteous appeals to see her dying boy did not quicken the journey much. She arrived on the 20th, but he had been buried the day before, his comrades, with the drum-corps of the 26th New York, following his body to the grave, and there they took the mother to show her where her boy lay. Her heart was nearly broken with grief, but the men consoled her as best they could, and, exhuming the body of the dead soldier, they put it in a rough box and the sorrowful mother took her precious clay home for final burial. Mrs. Hill subsequently returned to the regiment and faithfully nursed the sick and wounded men until the end of the war.

In the absence of Captain Myers, who resigned November 1, Captain Griffith took command of the regiment, all the field-officers being absent sick or wounded.

Late in October overcoats and other much-needed clothing were issued to the shivering soldiers, who were poorly clad to endure the chilling night winds of the season. On October 3 the division was reviewed by President Lincoln, attended by General McClellan and a small army of lesser lights, the tall form of the President being conspicuous as he gracefully rode along the lines, critically inspecting every soldier in the command. The appearance of the President was the signal for a hearty outburst of enthusiasm from the thousands standing at arms, and amid the thunder of artillery and music of the bands as they rang out "Hail to the Chief," the inspection and review ended and were pronounced a success.

On the 27th of October the expected marching orders came, and, striking tents, the boys bid farewell to this pleasant section of "My Maryland" and faced Dixieward, the drum corps leading off with "Carry me back to Old Virginny." The regiment had been strengthened by the return of some of its members who had been sick or wounded, and reported 331 present; but of these, thirty-one were sick and twenty-one on detailed duty, leaving less than 300 in line for action. On the 29th the brigade passed through Crampton's Gap and Burkettsville, encamping in the woods near Berlin, where it remained until the 30th, when Colonel McLean again led the regiment into Virginia, passing across the Potomac and through the little town of Lovettsville, and encamping for the night near the hamlet of Milton. Before crossing the Potomac all the sick were put aboard the cars and sent to Washington hospitals, in order that the army might not be encumbered when the time of battle arrived.

On the 31st of October, Colonel McLean mustered the brigade, and the next day the march was resumed to Waterford, resting there until the 4th of November, when the road was again taken, the command bivouacking beyond Broomfield. On the 5th only about five miles were made, but on the 7th the division passed through Warrenton, "tenting on the old camp ground," the identical spot encamped on the preceding August.

On November 10 the brigade was reviewed by General McClellan, and on the 12th proceeded to Bealeton, remaining there several days. General Gibbon now assumed command of the division and General Nelson Taylor of the brigade, which consisted of the 83d and 97th

New York, 13th Massachusetts, 11th and 88th Pennsylvania Regiments. While here Colonel McLean was compelled to resign his commission on account of sickness, the command of the regiment falling again upon Captain Griffith. A number of promotions were now made to fill vacancies in the field, Major Gile succeeding to the colonelcy, Captain Louis Wagner to lieutenant-colonel, and Captain Griffith to major; but the first two officers being absent, wounded, Major Griffith was in command.

On November 18 and 19 the brigade picketed the Rappahannock, and after destroying the railroad bridge, passed through Morrisville, encamping near White Oak Church on the 23d. , The weather now set in cold and stormy, making it extremely unpleasant for the soldiers, who were greatly exposed, and presaging evil to the further prosecution of the campaign, which rumor said was to be vigorously continued until the Confederate army was finally defeated.

On November 9, George W. Jacoby was detailed temporarily to act as attendant at the Warrenton Hospital, and on November 12, Surgeon Charles J. Nordquist was appointed chief medical officer of the division, and Reuben Sanders, John Nugent, and John Shonour were detailed on the 24th as division teamsters.

On November 24, Surgeon B. F. Hough, of the 97th New York, was appointed chief medical officer of the brigade. On December 1, Lieutenant Schell was detailed to proceed to Convalescent Camp and bring all convalescents, stragglers, and recruits to the regiment. On December 5, Sergeant Beath was detached for temporary duty in the quartermaster's office, and on the 7th, John Thomas, Albert Wise, and Henry Haywood were also temporarily detailed for duty at brigade head-quarters.

CHAPTER XIV.

FREDERICKSBURG TO CHANCELLORSVILLE: DECEMBER 12, 1862, TO MAY 7, 1863.

THE expected marching orders were issued on December 7, on which day the brigade broke camp and marched a mile or two towards Fredericksburg; but the movement was countermanded until the 11th, when the brigade went to the river-bank, but again returned to camp. On the 12th the great movement was begun in earnest, the division marching to the river with flying colors, hopeful of success in the forthcoming battle. The Union artillery in position on the north bank of the river maintained a heavy fire against the opposite shore during the attempt of the pioneers to lay the pontoons, but the enemy's sharp-shooters posted in the houses and cellars of the town effectually prevented the placing of the pontoons, until volunteers, rowing across the river, drove the Confederates off, when the bridge was finished. Lieutenant-Colonel Henry Baxter, of the 7th Michigan, was the leader of the volunteers who poled across the river, and to his conspicuous bravery on this occasion Baxter's brigade probably owes the commander who afterwards so creditably led it to the end of the war.

At Franklin's crossing, below the city, but slight resistance was encountered, the hills being some distance from the river and offering no very desirable positions for the Confederate cannon to successfully resist the laying of the bridges. The crossing was effected during the afternoon of December 12, after which, massing on the plain, the soldiers rested for the night; but the minds of the men were occupied with anxious thoughts of the coming contest with the concealed forces in the woods covering the heights in front. The chances of a successful result were earnestly discussed, but no comforting conclusion was reached when the difficulties of a direct attack against the strong position held by the enemy were considered, though every soldier resolved to do his whole duty to his flag and country. The weather had been wintry and the night was cold and cheerless; a bleak wind sweeping over the plain chilled the men to the bone, no fires being allowed for fear of drawing a hotter fire from the cannon of the inhospitable Southerners on the hills, and all that long, weary winter night, to many the last of this life, the men shivered and suffered in the darkness.

The morning of December 13 dawned quietly upon the opposing armies crouching like wild beasts ready to spring upon one another, but the bank of fog which hung over the scene like a cloud rendered any movement uncertain, and nothing could be done until this curtain was raised to reveal the stage on which this horrible drama of war was to be performed. Finally the fog lifted and the advance began about 9.30 A.M., the 13th Massachusetts skirmishers in the van and popping away briskly at the Confederate skirmishers, driving them back without ceremony all along the front. Taylor's brigade followed closely, supported by Lyle, with Root in reserve, these brigades composing Gibbon's division. The Union cannon in the rear opening a furious fire, the Confederate artillery quickly returned the compliment, giving the division the benefit of their experience as artillerists, and, judging from the accuracy of their aim, they were veterans at the business. The Confederate advance was slowly forced back over the stage road, but when near the railroad it halted and made a determined resistance, having batteries in position supported by infantry, whose fire covered every foot of ground over which Gibbon's division was advancing. Here Taylor halted, sending the 88th forward to a rise of ground to silence a battery which was particularly annoying to the division. Upon reaching the position the battalion opened a galling fusillade on the butternut gunners, who replied with canister, knocking over many of the men and sweeping part of the regiment back in some confusion to a ditch, where the men were rallied by the personal example of Major Griffith, Captains Harkisheimer and Shalters, Adjutant Foust, Lieu-tenants Napier, Schell, Rhoads, and other officers of the regiment.

About one o'clock a spirited charge was made upon the works along the railroad, some of the regiments, especially the 107th Pennsylvania and 16th Maine, capturing many Johnnies; but the

Confederate line was too strong for Gibbon to make any impression on, and the entire line was forced back over the railroad, after sustaining much loss, the regiment losing Acting Adjutant Kartscher and Lieutenant Fulton killed, Captain Harkisheimer badly injured in the groin (he had his haversack cut in two and the hilt of his sword hit by bullets), Captain Shalters and Lieutenant Napier wounded, and many non commissioned officers and privates killed and wounded. The 88th, together with the 97th New York, held the advance after most of the other regiments had fallen back and until ordered to take a position near the stage road in the rear. Here the men lay in the freezing mud all that dismal night, dreading the morning, while the ambulance corps was busy bringing the helpless wounded from the front and taking them to the hospitals in the rear.

The division remained here during the 14th (Sunday), and early Monday morning was called to arms, standing in this expectant position all day. On Monday night the regiment was sent on the skirmish line, and remained among the dead men in that gruesome place until three o'clock Tuesday morning, when, the army having recrossed the river, the regiment was ordered to fall back as quickly as possible. The boys, understanding the danger of the situation, lost no time in reaching the river, and arrived none too soon, as the pontoons were being taken up, the engineers supposing that all the troops were across. They had to run their boats back to take the men over.

So ended another disastrous battle, a sad chapter in the history of the regiment and a day that carried great sorrow to many loved ones whose kinsfolk were killed in this contest. Among those killed in the regiment were Lieutenants Kartscher and Fulton, who had not yet received their commissions, these documents arriving after the battle to find them beyond the influence of earthly honors. Private Nathan White, of Company I, was one of the bravest soldiers in the regiment; as the command was being withdrawn the enemy opened fire with canister, when White, turning towards their guns, facetiously called to them to "cease firing and come to a shoulder;" but at this moment a shot entered his head and he fell dead without a groan.

The following report was made by Major Griffith:

COL. S. H. LEONARD, Command'g 3d Brigade:

In accordance with orders, I herewith send a statement of the part taken by my command in the recent battle of Fredericksburg, Va.

Crossed the Rappahannock River with the rest of the brigade, being in position near the Bowling Green road, 13th Mass. being in the road as skirmishers; remained in the position until 9.30 A.M. of the 13th. The brigade was advanced into the field fronting the enemy, driving in their pickets and supporting our skirmishers. The men were ordered to lie down in the face of a heavy artillery fire. General Taylor soon ordered an advance on the rebel battery; amid a heavy shower of grape and canister we reached the brow of the hill; the centre of the right being swept off, the men commenced falling back, but the officers succeeded in rallying them in a trench, when we again took position on right of brigade, lying down. At two P.M. another charge was made, and silenced a rebel battery that was shelling us at railroad crossing.

The 2d Brigade ordered up to our support, I took position on their right. I retired with the 1st Brigade, marching out in quick time and in good order, having lost seven killed, thirty-four wounded, and one missing out of a total of only 183 officers and men when we advanced, and being under fire five hours.

Having no orders to fall back with our brigade, the 3d, I sustained my position on the right of the line, using all my ammunition, sixty rounds per man, and still retained the position, expecting to obtain support.

The officers and men behaved with great gallantry, and would particularly mention my Adjt. B. F. Foust and Lieut. Geo. B. Rhoads, command'g Co. B, whose good conduct greatly encouraged the men. Of the non-com. officers, Sergts. Geo. H. Fulton, Wm. H. Forbes, and Jacob Ninesteel were conspicuous and will be recommended for promotion.

D. A. GRIFFITH,

Maj. comdg. 88 Pa. Vols.

On December 16, 1862, the regiment returned to the old camp, marching through the mire in a heavy rain, weary, dispirited, and disappointed, though determined to make the best of the cheerless situation; but every soldier realized that the prospect was very gloomy. On the 19th the camp was removed to about four miles from Potomac Creek, and the men soon erected comfortable shelters from the nipping winter weather.

New Year's Day, 1863, dawned clear and crisp, finding the regiment encamped near Fletcher's Chapel, doing picket and camp duty and exercising at battalion drill in the mud as often as the powers that be thought expedient. On January 12, General John C. Robinson, having been assigned to the command of the division, reviewed the brigade, the regiment being commanded by Captain J. Parker Martin.

On January 12, Corporal Charles M. Clark was detached for special duty in the quartermaster's department; and on the 15th an additional detail, consisting of Matthias Pinyard, Peter Read, J. L. Wentzel, Alfred Dautrich, Jacob Fabian, and Harrison Eddinger, was made for the same duty.

Captain Wagner was now in command of the battalion, and in pursuance of orders, on January 18 he sent Dr. Shoemaker, A. P. Carter, and Albert Booz to Aquia Creek with the sick and disabled men of the command. On the 19th of January, Peter Read returned to the regiment from detached duty, and Levi Miller was detailed as teamster in the division ammunition train, until further orders.

As a sample of camp life the following order is given :

HEAD-QUARTERS, 2D DIV. 1ST A. C., Jany. 24, 1863.

GENERAL ORDER No. 11.

The regular routine of duties will at once be returned to. The signals for service will, until further orders, be sounded as follows :

, Reveille at daylight. Police call immediately after reveille. Breakfast at 7 A.M. Surgeon's call at 7.30 A.M. Guard mounting at 8 A.M. Drill (company or skirmish) at 9 A.M. Recall at 10.30 A.M. Dinner at 12 M. Drill (battalion or brigade) at 1 30 P.M. Recall at 3 P.M. First call for parade half-hour before sunset. Tattoo at 8 P.M. Taps at 8.20 P.M.

There will be dress parade every evening, regimental inspection every Sunday morning, and brigade inspection every Thursday morning at 8 o'clock.

By order

GENL ROBINSON, *Commanding.*

Up to this date the weather had been moderate,—not much snow and very little ice, but plenty of rain, making it soft and muddy underfoot. From the 15th to the 20th of January it was clear, with the wind just keen enough to remind one that it was winter time.

General Burnside was eagerly looking for an opportunity to deal the enemy a crushing blow and so restore the confidence of the army, which had been badly shaken by the unfortunate and deplorable battle at Fredericksburg. He had intended a movement on the lower Rappahannock about the last of December, but the President had peremptorily forbidden it, so he conceived a plan to cross the upper Rappahannock and force Lee to battle away from his formidable intrenchments. This movement, subsequently termed the mud march, was begun on the 19th of January, the weather being favorable to military movements, and everything indicated a successful campaign.

On the 20th the regiment struck tents and marched several miles towards the Rappahannock, then halted and bivouacked for the night, resuming the march at eight o'clock on the morning of the 21st ; but the weather now changed, a drenching cold rain falling in torrents, turning the ground first to the consistency of putty and finally to a sea of liquid mud. The troops struggled on in the sticky stuff; but soon the wagons were stalled, then the artillery stuck, and finally the men got mired, until it was not a question of getting to the enemy, but of returning to camp as speedily as possible. The rain continued all day and night, and when the order to countermarch was given the task of getting out of the mud was attended with almost insuperable difficulties. All the pontoons and artillery—in fact, every wheel—had to be bodily pulled from this slough of despond by the bedraggled soldiers, and the roads and fields were strewn with dead animals and wrecked wagons, frequently buried in the mire almost out of sight.

When the regiment reached the vicinity of Falmouth, the situation, at best, was discouraging ; the ground, or what had been firm ground, was now a sea of mud, and at every step the weary men sank to their ankles in the slime. No firewood ; an abundance of water everywhere, but none fit to use for coffee ; no dry ground on which to camp ; nothing but mud, mud on every hand. The men were in a pitiable plight, the attendant exposure filling the graves and hospitals more than would a battle. However, old soldiers can generally make themselves comfortable somehow ; so, after the arms were stacked in the Virginia mud, the men scattered in every direction searching for wood, water, pine boughs for bedding, etc., and

•

some of them finding a wagon-train, bribed the drivers for a night's lodging in the wagons.

During the night the wind shifted to the north, bringing a piercing cold blast which froze a stiff crust on top of the mud and also the dirt to the uniforms of the soldiers, so that in the morning they resembled a crowd of demoralized and forsaken graybacks rather than a brigade of honest Yanks; but the regiment eventually encamped near Fletcher's Chapel, and on the 24th the men were given some consolation by Paymaster Brua, in the shape of four months' pay.

The army now settled down for a rest and waited for something to turn up. Around head-quarters affairs were in a deplorable condition, General Burnside attributing, in a measure, the failure of his movements to the lack of co-operation and support on the part of some of his generals, who did not heartily concur in his plans of attacking the enemy, and he requested the dismissal of Generals Hooker, Brooks, Cochrane, and Newton, and that Generals Franklin, Ferrero, W. F. Smith, Sturgis, and others who had freely expressed themselves against his strategy be transferred to some other army. General Burnside did not charge that these subordinates had been derelict in the discharge of any duty, but that they simply lacked confidence in him as the chief of the army. The President, however, refused to relieve these officers, consequently General Burnside tendered his resignation, which was accepted, and General Hooker appointed his successor. It may be said here that the men had a high regard for Burnside, none doubting but that he had done his best; but the feeling was almost universal that he was not competent to command so large a body of troops as the Army of the Potomac.

"Fighting Joe" was favorably known, and at once proceeded to reorganize and discipline the entire army. Desertions were checked by issuing furloughs, the commissary was improved and better rations issued, each corps was designated by a peculiar badge, and many minor but important changes effected. So the remaining days of January and all of February and March passed, the army growing stronger and better every day; the drills and reviews showed a marked improvement in the bearing and appearance of the troops, and the men were quick to note the excellent spirit that had taken the place of the distrust and fear of the gloomiest period of the war.

General Hooker reviewed Robinson's division on the 2d of April, and on the 9th the 1st Corps passed in review before the President. In the mean time a number of changes had taken place in the regi-ment, which will be noted here.

About February 1, Captain Wagner was ordered to Georgetown for treatment of his wound, and Adjutant Foust, after being commissioned major, took command of the regiment. On February 3, Dr. John W. Rawlins was appointed chief surgeon, and on the 11th the morning report states that "Sergeant G. S. Nichols, having received commission as second lieutenant of Company G, returned said commission, refusing to recognize the promotion over the first sergeant, he being the second sergeant." On the same day Henry Reiff and William Ramich were detailed for duty in the quarter-master's department. Sergeant-Major Detre was commissioned adjutant, to date from December 4, 1862, an admirable selection, as he proved a most competent officer. Several sergeants also received commissions as lieutenants at the same time (February 24), among them being Sergeants Kram, Beath, Middleton, Houder, and Nunneville. On February 26, Surgeon Hayes was assigned to the division hospital and Dr. Shoemaker returned to the regiment. Neal Devine was detailed for duty in the bakery on March 4, 1863, and Daniel H. Clouser was ordered on extra duty with Brigade Quarter-master Jones. Dr. Rawlins was assigned to duty as acting chief medical officer of the brigade on March 10, and on the same day Robert Herron and Henry Raider returned from the hospital.

By a circular order from head-quarters Army of the Potomac, dated March 21, 1863, corps badges were given to each corps as follows: 1st Corps a sphere; 2d Corps a trefoil; 3d Corps a lozenge; 5th Corps a Maltese cross; 6th Corps a cross; 11th Corps a crescent; 12th Corps a star.

Lieutenant-Colonel Louis Wagner returned on March 19 and took command, remaining until May 14, when he was granted twenty days' leave of absence on account of disability. The consolidated morning report for April 1, 1863, shows the strength of the regi-ment, as follows:

Commissioned officers present 27
Non-commissioned officers present 74
Musicians present 13
Privates present 141

255
On detailed duty 23
Sick 19
In arrest 8

Total 305
Total present and absent 472

On this date Rest Parker was detailed as brigade teamster : it should be understood that all details for this kind of duty were for a short time only.

The commanding general having matured his plans for a grand movement against the Southern army, orders were issued to that effect, and the encampment broke up on April 28, the line of march being headed for the river below Fredericksburg. Upon reaching the vicinity of the crossing, on December 12, the column halted, and, throwing pontoons across, some of the troops marched over to the south bank, being received by a heavy artillery fire from the rebels, who as yet were in ignorance as to where Hooker intended to assault their lines.

The regiment, with the brigade, manœuvred in this vicinity during the 28th, 29th, and 30th, being mustered near the river on the 30th. Meanwhile, the rebs pitched their shell over in a most unfriendly manner and much to the discomfort of the men, whose time was fully occupied in answering to their names at the muster and dodging cannon-balls when they came too near. On the 1st of May the weather changed for the better, the sun shining bright and warm.

The strategy of the Union commander began now to fully develop. The 1st Corps was ordered up the river, where most of the army had already gone, and engaged the enemy back of Fredericksburg. The soldiers understood that Lee was now compelled to leave his intrench-ments and meet our army on equal terms, and the rank and file, always quick to detect an advantageous movement, were greatly elated at the turn affairs had taken, many believing that Lee had at last met his match and would suffer a defeat in the coming battle. Every-

7

thing appeared to be going along smoothly, and the troops were greatly inspirited, which feeling was intensified by a congratulatory order from General Hooker announcing that "The enemy must either ingloriously fly or come out from behind his defences and give us battle on our own ground, where certain destruction awaits him," and much more of the same sort; indeed, it has been asserted that the commanding general boasted that the "Almighty could not prevent him from obtaining a victory;" but these events indicate the truth of the proverb that "Man proposes, but God disposes," as also the fitness of a saying then much used, "Don't shout till you get out of the woods."

Lee, however, showed no disposition to run away; on the contrary, as soon as he understood Hooker's purpose, he put the bulk of his army in motion to attack the Union forces entangled in the dense woods above Fredericksburg known as the Wilderness, and to that point our march was directed, reaching Banks's Ford on the 1st of May and bivouacking there all night. Over the river the deep booming of cannon came rumbling through the trees, telling of a desperate struggle in the thicket in that direction. The division marched the following day (Saturday, May 2) to United States Ford, and, crossing the Rappahannock, moved towards Chancellorsville, the sound of battle becoming more distinct as the head of the column thridded the gloomy depths of the dark woods. Here the column halted for a short time; but orders having been received to hurry to the front, the march was again resumed.

As the column approached the field, news of the rout of the 11th Corps was received, and soon many of the stragglers were met, badly demoralized, and swiftly putting a safe distance between their own worthless bodies and the danger of the battle-field. During a fight the rear of an army is always encumbered by these wrecks of soldiers, some worthy ones wounded or sick, but many genuine skulkers who on some excuse have dropped out, and who glibly tell the sorrowful story of how "their regiment has all been cut up," as they quickly pike to the rear.

Arriving in proximity to the field, the division took position and intrenched, while through the woods in front the sullen rumble and roar of the cannon intermingled with the intermittent reports of musketry ; now in quick single shots, then gaining power and volume until it became a long, steady roll ; this was the music, the *crescendo* and *diminuendo*, of the battle-field, telling unmistakably that the fight was still on. Occasionally the bright flash of a bursting shell was seen, but too far off for harm ; and through the greater part of the night, in fitful swells, this infernal chorus was kept up, the distant huzzas of the loyal troops sometimes being heard above the loud roar of cannon and the sharp crackle of musketry. This night was an anxious and almost sleepless one to the men of the 1st Corps, lying on the fringe of the battle-field, and when Sunday morning came they expected to be ordered to succor their hard-pressed comrades of the other corps who had fought so well in the dense woods in front.

The contest was renewed at an early hour in the morning, a mile or more distant, and continued with unabated fury until near noon, when the sound of the conflict came nearer, the piercing " Ki-yi" of the rebel yell being often distinguished above the cheers of the Union soldiery as either side gained some advantage by a charge or countercharge. Long lines of wounded streamed down towards the ford,—true soldiers with powder-stained faces, shattered limbs, and bleeding bodies, bearing the badges of the 2d, 3d, 11th, and 12th Corps. The brigade threw out skirmishers in the woods in front and flank, the crack of the videttes' rifles giving warning that the time for action might come at any moment. While waiting here for orders, a request came from the brigade general for a detail of picked men to go carefully between the lines and recover some intrenching tools that had been abandoned a day or two before. The choice fell upon Lieutenant S. H. Martin, who, with twenty selected men, went outside of the lines, though in great danger, found the tools, and brought them in without losing a man. These same tools subsequently proved of great benefit, being used for throwing up works to protect the rear of our army while crossing the river in retreat.

The 300 men with the regiment, under command of Lieutenant-Colonel Wagner, anxiously waited all day, momentarily expecting to be ordered to the front, but no orders came. All day long the tumult of battle rattled and thundered a short distance in front, but at night the brigade still remained in the breastworks, staying here during the 4th and 5th, soaked by the rain and befouled by the mud ; but on the 6th the position was abandoned, the Rappahannock crossed, and tents pitched near Falmouth.

And so this brilliantly-planned but badly-executed campaign ended in a very discouraging manner ; and while the men felt that somehow they did not have a fair chance, that the movement ought to have been successful, yet it was noticeable that there was not the same bitter feeling manifested as followed the Fredericksburg slaughter. Though Hooker had not won a victory, he would not own a defeat, for a "congratulatory" order was issued to his army, praising it for what had been accomplished, affirming a renewal of confidence in its prowess, appealing to its pride, and stating that it had inflicted heavier blows than it had received, having placed 18,000 of the enemy's troops *hors de combat*, and much more of the same kind ; but to the intelligent reader, in the light of subsequent events, all this savors very much of braggadocio.

General Lee likewise issued an order to his army, but in a somewhat different spirit, and "recommended that the troops unite on Sunday next in ascribing unto the Lord of hosts the glory due unto His name."

In reviewing this movement, from which so much was reasonably expected, it is difficult to assign a reason for its failure, unless it was a rebuke from the Almighty to a commander who so contemptuously despised His power in so great a matter. It was the general opinion among the soldiers that this humiliating disaster was due to some cause other than even the rout of the 11th Corps, which command was made the scapegoat for the shortcomings of the whole army. In the "History of the 118th Pennsylvania Volunteers" is given an insight concerning one of the potent factors contributing to the loss of this battle :

A large tent had been pitched for the use of army head-quarters. The flaps open, its occupants and their doings were plainly in view. General Hooker, in reclining posture, still suffering from the blow he received from a falling pillar of the Chancellorsville house, was surrounded by a number of officers. The libations were quite imposing, and the beverage luxuriant and expensive. The light wines of France were apparently the exclusive tipple. The many abandoned

DAVID K. HARTZEL,
Company C.

CORPORAL HENRY TOWNSEND,
Company C.

LIEUTENANT JOHN WITMOYER,
Company H.

LIEUTENANT JAMES McCHALIKER,
Company H.

SERGEANT WILLIAM CHAMBERS,
Company D.
(Killed at Fredericksburg.)

bottles, the broken and empty baskets, the frequent popping of champagne corks, indicated a free and liberal allowance of this intoxicant.   An impertinent fellow, observing General Hooker as the only one of the party not upon his feet, inquired the cause, and a reply was made by an officer to the effect that he had been shot. "Shot in the neck," quickly responded the inquirer.   The smile with which his response was received assured him that he had not *shot* far from the mark.

And Chancellorsville was not the only battle that General John Barleycorn lost to the Union cause, though it has been strenuously denied that the commanding general was incapacitated from this cause.

Upon returning from this campaign the brigade lost the services of the 26th New York Regiment; their two years' enlistment having expired, the men of this command bid their comrades good-by and departed for home.   The 26th was a good regiment, composed of hard fighters who reflected great credit on their State.

CHAPTER XV.

ON May 7, 1863, the regiment marched in a heavy rain to White Oak Church, encamping in the wet and mud, but moved camp to another place near by on the 11th, and when nicely fixed received orders to pull up stakes and change to a more desirable location. The affairs of the country and the situation in the Army of the Potomac at this period were probably the darkest in the history of the war. Defeated, baffled, and thwarted time and again, it did sometimes appear that the Southern Confederacy might become an established fact; but notwithstanding all these discouragements, to the true men of this glorious army the final result of the war was never in doubt. Having a strong conviction of the righteousness of the Union cause, they offered their lives in its defence, leaving the result in the hands of Almighty God. If they had not won victories, they felt that the fault did not rest with the men in the ranks, but was due rather to the mismanagement of commanding officers, and hoped for better luck next time. The weather was improving and drilling was resumed, every needful preparation being made for the coming campaign. While at this place a number of promotions were made in the regiment, Sergeant G. M. Donnelly being promoted to sergeant-major, Sergeant Nichols to lieutenant, Sergeant Hanlon to lieutenant, Sergeant Booz to lieutenant, and on May 21, Captain Patterson was granted twenty days' sick leave.

On the 30th of May the corps was reviewed by General Reynolds, who warmly commended the troops for their excellent appearance. On June 1 the regiment had 326 present, the aggregate present and absent being 448. Major Foust was in command, Colonel Wagner having been forced to leave on account of his wound disabling him from active duty in the field. Camp rumors of all sorts spread fast and furious, everybody anticipating some great movement; but the wisest prophet was at a loss, and the knowing ones were as ignorant about the future as the dullest man in camp.

On June 4 orders to pack up came, but were countermanded, to be renewed and changed again on the 6th. On the 12th, however, final orders were issued, and, breaking camp, the brigade marched to the north, bivouacking near an old mill after a twenty-mile tramp. The march was resumed in the morning, the troops passing Grove Church and halting near Bealeton until ten o'clock on the morning of the 14th, when the tramp was continued. Manassas was reached at five o'clock, at which place a halt was made until the next morning, when the division proceeded to Centreville and formed line of battle, expecting the enemy to come through the mountain passes to attack Washington.

The division waited until the 17th for the Johnnies to turn up, but they not putting in an appearance, the march was resumed to Guilford Station, where a rest was taken until the 19th, on which day the command bivouacked at Goose Creek, after marching about fifteen miles in a heavy rain. The weary and besoaked men were soon rolled in their blankets, sleeping the slumber of the just; but at midnight the long roll beat sharp and clear in camp, causing every soldier to spring to arms. This proved a false alarm, however, and the men were soon resting again. The corps remained at Goose Creek until June 25, when the march was resumed, the command crossing the Potomac at Edwards Ferry and halting at Barnsville until the 26th; on that day the column passed through Stanleyville, and, crossing the Monocacy, reached Middletown on the 27th.

On the 28th the corps, with flying colors, marched through the loyal city of Frederick, at which place we were informed that General Meade had been appointed to the command of the army; this news excited no particular remark, as Meade was favorably known as the commander of that effective division, the Pennsylvania Reserves. The green fields and rolling hills of "My Maryland," with its loyal people, were a grateful contrast to the blighted plains and ruined homesteads of "Old Virginny," whose population was mostly bitterly opposed to the Union, giving the blue-coats scowls and black looks in place of the welcome extended by these patriotic Marylanders, and the soldiers of the Union army will ever kindly remember the beautiful little towns of this section, especially Frederick, Boonsborough, and Middletown.

A halt was made near Emmittsburg on June 29, but the march was resumed the next morning, and amidst the wildest demonstrations of joy the Pennsylvania line was crossed and the troops were in God's country, tramping the soil of the glorious old Keystone State, the first time for nearly two years that many of the boys had the privilege of being home again.

CHAPTER XVI.

GETTYSBURG : JULY 1, 2, AND 3, 1863.

THE first day of July, 1863, dawned clear and warm upon the 1st Corps, bivouacked in the fields near Marsh Creek. The 88th was on picket, and upon returning to the camp about nine o'clock, head of column pulled out on the Gettysburg pike. The morning was blistering hot, and the stifling clouds of yellow dust, settling on the ranks like a blanket, filled the eyes, mouth, nostrils, and entire person of the soldier with an impalpable powder, while the perspiration, running down the skin, ploughed furrows through the dirt. As the column neared Gettysburg the rumble and roar of cannon indicated that the Johnnies had been found, and soon the balls of smoke from the bursting shells were visible over the trees near the white cupola of the Seminary. Presently the crackle of the rifles was heard, mingled with the manly cheers of the Union soldiers and occasionally the shrill yelp of the rebels heard above the din of battle. The regiment had less than 300 men in line, led by Major Foust, the brigade numbering about 1200.

The division was held in reserve near the Seminary until about noon, at which time, heavy bodies of the enemy being reported by the cavalry as coming in near Oak Hill, Baxter was ordered to move in that direction. Major Foust called the regiment to arms, and, after loading, the brigade, following the ridge over the cut, preceded by Colonel Coulter with the 11th and 97th Regiments, soon reached the fields and woods near the Mummasburg road. Here, after some preliminary skirmishing by the advance, the regiment formed line of battle near the road, facing northeast. After alignment, skirmishers were sent into the woods to ascertain what the rebs were about; but no extended investigation was necessary, as the boys from the other side were coming right along, supported by O'Neal's Alabama brigade in line of battle, cocked and primed for a fight.

It is worthy of remark, in this connection, that the boys who wore U. S. on their blankets never appeared in better spirits for battle than at this moment; they were full of fight; not that they took naturally to that kind of medicine, but every man and boy felt that it was now or never, and all resolved to fight as they had never fought before.

When O'Neal's lines came in view the skirmishers at once opened upon them, and the enemy soon fell back into the woods, having sustained considerable loss. After these troops had been repulsed another line was observed approaching the road, through Forney's farm, taking Baxter directly in the left flank; this movement necessitated a change of front to the top of the hill, bringing the brigade behind a low stone wall nearly perpendicular to the road. And none too soon, for the field in front was swarming with Confederates, who came sweeping on in magnificent order, with perfect alignment, guns at right shoulder and colors to the front,—to many the dead march. Baxter's men behind the wall waited quietly for the enemy to come within range, word being passed along to aim low, and at the command a sheet of flame and smoke burst from the wall with the simultaneous crash of the rifles, flaring full in the faces of the advancing troops, the ground being quickly covered with their killed and wounded as the balls hissed and cut through the exposed line. These troops were Iverson's brigade of North Carolinians, and though they were badly shaken by this unexpected and destructive fire, they still essayed to advance to the charge; but so persistent and hot was their reception that they were compelled to fall back a couple of hundred yards to a little gully, where they rallied and opened a sharp fire on the Union line. This fusillade was maintained some time, during which the men kept well under cover.

Lying side by side behind the stone wall were Sergeant Evans, of Company B, and John Witmoyer, of Company H, industriously engaged in firing at the Confederates, sending back the leaden compliments with interest added. Being good marksmen, their balls struck in or near the opposing line, making it very lively for the "tar-heelers" in the gully. A color-bearer making himself very conspicuous by defiantly flaunting his flag in plain view, Evans

GETTYSBURG, JULY 1, 1863.

remarked, as he brought his piece to his shoulder, "John, I will give those colors a whack." At this moment Witmoyer heard the dull thud of a bullet, and turning quickly, asked Evans if he was hit. The sergeant did not reply, but slowly bringing his musket down, fell over dead, the ball having pierced his heart.

The fire from the Confederate infantry and artillery was rapidly thinning the ranks, but the boys made it very interesting for the gray line posted in the depression a hundred yards or more to the front, and the rebels suffered so much that they finally manifested a disposition to surrender, many of them throwing up their hats and in other ways indicating that they had had more than enough, and were willing to be taken back into the Union ; our officers, however, were suspicious as to their sincerity, many thinking it a trap. About this time General Baxter advised an application of cold steel, the supply of cartridges being exhausted ; acting on this hint, the regiment sprang over the wall with a shout, followed by most of the brigade, and, charging the rebs, ran over their line of battle, receiving the surrender of hundreds of prisoners and capturing the flags of the 23d North Carolina and an Alabama regiment, Lieutenant Levan taking one, which, in an impromptu speech, he presented to General Robinson, and Sergeant Gilligan, along with many others, capturing the other one.

But the brigade was now in a perilous position ; a galling fire in front and flank rendered the place too hot to hold, and the boys quickly realizing that their usefulness at this point was over, that pressing engagements called them to the stone wall, fell back without unnecessary delay, driving their willing captives before them. Here the contest was renewed against Ramseur's brigade in front and O'Neal's on the right, with Doles's brigade swinging in on the right rear, and under this musketry fire and the plunging artillery fire from the ridge, Baxter's line was rapidly melting. The men now running out of ammunition, Paul's brigade relieved Baxter's, which fell to the rear. Many of the regiment had been killed or wounded, among the latter Major Foust (Captain Mass succeeding in command) ; Lieutenants Ninesteel and Cuskaden ; Sergeants Shravely, Fraley, and Barber ; Privates Harry Read, Henry Ford, James G. Clark, M. Conover, George Toland, Henry Arnold,

Samuel Burkart, Michael Ruth, Mark Grigg, Henry Lloyd, Phil. Schriner, John Nice, William Bixenstine, Robert Wallace, and a score more, many killed, others weltering in their blood where they fell or limping painfully to the rear, their course marked by a trail of blood as they searched for the surgeons to dress their gaping wounds. In this procession of wounded men was Color-Corporal Bonnin, with the regimental flag, well to the rear; and though faint from loss of blood, he gamely carried the flag to the town, turning it over to the regiment. Then, finding he could go no farther, he crawled into a building to die, as he supposed; but he didn't die just then, and at the present writing is a lively specimen of a corpse, able to take his rations and to tell war stories with the best of the old boys.

The contest had been maintained for nearly three hours beneath the sweltering July sun, the men being without water, lips parched and smeared with powder; in short, they were completely exhausted, and dropped out one by one as the weary hours wore on. About three o'clock the enemy's fire increased and he advanced in overwhelming masses to crush the thin line of the 1st Corps on the ridge, a large force also coming across the Mummasburg road on the right and rear; then the shattered fragments of the regiments composing Robinson's division fell slowly back, firing as they retreated; but to make an orderly retreat was no easy matter, the advancing enemy pouring in a withering fire on front and flanks, knocking men down at every step. Near the railroad grading a battery of artillery, supposed to be Stewart's, was in danger of capture, and observing this, the men, encouraged by Captains Mass, Whitesides, Rhoads, Richards, and Schell, and Lieutenants Martin, Kram, Detre, Wagner, Boone, Levan, Beath, Grant, Gardiner, Nichols, Nunneville, and other officers, made a creditable rally, the gunners, after giving the Johnnies a few extra doses of canister, all escaping. Those of the fugitives who cut across lots and avoided the town reached the cemetery safely, but the unfortunates who tried to pass through the town were nearly all captured, the Confederates having succeeded in breaking the lines of the 11th Corps and occupying the town while the 1st Corps was still fighting near the Seminary.

While retreating, Lieutenant Beath overtook Private Little, of his company, who had been shot through the body while gamely fighting near the wall. In response to his piteous appeal the lieutenant remained with Little, assisting him to a hospital in the town. When the surgeon examined Little's wound he pronounced it mortal, saying that he would not live two hours. On hearing this the wounded man flared up in unrighteous indignation, and swore by many strange oaths that he would not die just yet, but would outlive the surgeon, which prediction, notwithstanding his horrible wound, he lived to verify. Through helping his disabled comrade, Beath had got into a scrape, being now in the hands of the enemy, and having recently won his shoulder-straps by hard service, he naturally objected to travelling Dixieward as a prisoner of war. He therefore offered his services in the care of the wounded, and in this capacity, having been decorated with the insignia of the hospital corps, was recognized by the Confederate authorities.

On the 2d the lieutenant visited the scene of the first day's battle and found our wounded men lying uncared for on the field, suffering untold agony from their festering wounds. After having assisted these unfortunates to the best of his ability, he entered the McPherson barn, which had been improvised as a hospital. Here the most distressing cases of suffering met his sight, the barn being filled with helpless soldiers, torn and mangled, who in the heat of the fight had been carried there by their comrades, and had lain since without care or attention of any kind. Their lacerated limbs were frightfully swollen and, turning black, had begun to decompose; the blood flowing from gaping wounds had glued some of the sufferers to the floor. He found a soldier wounded in one arm, and impressing him into carrying water, and tearing his own underclothing in ribbons, washed and bandaged their wounds to the best of his ability. In the evening he returned to the town and prevailed upon a surgeon to go out to the barn and care for these unfortunates.

After passing through the town, the remnant of the battalion rallied around the colors on the hill, Captain Whitesides taking command, and though scarcely 100 men were present, they were soon in line of battle, not very eager, but ready for another fight if called on. Many of the officers and men had been killed, wounded, or captured, among them Captain Mass, wounded and captured, Captain Schell and Lieutenants Boone and Grant, captured, with many others of the non-commissioned officers and privates, who went on a most unwilling excursion to rebeldom. These prisoners were offered their paroles, but patriotically refused for two reasons: first, that it required a large force of Confederates to guard them; secondly, they had strong hopes of being recaptured before they got to Dixie Land. If they had consulted their own personal comfort, every one of them might have avoided the horrors of the long captivity which they subsequently endured, some of them until the closing days of the war, many dying in the foul prison stockades in the South.

The night of July 1 was an anxious one for the men of the 1st Corps, as they extended their lines, preparing for the battle on the morrow; but the steady tramp of marching troops, with the rumbling of artillery, informed them that their comrades of the other corps were on hand, and that in the morning there would be troops enough present to successfully match the enemy. During the night the regiment was ordered to the left of Ziegler's Grove, where the men built a slight breastwork of fence-rails and stones; but the next morning, being relieved by the 2d Corps, the brigade marched over in rear of the cemetery and waited for orders.

Thursday, July 2, dawned hot and sultry. The scene on the hills back of the town was an animated one, troops and batteries marching and galloping here and there, taking positions and preparing for the day's bloody work. The tired men of Baxter's brigade, utterly worn out by the battle of the day before and by moving about all night, lay quietly on the hill back of the cemetery until afternoon, at which time the increasing and nearing roar of battle on the Union left flank indicated that Longstreet had overpowered the veterans of the 3d Corps and was forcing them back. To this point Robinson's division was directed, relieving some of the battered regiments holding that line, and, throwing out skirmishers, advanced towards the Emmittsburg road, searching for the enemy in the gathering gloom. The ground had all been fought over, the fields being strewn with the dead and wounded of both armies, the latter crying piteously for help, calling the names of comrades, company, or regi-

ment, in their frantic appeals ; one officer, said to be General Barks-
dale, of the Confederate army, alternately cursed and begged for aid.
Help was given to all the wounded within reach until the regiment
was relieved in the night, and marching to the vicinity of the cemetery, rested there until the morning of the 3d, listening, meanwhile,
to the noise of the conflict between the 12th Corps and Johnson's
division as the graybacks were forced out of Rock Creek Valley.

After this engagement a painful quietness ensued, but it proved
to be the calm before the storm. What mischief the enemy was con-
templating was difficult to fathom, but most of the men felt that
Lee hadn't been whipped enough yet, and that he wouldn't give
it up so ; and besides, the movement of troops and posting of batteries on the other side indicated that something was up. After a
sumptuous dinner of hardtack and water, the tired soldiers rested as
best they could in the hot sun until about one P.M., when the sullen
reports of two or three cannon within the Confederate line were heard,
and before their echoes had ceased to reverberate over the woods and
hills, a mighty rumble shook the earth as the cannon of the enemy
simultaneously opened on the Union position, the sky soon being
obscured by heavy clouds of white smoke, while the air was full of
hissing, shrieking, bursting shells, which appeared to fall everywhere
in the Federal lines. For a few moments our cannoneers failed to
respond, but then opened furiously, and in this iron tempest, amid
the hissing and screaming projectiles, the regiment was called to
arms, being marched down the hill to a clump of trees known as
Ziegler's Grove.

The cannonading, together with the shrieking and bursting of
the shell and solid shot as they tore madly through the air, made
a terrible noise, and when these missiles struck the ground they
threw up a cloud of dust as high as the trees, sometimes striking
among the crouching soldiers or ripping through the batteries, tearing men and horses to pieces and scattering death in every direction.
For about two hours this horrible duel continued, over 200 cannon
being engaged, the shots sometimes counting from four to eight in a
second, never less than one or two. To the men, who crouched behind the hillocks or trees that afforded the smallest protection, or
flattened themselves on the ground in the least possible space, it

seemed as if this horrible racket would never cease ; but about three o'clock, General Warren, from Round Top, reporting to Meade that the Union cannon, while doing the enemy but slight harm, were filling the plain with a cloud of smoke, through which they could approach unobserved, the order to cease firing was given. Presently the Confederate fire also ceased, and over the fields beyond the Emmittsburg road the gray brigades of Pickett and Pettigrew, with flaunting red battle-flags and the sunlight sparkling on their polished rifle-barrels, were in full view, the lines extending to the right and left as far as could be seen. When their lines had fairly uncovered, the Union artillery opened a terrific fire, first with solid shot and shell and afterwards with single and double charges of canister, ripping through their ranks, tearing men to pieces, and causing them to waver; but they gallantly closed up and, after crossing the Emmittsburg road, broke into a run to charge the Union line. As soon as they were within easy rifle range the infantry opened a withering fire ; but they came on, though now badly shattered, striking the Philadelphia Brigade a short distance to our left, when Baxter was ordered to the rescue, and upon reaching the scene found the spirit of the charge broken, but captured many prisoners, guns, and flags, the remnant of the charging column scattering in wild confusion over the plain, intent only upon getting safely back to their lines. General Lee had moved his queen and lost. When the result was known a mighty shout went up from the Union troops, spreading from regiment to regiment along the entire line.

After the terrible repulse of Pickett and Pettigrew there were intense excitement and consternation in the Southern ranks. They had been fairly whipped, every attack having utterly failed. Their army was literally cut to pieces, the field of the first day's *rencontre* being still encumbered with their killed and wounded, while the ground over which Longstreet had fought on the 2d and 3d and the woods along Rock Creek were strewn with dead and dying, torn and mangled Confederates, every house and barn also being filled with these disabled soldiers, with but scant means among their friends to alleviate the suffering on every hand. Lee had staked the life of the Southern Confederacy on this field and lost, and his soldiers realized the perilous position they were in. They began to retreat from

Gettysburg on the night of July 3, their artillery and wagon train taking the Chambersburg and Millerstown roads, the infantry going over the railroad grading, the stragglers and slightly wounded taking any and every path and anything else they could carry away with them.

Dr. Rawlins, our regimental surgeon, and Hospital Steward Frank Murphy had kindly remained on the battle-field of the first day to attend the wounded of the regiment, the doctor being at the Shead House, on Oak Ridge. Here he was a close observer of the movements as well as of the spirit of the Confederate troops. After their disastrous repulse on the 3d they gave it up, having lost all appetite for more fight; the retreat commenced at nightfall of the 3d, the only troops visible on this part of the field on the morning of the 4th being Ramseur's brigade, which was spread over a long line to give the appearance of a large force. On the night of the 4th they withdrew, leaving only a strong rear-guard to act as sharp-shooters and delay the Union advance as long as possible.

Many of our men who were within the Confederate lines during these fearful days kept their eyes and ears open, thereby learning much of the feeling among their troops. The rebels fully expected a victory, and were slow to admit a reverse when repulsed, but always claimed to have the Yanks just where they wanted them; that Uncle Bob would lead them into Philadelphia yet. Standing on the steps of the Lutheran Church were a group of wounded Union sol. diers, chaffing with some Johnnies on the sidewalk, when a great lanky Confederate, dressed in a citizen's black suit topped with a high silk hat, rode up and tauntingly asked the Federal soldiers "How he would pass for old Abe Lincoln." No sooner had the words been spoken than a Union soldier standing on the steps un-expectedly gave the counterfeit a crushing blow in the face which threw him off his mule into the street. The Southerners, espousing the cause of their friend, grasped their arms, and for a while it ap-peared as if there would be a skrimmage; but in the midst of the uproar a Confederate major rode up and ordered the butternuts to their regiments.

After the repulse on the 3d the Union lines were strengthened, but no further attack being made, the 88th went on the skirmish line at nightfall, having a hot time with the enemy's videttes. Next morning the regiment was relieved, but again advanced to the front line on the afternoon of Saturday, the 4th.   There were probably but few Confederates on hand, but those who were there opened a sharp fire on the regiment, which was promptly returned, though a heavy rain drenching the men and flooding the ground made sharp-shooting very uncomfortable work.

The following day was spent in burying the dead, bringing in the wounded, and counting heads to ascertain who were present and who absent.

EXTRACT FROM GENERAL HENRY BAXTER'S REPORT OF THE BATTLE OF GETTYSBURG.

We heard cannonading, and marched as rapidly as possible, arriving at 11 A.M.; the 11th Pennsylvania and 97th New York continued their march, moving to the front.   The remaining four regiments were ordered forward and formed on the right of the two already sent.

Indications being that we should be attacked on our right, I at once changed front by filing to the right and forming forward on first battalion.   I sent skirmishers forward, but the enemy now appearing on our left, I had to change front to the left, and moved to the crest of the hill, bringing us before the enemy, when the brigade opened a most deadly fire, soon causing them to give way.   Another line took the place of that repulsed, and at this time they appeared on our right flank, making it necessary for the 90th to change front to meet them.   Again they were repulsed and again re-enforced.   The 97th and 83d New York and 88th Pennsylvania made a charge, capturing many prisoners, the 88th taking two battle-flags and the 97th one.

We were relieved by Paul's brigade, having been engaged over two hours, and then ordered to support Stewart's battery until ordered from the field. . . .

About 5 o'clock the brigade moved from Cemetery Hill to the left, near and parallel with the Emmittsburg road, remaining in this position until about 10 o'clock of the 2d, being relieved by Webb's brigade of the 2d Corps; moving to the rear until about 4 P.M., then to the right a short distance to support a battery of the 11th Corps, remaining here till about 6 o'clock, losing men from the enemy's shells and sharp-shooters.   We were now ordered to the left to assist the 3d Corps, losing men killed and wounded from the enemy's shells.

Sent skirmishers to the front, when, after dark, were ordered to support the 11th Corps near the position we last left, where we remained until the morning of the 3d, when we again supported the batteries of the 11th Corps.

About 9 A.M. we went to the right to support the 12th Corps, and about 1 P.M. to the right and front of Cemetery Hill in support of batteries; under a heavy fire nearly two hours.

LIEUTENANT CHARLES HUNTER.

LIEUTENANT ROBERT P. BEATH,
Lieutenant-Colonel 6th Regiment U. S. C. T.

LIEUTENANT GEORGE E. WAGNER,
Brevet Colonel U. S. Vols.

LIEUTENANT MORTIMER WISHAM.

CORPORAL HARVEY MYLES.

We were then ordered to the left and rear of Cemetery Hill, and then to the left, and on the right of Hays's division of the 2d Corps, where we at once formed line of battle under one of the most galling artillery fires ever witnessed.   Threw out skirmishers, who drove back the enemy. . . .

The brigade went into the battle on the 1st with a few less than 1200 . . . and lost 645, the heavy loss being on the 1st.

H. BAXTER,

Brigadier-Gen. commanding 2d Brigade.

The following table taken from the official records tells the story of the losses in Robinson's division :

1ST BRIGADE, GENERAL PAUL COMMANDING.

	Killed.	Wounded.	Missing.	Total.
Staff		2	3	5
13th Massachusetts 7		77	101	185
107th Pennsylvania 11		56	98	165
104th New York 11		91	92	194
94th New York 12		58	175	245
16th Maine 9		59	164	232
Total 50		343	633	1026

2D BRIGADE, GENERAL HENRY BAXTER COMMANDING.

	Killed.	Wounded.	Missing.	Total.
Staff			1	1
12th Massachusetts 5		52	62	119
9th New York State Militia (83d) 6		18	58	82
97th New York 12		36	78	126
11th Pennsylvania 6		64	62	132
88th Pennsylvania 10		54	42	106
90th Pennsylvania 8		45	40	93
Total 47		269	343	659

CHAPTER XVII.

A DISCURSIVE CHAPTER ON THE FIRST DAY AT GETTYSBURG.

POSITIONS OF THE UNION ARMY ON JUNE 30, 1863.

ON the evening of June 30 the various commands comprising the Army of the Potomac were at distances ranging from five to thirty-five miles from Gettysburg, Buford's cavalry occupying the town. The 1st Corps was five miles distant, near Marsh Creek; the 11th Corps near Emmittsburg, about ten miles away; and the 3d Corps at Bridgeport. These corps formed the left wing of the army, under the personal direction of General Reynolds. The 2d Corps was at Uniontown, the 5th at Union Mills, the 6th at Manchester, the 12th at Littlestown, and Gregg's and Kilpatrick's cavalry were between Manchester and Hanover, chasing Stuart's Confederate troopers and trying to prevent them from joining Lee's army. Stuart and Kilpatrick came together on the morning of the 30th, between ten and eleven A.M., at Hanover, and had a spirited contest, resulting in Stuart heading towards York, in his blind effort to find Lee, with Kilpatrick in pursuit. This was a fine piece of work by Kilpatrick, for had he allowed Stuart to go to Heidlersburg, the latter would have joined Early's division on the morning of July 1 and been present at the opening of the battle. General Meade's plan was to take a defensive position on the Pipe Creek line, if no better offered, and the selection of Gettysburg for the greatest battle in America was an unforeseen feature of the campaign.

CONFEDERATE POSITIONS ON JUNE 30.

General Lee, upon discovering that the Army of the Potomac was after him, on the 28th of June directed his divisions to discontinue their march towards the Susquehanna and concentrate on Gettysburg, and in compliance with that order the rebel army, on June 30, was approaching the town, Heth being the nearest, at Cashtown, seven

or eight miles west of Gettysburg; Rodes and Early near Heidlersburg, ten miles away; the other divisions following Heth on the
Chambersburg road; and Stuart's cavalry near Hanover, on his wild
foray east of Meade's army.

BUFORD TO THE RESCUE.

Buford's division comprised the following troops: Gamble's
brigade (the 8th Illinois, four companies of the 12th Illinois, six
companies of the 3d Indiana, and the 8th New York); Devin's
brigade (6th and 9th New York, 17th Pennsylvania, and three companies of the 3d West Virginia Cavalry, with Calef's Battery A,
2d U. S. Artillery); in all, about 3000 strong. This force reached
Gettysburg about noon, just as Pettigrew's Confederate brigade was
approaching from the west. Buford scared Pettigrew off, who told
Heth that he had encountered cavalry and infantry and thought it
best to retire.

Buford immediately scouted the country and reported very accurately the location and probable intentions of the Confederates.
He found the town in a ferment of excitement caused by past and
prospective requisitions from the Johnnies, and his troopers were
hailed as deliverers by the delighted people. They were just in time,
for Pettigrew's errand was to search the town for army supplies
(shoes especially) and return the same day.

THE FIRST SHOT.

Wednesday, July 1, 1863, opened very warm, and the summer
sun cast its bright rays upon Buford's skirmishers, as they watched
among the clover and wild flowers for the Southern soldiers to come
down from the mountains.

Heth left camp near Cashtown about five o'clock, in time to
make a full day, and soon ran against an outpost of the 8th Illinois,
posted on the hill a few hundred yards east of Marsh Creek, and
here the first shot was fired by Captain Jones, of that regiment.
The videttes fell back to the skirmish line, and soon Marye's battery
opened the ball for the Confederates, Calef presently taking it up
for the Federals. The first soldier killed was Henry Raison, of the
7th Tennessee. The cavalry dismounted and formed line of battle

near the McPherson barn, to the right and left of the Chambersburg road.

When Heth found that his skirmishers were having trouble in front, he deployed Archer's and Davis's brigades, and a little past ten o'clock sent them over the creek to see what was in his front.

WADSWORTH TO THE FRONT.

Wadsworth's division left its bivouac, some four or five miles from Gettysburg, about eight o'clock ; but Heth, starting at five o'clock from Cashtown, reached the field first.

General Reynolds, leaving his column, hurried to Gettysburg as soon as he heard the cannonading, and with Buford hastily surveyed the field. There was no time to be lost if the Confederate advance was to be checked, so leaving Buford to encourage his carbineers to hold out a little longer, Reynolds rode back to meet Wadsworth's division, the brigade flag of General Cutler, being in plain view as that command crossed the fields near the Codori house, the Iron Brigade a good second, just as Archer and Davis were crossing the run and driving the cavalry. Cutler, being on the right, deployed first, sending the 14th Brooklyn (84th New York) and the 95th New York along the Chambersburg road to support Hall's battery, which relieved Calef, the object of this movement being to meet Archer's left regiment near the toll-gate. He then sent the 76th New York, 56th Pennsylvania, and 147th New York, in the order named, from the right across the grading to meet Davis, who was forcing the cavalry in that direction.

While Hall's battery and the 14th and 95th Regiments were disputing Archer's advance near the Chambersburg road, the Iron Brigade came across the Hagerstown road on the double-quick and went straight for McPherson's woods.

CAPTURE OF ARCHER.

Reynolds directed the advance, while Doubleday urged the importance of holding the woods to the last. The black hats were full of fight, saying, "If we can't hold it, where will you find men who can ?"

Archer says that his brigade was at some disadvantage in crossing the creek, but his men rushed across with a cheer (yell) and opened fire when about fifty yards from the Union line. The contest had been maintained but a short time when a heavy force opened a cross-fire on his right flank, rendering the position untenable and forcing the brigade back across the creek, where it reformed in rear of its supports.

To properly comprehend the movement of the Iron Brigade in its charge upon Archer, it must be understood that it approached the field in column in this order: 2d and 7th Wisconsin, 19th Indiana, and 24th Michigan ; the 6th Wisconsin was in reserve near the Seminary. These troops went in on the double-quick, loading as they ran, and deployed as stated, with the 2d Wisconsin on the right, facing the woods. The brigade soon advanced, the left regiments swinging clear around into the woods in rear of the Tennesseeans. After pushing about fifty yards into the timber it received a terrific fire from Archer's troops, which knocked over scores of men ; but the advance was irresistible, and though the Confederates made a gallant stand, the Hoosiers, sweeping in from front and flank, routed them, and those who were not disabled or captured fled to their supports across the creek without delay, leaving General Archer a captive. Meredith's left regiments followed the fugitives across the run, but soon returned, forming a new line in the woods, with the 2d Wisconsin on the right and the 19th Indiana on the left.

Though this movement resulted in a brilliant success for the Union arms, it was attained at the cost of Reynolds's life, he being killed by a sharp-shooter's bullet just as the advance began. So died, honored and respected, in defence of his native State, one of the ablest generals in the Army of the Potomac.

CUTLER AND DAVIS.

But while this wing of Wadsworth's division was engaged with Archer's men, Davis was making it very interesting for the other wing north of the cut in the old railroad grading. As Davis advanced he observed Cutler's men forming on a ridge in his front, and about 10.30 A.M. he opened on them before they were fully

aligned. The fire was promptly returned and continued with great
spirit by both sides, the Confederates rushing on with the greatest
recklessness, evidently expecting the Union soldiers to fall back,
while the blue-coats evinced no disposition to do so, but faced the
music like good soldiers striving to earn their thirteen dollars per
month, worth in gold at this date about seven dollars. Davis had
the advantage in numbers, however, his left considerably overlapping
the 76th New York, and when the 55th North Carolina advanced, it
took Cutler in flank and rear, and though the 76th attempted to
change front to right to meet this galling cross-fire, it was unavailing,
both that regiment and the 56th Pennsylvania being forced back to
the woods with heavy loss, including Major Grover, the commander
of the 76th. In the *mêlée* the 147th New York, in line nearer
the railroad cut, having its commanding officers disabled, did not
get the order to retreat, and was almost surrounded before it was
forced off the field. The 76th and 56th rallied near the woods, but
the Confederates broke their line again, forcing them over the hill.
When near the town, however, they formed once more, quickly
advancing up the hill to renew the fight, and this time with better
success, for Davis, being attacked on his right, had more on his hands
than he bargained for.

The final dressing down that Davis received occurred in this way.
When Cutler's two left regiments, the 14th and 95th, were apprised
of the peril of their comrades, they left Archer's men to the paternal
care of the Iron Brigade, and, facing about, double-quicked along
the pike towards the town until they were on Davis's flank; then,
by change of front, formed line facing the railroad grading. The
6th Wisconsin coming in on the right of Cutler, the entire line
made a rush for Davis, who had changed front and occupied the cut
to meet this threatened attack. The Confederates made a resolute
stand, but the flanking process so successfully practised on Archer
was again applied here with like result. While the main line swept
on in a front attack from the Chambersburg road, a detachment of
the 6th Wisconsin took position across the cut and enfiladed the
Confederate line. The Mississippians were not easily whipped, but
a further sacrifice of their gallant men in an attempt to check this
impetuous attack would have been useless, and those that could do

so retreated along the grading and over the fields to the friendly side of the creek; but hundreds were shot and several hundred more captured, including most of the 2d Mississippi with its officers and colors, the latter being taken by the 6th Wisconsin.

In the above condensed sketch of this preliminary combat the writer is conscious that but an imperfect description has been given, and hopes that no one will imagine that it was a spiritless affair. The Confederates at first exposed themselves with a freedom bordering on bravado, while the defence and counter-attack by Wadsworth were most obstinate and irresistible, the result being that both sides were terribly used up in this savage encounter, the Confederates losing over 1000 men and the Union loss being almost as heavy during this half-hour's murderous work.

CAPTAIN HALL'S GALLANT FIGHT.

As mentioned above, Captain Hall's battery accompanied Cutler's left to meet Archer's attack on the Chambersburg road. He went into battery near the barn, and about 10.45 A.M. talked back to Pegram's batteries at 1300 yards' distance. Hall was holding his own; but when the infantry was withdrawn to attack Davis he was left without support, being assailed by a swarm of sharp-shooters from the grading, who shot his horses and gunners. Though he gave them unstinted doses of canister, he could not fight skirmishers; so after losing twenty-two men and thirty-four horses he dragged his pieces to the rear, leaving one gun, which was subsequently recovered.

Thus ended the first round of the first day at Gettysburg, fought by two brigades of infantry and two Union and several Confederate batteries, comprising a little less than 4000 men on each side; but the Johnnies were beaten at all points, and retired discomfited to the friendly cover of the woods across the creek.

HETH REFORMING HIS LINES.

When the discouraged stragglers from Archer's and Davis's brigades came streaming to the rear, they were rallied with much trouble and again faced to the front. Heth now realized that there was serious work ahead, and, while his other brigades and supports were forming, he treated the Union lines to a lively cannonade from his numerous batteries. He posted Davis's battered brigade on his left near the grading, then Brockenbrough's Virginians (the 55th, 47th, 40th, and 22d Regiments) as named from the left, then Pettigrew's strong brigade of North Carolinians (the 11th, 26th, 47th, and 52d) from the left to right, with the remnant of Archer's brigade on his extreme right, near the Hagerstown road. Pender's division formed in rear of Heth, Lane's brigade on the right, Colonel Perrin with McGowan's brigade in the centre, Scales on the left, and Thomas in reserve. On the morning of July 1 these two divisions mustered not less than 13,000 men.

On the ridge near Herr's tavern General Hill had at this time about forty guns in action, commanding all the ground occupied by the Union troops, and while waiting for Ewell he kept his gunners busy battering the Federal line.

RODES TO THE RESCUE.

Rodes's division, of Ewell's 2d Confederate Corps, when about four miles distant, heard the cannonading, and leaving the Newville road, struck across Oak Ridge, arriving within sight of the fight about noon. Upon surveying the field, it became evident to Rodes that by keeping along the wooded ridge he could strike the Union force facing Hill's corps upon the flank, and that, moving under cover, he could engage them at great advantage. He therefore sent Blackford's battalion of sharp-shooters and Doles's brigade to his left, near the Carlisle road, to watch for Early and to keep Devin's troopers in check. Then, with O'Neal on the ridge, Iverson on his right near the Mummasburg road, and Daniels and Ramseur coming up, he sent his four batteries under Colonel Carter to the front, to seek for a good position to rake the Union lines. Rodes's division was one of the strongest and best in the Army of Northern Virginia, reporting, on June 30, aggregate present 9098; effectives, 8125, not including the artillery; and this experienced division, secretly marching down on the bare flank of the Union corps, threatened swift disaster to it. Rodes's experienced mind comprehended that he held the key of the field, and he felt confident that when he got ready to launch his powerful brigades against the Union line he would knock it to pieces. Off to the east clouds of dust assured him that "Old Jubilee" would soon be on hand, and he hastened his preparations to strike his opponents, feeling satisfied that if he needed help Early would be quick to the rescue. To reach the Union troops fighting Heth it was necessary for Rodes to change direction to the right, and while performing this movement Carter's batteries opened on Cutler, near the cut. Rodes's preparations were almost completed, when, to his surprise, Union troops appeared in his front, the 11th Corps debouching from the town, together with Robinson's division of the 1st Corps.

ROBINSON TO THE FRONT.

Robinson's division arrived between eleven and twelve o'clock, Baxter leading Paul. These troops halted near the Seminary, part of them erecting a frail barricade of fence-rails which proved very serviceable as a rallying-place for the retreating troops later in the day. This flimsy breastwork comprised all the works on either side during the first day's fight.

About noon the cavalry reported Rodes approaching Oak Ridge. This necessitated the prolongation of the Union line to the right, and Colonel Coulter, with the 11th Pennsylvania, and Colonel Wheelock's 97th New York were sent along the ridge to a point near the Mummasburg road. Baxter soon brought up the rest of the brigade, Paul following about an hour later, and forming his command on Baxter's left and rear. These were the troops that Rodes had observed in his front, and because of their advance through the woods he did not discover them until they uncovered, probably less than 500 yards from his point of observation.

The ground occupied by Robinson is much lower than Oak Ridge and was completely commanded by Rodes's cannon, the position being untenable for the Union artillery while Rodes held the hill. Stewart's battery at the cut was the nearest artillery to this point.

ARRIVAL OF ROWLEY'S 3D DIVISION.

Biddle's brigade, of this division, came in on the Hagerstown road, while Stone arrived by way of the Emmittsburg road, in advance of the 2d Division, between eleven and twelve o'clock. Stone's 2d Brigade was posted along the Chambersburg road, near the McPherson buildings and between the Iron Brigade and Cutler's brigade, the former being in the woods and the latter, at this hour, in the fields north of the cut, on the ground where it had contested with Davis an hour earlier. Rowley's division was composed of Pennsylvania troops, with the exception of the 80th New York (20th New York State Militia), a veteran regiment of hard fighters. Biddle's brigade was sent to the extreme left of the 1st Corps, and before the final Confederate advance occupied several positions near the Hagerstown road, changing its lines as new opponents were discovered.

THE ARTILLERY ON HAND.

As before noted, Calef's (Tidball's) horse artillery, A, 2d United States, six 3 inch rifles, and Hall's 2d Maine, six 3-inch rifles, took a prominent part in the opening exercises. The rest of the 1st Corps artillery, consisting of Stewart's, B, 4th United States, six 12 pounders; Reynolds's, L, 1st New York, six 3·inch rifles; Cooper's, B, 1st Pennsylvania, four 3·inch rifles; and Stevens's 5th Maine, six 12 pounders, arrived, under command of Colonel Wainwright, and massed in front of the Seminary. Including Calef, these batteries comprised thirty-four guns. He posted Cooper in an oat-field about 350 yards south of the Chambersburg road, Stewart on both sides of the cut, Reynolds on the McPherson farm to assist Calef, Stevens near the Seminary, and Hall in reserve. Reynolds's battery was divided, one section being posted near the farm-house and the other, under Lieutenant Wilbur, in a peach-orchard south of the road. The latter was badly hammered when Carter's three batteries opened on it from Oak Ridge, being frequently compelled to change position ; but later on these guns proved very embarrassing to Daniels and the other brigades of the enemy advancing along the railroad.

THE 11TH CORPS ON THE FIELD.

General Howard, commanding the 11th Corps, arrived on the field about eleven o'clock, and, being informed of Reynolds's death, took command, turning the corps over to General Schurz. Making a hasty examination of the positions, he approved of Doubleday's plan of defence, and ordered Schurz to post his troops on the right of the 1st Corps.

Major Thomas W. Osborn, commanding the corps artillery, when within a few miles of the town, received notice to move the artillery to the front as soon as possible. The following batteries composed the command : G, 4th United States, Lieutenant Wilkeson, six light 12-pounders ; I, 1st Ohio, Captain Dilger, six light 12-pounders ; K, 1st Ohio, Captain Heckman, four light 12 pounders ; I, 1st New York, Captain Wiedrich, six 3-inch guns ; and 13th New York, Lieutenant Wheeler, four 3 inch guns. Total, twenty-six guns. Dilger reached the town first, and was ordered by Schurz to the front and 300 yards beyond the town, where he at once became engaged. The fire becoming very hot, Wheeler went to his support, both batteries being in position in the fields between the Mummasburg and Carlisle roads. These batteries first engaged Page's battery, which, suffering heavily,—losing thirty men and seventeen horses,— was finally succored by Carter and Reese. This combined force proved more than a match for the Unionists, and treated them to an unmerciful pelting of shot and shell.

Wilkeson arrived about eleven o'clock, going into battery near the poor-house and subsequently advancing to Barlow's Knoll. At this hour Heckman and Wiedrich were in reserve on Cemetery Hill.

THE INFANTRY ON HAND.

The 3d Division, commanded by General Schimmelfennig, reached the town after twelve o'clock, Barlow's 1st Division next, Steinwehr, with the 2d Division, bringing up the rear and going into position on Cemetery Hill. When Schurz arrived, Robinson's division was moving by the flank along Oak Ridge,.and Devin's cavalry was deployed over the fields to 'the north of the village, skirmishing with Blackford's sharp-shooters.

Howard concluded that Cemetery Ridge was the only tenable position for the limited force present, but, unwilling to draw his forces back without a fight, because of the harmful effect on the soldiers, who were anxious to meet the enemy, he, as a temporary measure to relieve the increasing pressure on the 1st Corps, ordered his 1st and 3d Divisions to seize Oak Ridge. The occupation of the ridge at this time appeared to be feasible, no considerable Confederate force being visible; but in reality the movement was impracticable, as Rodes's division was already in possession, the thick woods and the altitude masking its movements.

General Schurz, conforming to Howard's plan, directed his 3d Division to form in two lines on the right of the 1st Corps, and the 1st Division to the right of the 3d; then, with Dilger's and Wheeler's batteries to the front, he advanced towards Oak Ridge. He also requested a brigade of the 2d Division to be posted in reserve at the dépôt, to protect his right flank; but in Schurz's absence, Barlow, eager for a fight, and anxious to obtain a more advanced position, moved his division to the hill now known as Barlow's Knoll, brushing Doles's sharp-shooters from his path. At that moment this appeared to be the correct thing to do, but subsequent developments proved the movement to have been an error, as it uncovered his right flank to Early's attack and caused the 3d Division to make a corresponding advance to cover Barlow's left. At best, the corps presented a thin and broken line, too feeble to resist the grand attack that was presently to be made on its scattered battalions.

A SURVEY OF THE FIELD BETWEEN ONE AND TWO O'CLOCK P.M.

The general positions about this time were as follows: On the Union side, Biddle's brigade was on the extreme left, along the Hagerstown road, trying to get out of range of Carter's and McIntosh's guns, Cooper's battery replying; then came the Iron Brigade in the woods and Stone's brigade contiguous to the Chambersburg pike, Reynolds's battery in their rear, Stewart's battery and the 6th Wisconsin at the cut, Cutler's brigade in the woods to the right, and Baxter prolonging the line to the Mummasburg road, with Paul in support; Stevens's and Hall's batteries and the 151st Pennsylvania near the Seminary. The 11th Corps was taking ground in this way: Dilger's and Wheeler's batteries to the right of the Mummasburg road, exchanging shots with Page on Oak Hill; Amsberg's and Kryzanowski's brigades coming up in support of the artillery, while Barlow's division—Gilsa's brigade in advance, Ames in support—was pushing out beyond the poor-house in support of Wilkeson's battery, which was carefully feeling for the enemy. Steinwehr's division was approaching the town, and the cavalry was on the flanks, Gamble to the left, Devin on the right.

Along the Confederate line the remnants of Archer's brigade had been got together and posted on the extreme right, along the Hagerstown road ; then came Pettigrew, Brockenbrough, and what was left of Davis's brigade, this brigade prolonging the continuous line to the railroad grading. Behind Heth's division, Pender's division was coming in, Lane's brigade on the right back of Archer, Perrin in rear of Pettigrew, Scales in rear of Brockenbrough, and Thomas behind Davis. Anderson's division was at this time marching in on the pike, the head of column near Marsh Run. Along Heth's front numerous batteries from Pegram's and McIntosh's artillery brigades were advantageously posted, of which more anon. Connecting with the left of Heth was Rodes's division, Daniel's brigade on the right, Iverson along the Mummasburg road, O'Neal on Oak Ridge, Doles near the Carlisle road, and Ramseur in reserve. East of Rock Creek, Early was forming along the Harrisburg road, Gordon's brigade on the right, Hays in the centre, Hoke on the left, and Smith in reserve. Jones's battalion of artillery was on the left of the road, exchanging shots with Wilkeson's 11th Corps battery.

POSITIONS OF THE CONFEDERATE BATTERIES.

The batteries on Hill's line were ably commanded by Colonel Walker, chief of corps artillery, and, owing to their excellent position and superior weight of metal, made it very uncomfortable for the Federal artillery, it being impossible for any advanced Union battery to remain long in one position. These batteries were located about as follows : Wallace's 3-inch rifles on the right, back of the springs, then Rice's Napoleons, Marye's battery, and the Whitworths near the road. North of the road were McGraw's, Crenshaw's, Maurin's (six 3-inch rifles), and Brander's on a hill east of the run. There were several batteries in reserve because they could not get in line, but subsequently Johnson and Hurt went into action near the Hagerstown road. These batteries comprised upward of fifty guns. Carter's batteries were posted on Oak Ridge : Captain Carter, with two 10-pounders and two 12-pounders, on the right ; then Fry's two

10-pounders and two 3 inch rifles, firing on the 1st Corps; and Page, with four 12-pounders, contesting with the 11th Corps, soon re-enforced by Reese's four 3-inch rifles, these two batteries being planted on the eastern slope of the ridge.

Early's batteries east of Rock Creek were in action south of the road: Garber's four 12 pounders on the right, Green's two 10-pounders and two 3-inch rifles in the centre, and Tanner, with four 3-inch rifles, on the left. About eighty guns were engaged on the Confederate and sixty on the Federal side, including Calef's, Heckman's, and Wiedrich's batteries, the last in position on Cemetery Hill.

HETH TO THE ATTACK.

After a furious cannonade, about two o'clock P.M. Heth pushed his division over Willoughby Run to the attack, Pender in close support to prevent a repetition of the disaster happening to Archer and Davis. Pettigrew's strong brigade, numbering about 2500 men, really sustained the brunt of the fight for some time. These troops moved forward in good shape and in quick time, their left—the 11th and 26th North Carolina regiments—entering the woods and running against the Iron Brigade, the other regiments to their right receiving the fire of Cooper's battery and Biddle's brigade.

The Iron Brigade was composed of stubborn fighters, but the rebel line flanked the 19th Indiana, forcing it back and exposing the left of the 24th Michigan, which changed front under a withering fire to face the Confederates; the result was that both regiments were pressed back, forming a short distance in the rear. Major Jones, commanding Pettigrew's brigade, says he broke two lines, but these broken lines—not fresh troops, but the same regiments— rallied in the rear.

While the left of Pettigrew's command was gradually forcing the flank of the Iron Brigade back, his right regiments attacked Biddle's brigade in the fields. Biddle had placed the 121st Pennsylvania on the left, not reaching the Hagerstown road, then the 80th New York and 142d Pennsylvania, with Cooper's battery between the last two regiments. The 121st Pennsylvania formed the extreme left of the 1st Corps infantry, the brigade being well posted on the crest, and

JULY 1 1863.
POSITIONS 3-3:30 P.M.
— UNION
— CONFEDERATE

when Pettigrew advanced against these troops they confidently awaited the attack, feeling able to repel any direct assault against their front. Colonel Gates, of the 80th New York, had sent two of his companies to occupy a house and barn west of the run, which post they held until nearly surrounded, when they escaped through a ravine and rejoined the regiment on Cemetery Hill. As the Confederates marched up the hill, Cooper's guns opened fiercely on them, and when their faces appeared above the crest they received the infantry fire, which checked their line; but the 52d and 47th North Carolina, swinging around, flanked Biddle, pouring in a raking fire which crumbled his line to pieces. In face of this withering enfilade that took them in the left and was working to their rear, Biddle's men tried to change front to the left, and though in the noise and confusion it was impossible to successfully execute the movement, still, the left was refused and the Carolinians held in check for some time. About the time Pettigrew's right was in contact with Biddle and the Iron Brigade, forcing them both slowly back, the 151st Pennsylvania was ordered up to fill a gap between the brigades. This was the only regiment that Doubleday had in reserve, and when it went in there was not a battalion on the field but what was in the front line.

The 151st was posted partly in the field and partly in the woods, connecting with the left of the Iron Brigade and facing the 26th North Carolina. Colonel McFarland, of the 151st Pennsylvania, had cautioned his men against random firing, directing each man to take deliberate aim at the enemy, and in the hour of close and deadly fighting that followed this was strictly observed. The commanding officer of the 26th North Carolina says that the fighting on this line was terrible,—

our men advancing, the enemy stubbornly resisting, until the two lines were pouring volleys into each other at a distance not greater than twenty paces. At last the enemy were compelled to give way. They again made a stand in the woods, and the third time they were driven from their position.

To fully comprehend the tenacious stand made by the Union soldiers, reference is made to Heth's report, which says,—

9

When the 26th North Carolina encountered the second line of the enemy, his
dead marked his line of battle with the accuracy of a line at dress parade.

In this murderous impact against the left of the Iron Brigade and
the right of Biddle's brigade the 26th North Carolina lost more than
half of its men in killed and wounded, including nearly every officer
and eleven men carrying the colors. This frightful loss may be best
realized when it is known that this regiment carried into action over
800 men. Its total loss at Gettysburg was 588, only 216 escaping
unharmed, and of these there were but eighty left for duty on July 4.
Though this command suffered so severely, the regiments it fought
fared almost as badly. The 24th Michigan went into battle with 496
men, and lost 363. The 151st Pennsylvania numbered 467, and
lost 337.

In the mean time, Brockenbrough's Virginians had continued the
advance, the left of their line nearly reaching the Chambersburg
pike ; but they could make no impression on the right regiments of
the Iron Brigade in the woods and the 150th Pennsylvania near
McPherson's barn until the Federal flanks were turned, when they
advanced with better results. Finally, after nearly two hours' persistent and deadly fighting, the Union left was gradually forced
back until a final stand was made in the woods near the Seminary.
It was about four o'clock when the broken lines rallied at the western edge of the grove, and, notwithstanding their appalling losses,
prepared to dispute the farther advance of the enemy.

THE FIGHT ON THE CHAMBERSBURG ROAD.

The Bucktail Brigade, consisting of the 143d, 149th, and 150th
Pennsylvania, defended the position around the McPherson buildings and as far as the railroad cut ; behind them Reynolds's battery,
divided into two sections, was posted. The line first formed a right
angle facing north and west, the 150th and 143d to the left of the
road, extending nearly to the Iron Brigade in the woods, the 149th
in the road, facing north. This line was maintained until Brander's
battery opened on the apex and Rodes enfiladed the right from Oak
Ridge, causing Cutler to retire to the cover of the woods on
Seminary Ridge.

When Cutler fell back, Stone moved the 143d, under a hot fire, to the right of the 149th, protecting his flank and prolonging the line to the rear along the pike. Colonel Stone says the grand advance of the enemy began about 1.30 P.M. "I traced their formation for at least two miles, a nearly continuous line of deployed battalions, with other battalions in mass in reserve." These were Rodes's troops, coming from Oak Ridge, and the left of Heth's and Pender's divisions in the vicinity of the Chambersburg pike. Daniels's brigade of North Carolinians marched direct for Stone's men in the angle of our line. On June 30, Daniels had 2565 men present, and to meet these Stone had in his three regiments 1312 men. Besides Daniels's well-sustained attack, he had to resist the intermittent assaults of Davis and Brockenbrough, who charged occasionally, seeking a vulnerable place in his lines. Daniels first moved the 2d and 45th North Carolina against the cut occupied by the 149th Pennsylvania, then he directed the 43d and 53d North Carolina to the left and the 32d to the right to flank the cut and take the barn, and when the bucktails and tar-heels met, then came the tug of war. Colonel Dwight planted his colors twenty paces on the left, his men being deployed in the cut in single line, their arms resting on the bank, with orders to fire at their opponents' knees. Dwight reports,—

My position was undiscovered by the enemy until he reached a fence twenty-two paces in my front, when he saw my colors flying, directing his fire on them, my regiment not suffering therefrom, as it was directed at the colors. I now fired by battalion; its effect on the enemy was terrible, he being brigade *en masse* at nine paces interval.

This telling volley broke the Confederate line, but with indomitable pluck they again marched up and made another desperate assault on the cut; the defenders, however, reserving their fire as before, again hurled them back. But the 149th was finally forced from the cut by the fire of a battery in an orchard about half a mile away and by that of the 32d North Carolina, which, crossing the cut, flanked the line. In falling back the 149th was forced to leave its colors, and it may be interesting to relate a Confederate account of the capture of a flag, supposed to be this one, by Captain W. R. Bond, of Daniels's brigade. He says,—

A Federal regiment had its colors and guard a short distance in advance of its line. These colors Sergeant Price, of the 42d Mississippi, and half a dozen of his comrades determined to capture. Moving on hands and knees till they had nearly reached the desired object, they suddenly rose, charged and overcame the guard, captured the flag, and were rapidly making off with it when its owners fired upon them; all were struck down but the sergeant, and as he was making off, a young staff officer of my command, having carried a message to Heth, was returning by a short cut, and seeing a man with the stars and stripes, without noticing his uniform, thought he, too, would capture the flag. Dismounting among the dead and wounded, he picked up and fired several muskets at Price, but missed him.

Daniels, finding it impossible to cross the cut at this point, ordered the 45th and 2d back some forty paces to a hill which afforded some shelter, and from this position kept up a lively fusillade. He then, after a close examination of the field, pushed the 32d across the grading, "in front of some troops of Hill's corps (Davis's brigade) who were lying down in line of battle, but would not advance."

Colonel Brabble, commanding the 32d, reports,—

About four o'clock [?] advanced and met the enemy near a railroad cut, the right supported by a regiment of Davis's brigade. Beyond the cut was a large stone barn [McPherson's]. Upon a hill between us and the town was a battery which commanded our front. The brigade made an advance to dislodge him from the barn, but the cut was too difficult to cross, and the 32d fell back. After a short time this regiment charged up to the barn, but, being unsupported, fell back again.

Daniels had been brought up with a short turn; he could go no farther. At this critical moment Pender's fresh division went into action over Heth's exhausted men, and Daniels taking up the advance, his men, with a chorus of terrific yells, rushed again upon the Pennsylvanians and drove them back. The impact of Pender's 6000 or 7000 well-rested soldiers, in conjunction with Daniels's veterans, was too much for the worn-out Federals in that vicinity, and they were glad to get away.

In the defence of this point, Reynolds's, Cooper's, and Calef's batteries played a very important part. The cannoneers stood manfully by their guns, and when one place got too hot they took up another less exposed position, pelting the Confederates with a fire that seriously retarded their progress. Colonel Stone was wounded, and his successor, Colonel Wister, says of this stage of the battle,—

Under a furious musketry fire, the enemy began another advance, mainly against the 149th and 143d. To meet this attack from the north, I divided the 150th into two wings, the right under Lieutenant-Colonel Huidekoper, the left under Major Chamberlain. The right wing changed front forward on first company facing the cut, and behind a fence waited the rebel charge on the flank of the 143d and 149th, which had repulsed a front attack. At a distance of fifty yards a staggering volley was poured into the rebels, followed by a charge of the 149th and this wing of the 150th, the colors of the 149th being recaptured. The line then fell back to its former position, and the fire from the left increasing, the right wing changed front to rear to meet this new attack.

Colonel Dana, of the 143d, assumed command after Wister was wounded. He officially reports,—

> The brigade went into position about eleven A.M. and fought until about four, when the loss among officers and men made it necessary, to avoid capture, to retreat. Facing to the rear, the line was withdrawn in good order some distance, where it halted and fired. Moving thence to a peach-orchard, the brigade again halted and, with some artillery, the fire was renewed.

The result of this desperate contest was that Daniels lost about one-third of his men and Stone's brigade was almost annihilated, losing two-thirds of its number in this and the subsequent stand near the Seminary.

RODES'S DESCENT ON ROBINSON.

Leaving the left of the 1st Corps falling slowly back to the Seminary, we will cross the cut and observe the tug of war between Rodes and Robinson. We have noted the arrival of Rodes and seen him advancing on the right of the 1st Corps; he justly congratulated himself on surprising his opponents, as he could see no troops facing him, and but a desultory artillery fire was in progress between Heth and the Union left; but before he could attack, Robinson appeared on his front and the 11th Corps moved up from the town, Robinson taking the very ground he had intended to occupy. Being thus threatened in two directions, Rodes resolved to hold the 11th Corps with Doles's brigade until Early could assist, and to crush Robinson with his other three brigades. Taking Baxter's advance as a menace, he determined to settle him by assailing him on the right with O'Neal's brigade, while Iverson attacked in front, Ramseur in close support.

O'Neal promptly advanced in the following order: the 6th, 12th, and 26th in line, the 3d moving to the right and the 5th to the left. Iverson formed his North Carolinians to the right of O'Neal's Alabamians, near the Mummasburg road, the 12th first, then the 23d, 20th, and 5th Regiments in the order named, his left reaching the road, but leaving a considerable space to O'Neal's right. Rodes purposed that the attack should be simultaneous, but, happily for Baxter, this part of the program miscarried. Baxter says that he carried into action less than 1200 men, and Paul had about 1300. Opposed to these, O'Neal was swinging around on his right with 1800, Iverson on his front with 1500, and Ramseur in reserve with about 1200 more. If this blow had been delivered as intended, it is safe to say that Robinson's retreat would have been forced in short order. But O'Neal had many difficulties to overcome; marching over the hill, through the brush, over fences and rocks, and, being in the advance, he came in collision with Baxter before Iverson came up. To meet O'Neal, Baxter changed front to right, forming along the road and presenting a firm front. His men received the enemy courageously, and the result was, to quote Rodes's words, "that the whole brigade was repulsed quickly and with loss."

O'Neal reports,—

They found the enemy strongly posted, and after a desperate and bloody fight of about half an hour were compelled to fall back.

Colonel Pickens, of the 12th, says that they were engaged about fifteen minutes, and were flanked and in danger of being surrounded, so they had to get out. This flank fire came largely from the 45th New York and Dilger's battery, of the 11th Corps. O'Neal's soldiers hurriedly made for the rear, and were with difficulty rallied beyond the range of the Union fire.

O'Neal had scarcely gone when Baxter saw Iverson's Confederates menacing his left and rear, and to meet this attack he changed front to the left, moving up to the crest of the hill behind a low stone wall, and there waited until the enemy got within range.

Those who have observed this point will remember that back of the position which Baxter occupied there is quite a descent, but in front of it the ground is nearly level, and over this plateau Iverson's brigade was advancing. Baxter's regiments behind the wall were posted in this order : the 90th Pennsylvania on the right, the right battalion refused along the Mummasburg road, the colors in the point of the angle ; then the 12th Massachusetts, 88th Pennsylvania, 9th New York, 94th New York, and 11th Pennsylvania. To the left of Baxter's line some of Paul's and Cutler's regiments came forward to the edge of the woods and opened a savage fire on Iverson's right. Iverson had halted while Carter's guns shelled the Union position, hence the delay in moving at the same time as O'Neal. This done, he received orders to "advance to meet the enemy who are approaching to take the battery." Before he got fairly in motion, O'Neal had been repulsed, consequently Baxter had abundant opportunity to receive him with the best he had in the shop. Expecting to be fully supported, Iverson confidently marched to the attack with a line as straight as if on parade, apparently unaware of the hostile troops crouching in the shadow of the low stone wall in his front.

When the Carolinians were about 100 paces distant, Baxter's men arose and poured a withering fire into their faces with terrible effect. Hundreds of the Confederates fell at the first volley, plainly marking their line with a ghastly row of dead and wounded men, whose blood trailed the course of their line with a crimson stain clearly discernible for several days after the battle, until the rain washed the gory record away. Those who were uninjured broke to the rear, taking refuge from the pitiless storm in a little gully or depression about 200 paces from the Union line.

A deadly duel at once began between the opposing lines, until Iverson's men, seeing that they were left to their fate, lost heart and evinced a disposition to surrender. Just at this time Baxter, riding behind his brigade, ordered his men to give them the cold steel ; his soldiers promptly responded, and, led by the 88th Pennsylvania, the entire line, facing in this direction, made a rush for Iverson's men in the gully. This charge resulted in the capture of nearly all of the 5th, 20th, and 23d North Carolina, the 88th Pennsylvania taking in the 23d, colors and all, and the flag of another regiment ; the 97th New York captured the 20th and its flag, but this standard was retaken by Daniels later in the day, its captor staying too

long to show his prize, and when he got ready to go to the town
he ran into Daniels's men, who kindly and promptly relieved him
from any further responsibility for that flag.

Iverson says of this affair,—

Colonel O'Neal having been instantaneously driven back on my left, upon which
the enemy charged in overwhelming force upon and captured nearly all that were
left of my brigade. When I saw handkerchiefs raised and my line still lying
down, I characterized the surrender as disgraceful; but when I found that 500
of my men were lying dead and wounded on a line as straight as a dress parade,
I exonerated the survivors. I endeavored, during the confusion among the enemy
incident to the capture of my men, to charge them with the 12th North Carolina
and 3d Alabama, but in the noise and excitement my voice could not be heard.

General Ewell says,—

The unfortunate mistake of Iverson at this critical juncture, in sending word to
Rodes that one of his regiments had raised the white flag and gone over to the
enemy, might have produced the most disastrous consequences.

The survivors of Iverson's command fell back in great disorder, but
were rallied and placed with Ramseur's brigade, where they fought
creditably until the day was decided. General Robinson claims to
have taken 1000 prisoners; but Iverson reports a total loss of 820,
of which only 308 were missing. These last figures are evidently
too low, as the official report of the 97th New York gives 213 of the
20th North Carolina as captured by it, and the other regiments engaged in the charge all report large numbers taken, but it is likely
that many of these subsequently escaped. After the charge, Baxter
fell back to the fence. and, being out of ammunition, Paul relieved
him.

General Rodes was intensely disgusted at the disastrous result of
this move, and though he had lost over 1000 of his best troops, he
quickly formed his broken lines and, with Ramseur's fresh brigade
in place of Iverson's, and O'Neal coming down the ridge, promptly
came to the front once more. To meet this new attack Paul's brigade formed on the hill a little in rear of Baxter's first position,
the 13th Massachusetts on the right, posted on the slope facing the
Mummasburg road, then the 104th New York, 16th Maine, 107th
Pennsylvania, and 94th New York on the left. While this line

obliqued somewhat down the hill, the locations given above are nearly correct; still, there were many changes in the surging line, some of the regiments charging to and across the road in a vain effort to shake off Rodes's grip.

THE 1ST CORPS AT FOUR O'CLOCK.

It was near four o'clock, and the 1st Corps had been forced back to the vicinity of the Seminary woods, having lost about 2500 men killed and wounded, but up to this time few had been captured. Not counting the cavalry, it is estimated that scarcely 2500 men formed the ragged line of blue that rallied along the edge of the woods when the last grand rebel advance swept the ground. Many had carried their wounded comrades to the rear, some had straggled, and others had been detailed for various purposes, thus sensibly diminishing the fighting strength of the corps. But the Confederates had suffered more than their opponents, Heth having lost over 2000 men, most of his brigades being completely used up; Rodes's division had also lost heavily (more than 1500 men), the Confederates paying dearly for every foot of ground gained.

General Ewell was seriously impressed with the situation. He says,—

All of Rodes's troops were now engaged. The enemy was moving large bodies of troops from the town against my left, and affairs were in a very critical condition, when Early, coming up on the Heidlersburg road, opened a brisk fire upon large columns moving against Doles' left, and ordered up Gordon, etc.

Indeed, if Early had not arrived at this opportune time for the Confederates, the result of the first day at Gettysburg might have been very different. Up to this hour 15,000 Confederates had failed to drive the 9000 soldiers of the 1st Corps more than a quarter of a mile, though they had attacked with much spirit and maintained the assault with the greatest pertinacity; but if the three divisions of Heth, Rodes, and Pender had made a united advance any time after one o'clock they would have overwhelmed the 1st Corps and literally swept it before them.

ARRIVAL OF GENERAL LEE.

General Lee, accompanied by General Pendleton, chief of artillery, arrived near the crest of an eminence about two o'clock, and, dismounting, took a position overlooking the field. The battle was raging fiercely; Carter's and Jones's batteries were at that time vigorously playing on the Union line that had been pressing Hill's corps, and when the Federal guns were turned upon their new assailants, they were enfiladed by the battalions of McIntosh and Pegram, posted in front of Lee on the right and left of the road. Lee suggested posting batteries on the right to enfilade the valley between the Union line and the town and the Union artillery next to the town. Ten batteries (including Johnson's and Hurt's) and Garnett's and Poague's battalions were hurried towards the desired position; but the infantry supports not being thought strong enough, action was suspended until the Union line had fallen back. If this strong force of artillery had taken position at this point, south of the Hagerstown road, earlier in the day, it would have raked the valley in rear of the Union line with a fire under which every living thing would have perished.

EARLY ATTACKS THE 11TH CORPS.

The head of Early's column arrived and formed line east of Rock Creek about one P.M. Gordon's Georgia brigade, the 60th Regiment in advance, then the 31st, 13th, 61st, and 38th, in the order named, the 26th in the rear, formed on the right, above the bridge ; Hays's Louisiana brigade, the 5th, 6th, and 9th Regiments taking position on the right of the road, the 7th and 8th to the left ; Hoke's (Avery's) North Carolina brigade formed on the left of Hays, the 6th on the right, 21st in the centre, and 57th on the left. Smith's brigade was supporting the artillery, but, not sustaining any loss, may be considered out of the first day's fight.

When he had his command well in hand, Early moved forward, Gordon on the lead, crossed the creek above the bridge, and with an unearthly chorus of savage yells, the rebels went straight for Gilsa's brigade, deployed on the banks of the creek and on the hill. They were just in time, as Ames and Amsberg were flanking Doles, who was stoutly contesting the ground, biding his time until Early should burst like an avalanche on the flank of his assailants. Doles had posted his 1400 Georgians in a good position, well supported by Rodes's cannon on Oak Hill, his front covered by Blackford's sharpshooters, and successfully parried every thrust of his opponents until Early came bravely to the rescue.

POSITIONS OF THE 11TH CORPS.

Gilsa's brigade faced Gordon, on the outer slope of Barlow's (Blocher's) Knoll, the 54th and 68th New York stretched along the banks of the creek, the 153d Pennsylvania on the hill; the 41st New York was absent on a scout. Ames was formed somewhat *en echelon* in rear of Gilsa, and was aiming to strike Doles's left flank. The brigade was formed with the 17th Connecticut on the right, then the 25th, 75th, and 107th Ohio; but four companies of the 17th were skirmishing near the railroad bridge, and most of the 75th were away on a reconnoissance. Wilkeson's battery assisted Barlow in defence of the position; but Wilkeson met a soldier's death early in the action, the command devolving on Lieutenant Bancroft, who, with Lieutenant Merkle, skilfully handled the guns until the retreat. Kryzanowski's brigade prolonged the line to the Carlisle road, two companies of the 58th New York on the right, then the 26th Wisconsin, 75th Pennsylvania, 82d Ohio, and 119th New York. Amsberg extended the line, supporting Dilger's and Wheeler's batteries, towards the Mummasburg road, the 45th New York and 61st Ohio skirmishing, the 157th New York, 82d Illinois, and 74th Pennsylvania in line.

A CONFEDERATE VIEW OF THE 11TH CORPS LINE.

Colonel Swallow, of Early's division, says he reached Rodes about one P.M., and could see the two divisions of Howard's corps getting into position. They seemed greatly scattered. The division in front of Rodes seemed to stand alone and totally unconnected with Reynolds's right, there being a wide space, extending through the line of battle to the Union rear. The Federals in front of Early were in the same order, standing alone, not connecting with the other division. Some Confederates who had been captured by Reynolds about noon had been recaptured. Rodes was informed by them that Heth and Pender were in the Union front. He at once sent a courier to Heth, requesting him to press the enemy vigorously, and sent this message to Early: "Heth and Pender are in Reynolds's front. I can burst through the enemy in an hour." Early replied, "All right; burst through." It was now nearly two o'clock, and when Swallow told Early that Howard's corps was in his front, he laughed and said, "Why, these are the very same chaps that our fellows routed at Chancellorsville." Early now began to press the enemy, and from signs not to be mistaken by a soldier, was satisfied that the utter defeat of the enemy was certain.

DEFEAT OF BARLOW'S DIVISION.

We left Doles in a critical position, with a brigade of the 11th Corps menacing either flank; but Gordon's attack relieved Doles, who then advanced, taking the hill at "3.30 P.M."

But to return to Early's march. He reports,—

> Gordon, about three P.M., was ordered to the support of Dole, who was being pressed by the enemy; and as soon as Gordon was fairly engaged, Hays and Hoke were ordered forward, the artillery, supported by Smith, to follow.

Gordon says,—

> The enemy had succeeded in gaining a position upon Doles's left, causing him to retreat. The enemy made a most obstinate resistance, until the colors on portions of the lines were less than fifty paces apart, when his line was broken [Gilsa's] and driven back, leaving the flank which this line had protected [Ames's] exposed to my fire. An effort was made by the enemy to change his front and check our advance, but failed, this line, too, being driven back. . . . I was here ordered to halt.

Avery crossed the creek to the left of Hays, striking Barlow's discomfited battalions, who made a futile stand, Avery reporting, "The enemy stubbornly holding their position until we had climbed over the fence in their midst."

Hays drove all before him until he reached the railroad, at which place he came within range of Heckman's guns, which checked him for a time, when he changed front forward on first company, first battalion, of part of his brigade, to face Heckman's and Coster's brigade, then deploying from the town. He routed Coster, captured two of Heckman's guns, and drove the fugitives into the town, following them closely and taking prisoners at every step; finally resting his lines on one of the streets, with Hoke's (Avery's) brigade on the left.

THE STAND OF THE 11TH CORPS.

The Confederate account of the overthrow of the 11th Corps having been briefly given, we will now consider the other side. General Howard reports that at 4.10 P.M., finding he could hold his position no longer, he sent a positive order to the 1st and 11th Corps to fall back gradually, disputing every inch of the ground, and form on Cemetery Hill. With respect to the attack on Barlow's division on the knoll, Ames says he was driven from this position, the men of Gilsa's brigade running through his lines, creating considerable confusion. Doubtless, Gilsa's men came back with little regard to tactics, and this unfortunate break was the beginning of the crumbling of the Union right flank ; but the rout was inevitable ; if they had not retreated, every one would have been killed or captured when Hays and Avery swung around in their rear. This break took Ames's troops in flank and rear, and though they tried to change front to fight Early, it was too late ; he gave them no opportunity to get in shape to make a successful defence.

Barlow had many good regiments, and they made a gallant stand, as the figures show. A little to the left of Hays, a tattered Federal regiment faced about and tried to make a stand, led by a mounted officer, who, riding among them, waved his hat and sword, shouting, "Don't run, men ; none but cowards run." Some of the Confederates, admiring his pluck, cried out, "Don't shoot that man ;" but a volley brought him down, and his heroic command was scattered by the advancing battalions of Hays and Avery.

DOLES'S ATTACK ON SCHIMMELFENNIG.

We left Doles's brigade in line from Oak Hill to Rock Creek. When Gordon's battle-flags burst through the bushes skirting Rock Creek, Doles promptly took up the advance, moving forward his left near Barlow's Knoll and his right west of the Carlisle road, connecting with O'Neal's brigade. When Barlow's division broke, Doles struck Ames's flank, which he pursued until threatened by Schimmelfennig on his right. He reports,—

While we were in pursuit of the enemy a strong force appeared on our right. We changed our front to meet this force. Attacked and routed it, pursuing it across the plain, but few escaping.

All this reads smoothly enough, but it is more than likely that he did not have so easy a job as it appears. When the 1st Division was overwhelmed, the 3d Division was exposed to a flank attack as well as Doles's front fire, and whenever these troops formed line their right crumbled from Early's vigorous fire from that quarter. Major Wills, of the 119th New York, says,—

> Our regiment did not yield, but stood firmly until the 1st Division had fallen back and Amsberg's brigade on our left had disappeared; then we retired.

Major Ledig, of the 75th Pennsylvania, states,—

> About two o'clock the whole brigade advanced near half a mile and opened on the enemy. The 82d Ohio, on my left, was flanked and gave way. I directed the fire left oblique, and began to retreat behind a fence. During this short period—say fifteen minutes—I lost 111 killed and wounded.

Dilger and Wheeler fought their batteries skilfully, only limbering to the rear when in danger of losing their guns, and going into battery at every favorable position to check the Confederate advance.

COSTER IN THE BREACH.

It has been stated that General Schurz desired, earlier in the day, that a reserve brigade be posted near the dépôt, to take in flank any Confederate force threatening the line he proposed to establish ; but we have seen how that line was advanced half a mile or more, thus rendering the proposed plan impracticable.

Coster's brigade, composed of the 134th and 154th New York, 27th and 73d Pennsylvania, was posted here when the corps was falling back, and, with Heckman's battery, made a gallant but vain effort to stay the victorious march of the Confederates, who were pressing the fugitives closely. Coster posted the 73d in reserve at the edge of the town and hurriedly pushed the rest of the brigade— the 134th on the right and the 27th on the left—some 200 yards out in the fields between the railroad and the Harrisburg road. Heckman went into battery to the left of the road, the Confederates being in range at once. He writes,—

My battery was engaged thirty minutes; during that time I expended 113 rounds, mostly canister. The enemy had gotten very close, when the order was given to limber up, but too late to save my whole battery, two pieces being left.

But although these regiments and batteries of the 11th Corps made a creditable stand, it is remarkable, when compared with the 1st Corps, how little damage they inflicted upon their opponents. The loss of the corps, including about 1400 prisoners, aggregates nearly 2700 in the first day's operations. Early officially reports his loss on this day at 586, and if to this be added about 160 for Doles and 54 for O'Neal and the artillery, the Confederate loss will amount to about 800, less than 100 of this number being captured.

RODES OVERWHELMS PAUL.

As soon as the remnants of Iverson's and the shattered battalions of O'Neal's brigades were rallied, they were aligned with Ramseur and a general advance made on Paul's exhausted troops, holding the hill formerly occupied by Baxter, who was now reforming near the cut. Ramseur reports that about four o'clock he advanced, sending the 4th and 2d North Carolina to the left of the road and the 30th and 14th North Carolina to the right. He "found three regiments of Iverson's command almost annihilated, and the 3d Alabama, of O'Neal's brigade, coming out of the fight from Iverson's right." He took this regiment and the 12th North Carolina, which had escaped the general ruin, and, re-enforced by O'Neal, coming down and around the base of Oak Hill, made a fierce attack on Paul, striking him in front and right, this being the identical movement attempted an hour or two before. Ramseur says,—

With these regiments I turned the enemy's strong position in a body of woods, surrounded by a stone fence, by attacking *en masse* on the right, driving him back and getting in his rear. The enemy, seeing his flank turned, made but a feeble resistance to the front attack.

Paul and the fragments of Baxter's command did not abandon the hill in the way that Ramseur infers, but clung to the woods with a bull-dog grip. The 13th Massachusetts held the right of Paul's brigade, and when Rodes's men got too close, repulsed them by a bayonet charge, taking 132 prisoners, but was quickly charged in return by Ramseur and O'Neal, and being almost surrounded, lost three-fourths of its number before it got clear.

In their desperate efforts to shake off the Confederate grip the 94th and 104th New York also charged, Colonel Prey reporting,—

my line running obliquely to the crest, where the enemy was posted behind a wall, covered by thick brush, the fire from the wall taking us on the flank as the line advanced. The three left companies gained the wall and dislodged the enemy. I then advanced my line to the Mummasburg road, taking thirty-five or forty prisoners.

Robinson says that he held the hill till nearly five o'clock, when the troops retired fighting, the 16th Maine making a last obstinate but hopeless charge to the road ; but nearly all were shot or captured, and the survivors, finding their retreat cut off, destroyed their flag to prevent its capture, dividing the ribbons. When the decimated battalions of Paul's command finally fell back, they discovered the enemy in every direction, having to run the gantlet of fire from Doles on one flank, Pender on the other, and Rodes bringing up the rear.

It was now after four o'clock, and we shall turn our attention to the last stand made back of the Seminary, which occurred about the time Robinson was driven from the woods north of the cut.

THE LAST STAND OF THE 1ST CORPS.

We have followed Biddle's, Meredith's, and Stone's brigades to their last stand back of the Seminary buildings. If these troops had fallen back at once to Cemetery Hill, the loss in prisoners when they were finally forced off would probably have been prevented ; but good soldiers always stand by their guns, and when the artillery unlimbered the dough-boys promptly formed line in support. It was probably after four o'clock when Pender advanced to the last assault. General Wadsworth says it was about 3.45 ; Cutler and Biddle note it as about four ; Colonel McFarland says 4.20 by his watch ; Dana, after four ; Robinson and Captain Cooper, about five ; while on the

Confederate side, Colonel Grimes and Major Engelhard place it at about four, and Perrin, after four. The Union line was formed in much the same order as when near the creek : Biddle on the left, then the Iron and Bucktail Brigades, and Cutler on the right near the cut, with Baxter back of Stewart's right sections, and Paul trying to stem the tide near the Mummasburg road. On the extreme left, Gamble had dismounted parts of the 8th New York, 3d Indiana, and 12th Illinois cavalry, to cover the flank of the 1st Corps.

WHY SEMINARY HILL WAS HELD.

The desperate and hazardous stand on this line may be explained in this wise. Chief of Artillery Wainwright having heard General Doubleday speak of holding Cemetery Hill, and not then knowing of such a place, confounded it with Seminary Hill, and, loyal to his chief, planted his guns in what he supposed was the right place, concentrating twelve cannon in a space hardly five yards apart, Reynolds being on the left, then Cooper and Stevens, with Stewart astraddle of the cut.

THE MARCH OF THE CONFEDERATES.

About four o'clock Pender determined to go in again, and passing over Heth's exhausted and greatly-reduced division, with Lane on the right, then Perrin, with Scales on the left and Thomas in the rear, made for the blue line in the shade of the trees. Perrin especially handled his brigade with good judgment, and being in a position to turn and smash the Union flank, he worked his troops for all they were worth. Forming his men, he instructed them not to fire until he gave the order, and with Scales on his left and Heth's division at his back, rushed to the assault. He soon encountered a furious storm of musketry and shells from the Union batteries to the left of the road ; but his instructions were strictly observed ; not a gun was discharged ; the brigade receiving the fire without faltering, rushing up the hill at a charge, and soon forcing the Union lines. Perrin reports,—

We continued the charge without opposition, except from their artillery, which maintained a constant and most galling fire upon us, until we got within 200 yards of their position about the College. While crossing the last fence, about 200 yards from the grove near the College [Seminary], the brigade received the most destructive fire of musketry I have ever been exposed to. We continued to press forward, however, until we reached the edge of the grove. Here the 14th [all South Carolina regiments] was staggered for a moment by the enemy's musketry. It looked to us as though this regiment was entirely destroyed. Here I found myself without support either on the right or left, Scales having halted to return the enemy's fire. This gave the enemy an enfilading fire upon the 14th. I now obliqued the 1st Regiment to the right to avoid a breastwork of rails, behind which the enemy was posted, and then changed front to the left, and attacked in flank. This caused the whole of their artillery on our left—at least thirty pieces— to limber to the rear. Much of their artillery would have been captured, but the 1st and 14th, in their pursuit, again met a force of the enemy's infantry, strongly posted behind a stone wall near and to the left of the College. While the 1st and 14th were driving him from his breastworks, the 12th and 13th Regiments obliqued to the right and charged a stone fence to the right of the College, from which he had kept up a constant and withering fire of musketry upon the front and right flank of the brigade.

This wall was defended by the dismounted cavalry.

Such is Perrin's vivid account of the part he took in this fight. His firm advance swept all the Union defenders from the Seminary grounds.

Scales's share in the work, with his North Carolina brigade, is embodied in the following report:

We passed over them [Heth's men], crossed the ridge, and commenced the descent just opposite the Seminary. Here the brigade encountered a most terrific fire of grape and shell on our flank and grape and musketry on our front. Every discharge made sad havoc in our line; but still we pressed on at double-quick until we reached the bottom, a distance of about seventy-five yards from the ridge we had just crossed and about the same distance from the College in our front. Here I was wounded. Our line had been broken up, and now only a squad, here and there, marked the places where regiments had rested.

That night only 500 of Scales's men, "depressed, dilapidated, and almost unorganized," could be mustered, so severely had they been handled by the battered and broken battalions of the 1st Corps.

THE UNION CANNONEERS STANDING TO THEIR GUNS.

The Union artillery took so important a part in the final defence of Seminary Ridge that it would be an injustice not to notice its heroic stand. The 5th Maine was in position to the left of the Seminary, opening first with spherical case and shell, then with canister, giving the Confederates hot doses until it was long past quitting-time. Battery L changed position frequently, greeting the advancing lines with canister, repulsing several charges, and finally retiring under cover of the cavalry. Cooper opened with case-shot and shell until canister range was reached, giving them unstinted rations of that until he was driven from his position. Hall's 2d Maine had been so badly used in the morning, that after an unsuccessful attempt to find a good position from which to again engage the Confederates, it was sent to the town and rendered invaluable aid in the final retreat.

Probably the fiercest battery fighting at Gettysburg was done by Stewart's B, 4th United States, and is vividly described in the "Cannoneer," written by Private Buell, of that company, and published by the *National Tribune*, Washington, D.C. That battery had not been actively engaged until the corps had been forced back to the hill; then came its turn for a share of the sport. The command was in half battery on both sides of the cut, the right under Stewart and the left in charge of Lieutenant Davison, whose guns were in Thompson's yard, pointing west. When the enemy got within range the battery opened an effective fire with canister, single, double, and finally triple charges, and with such deadly aim that Scales's brigade was broken up with fearful slaughter and Daniels was held in check for probably half an hour. Lieutenant Davison, though bleeding from two wounds, one ankle being shattered, refused to order the guns off, but, supported by a cannoneer, hobbled among his gunners, exhorting them to feed the canister to the approaching lines of gray, until the guns were so hot that the thumb-leathers were burned to a crisp. When Scales got too close, he ran his guns forward to the road, enfilading the enemy's lines with a terrific storm of double canister until the rebs hustled to the rear in confusion.

Stewart, with his guns north of the cut, made it red hot for any of the Johnnies who dared come within range, but the converging fire became so destructive that he was finally obliged either to limber to the rear or lose his guns.

Colonel Wainwright reports,—

All the batteries were limbered to the rear, and moved at a walk down the Chambersburg pike until the infantry had all left. By this time the enemy had lapped our retreating columns and opened a severe fire from behind a paling fence within fifty yards of the road. The batteries now broke into a trot, but too late to save everything; Reynolds's last piece had a horse shot, and just as he disengaged it, three more of the horses were down, so it was impossible to bring it off.

It was a wonder that any of these guns escaped ; a rush by the rebs would have taken them all in; but the pursuing lines came on so cautiously that they all got safely off, with the exception noted.

In the last stand made back of the Seminary, portions of all the regiments rallied behind the rail barricade which Robinson's men had hastily thrown up in the morning, and when flanked from this slight defence, they retreated as best they could. The 7th Wisconsin retired by right of companies to the rear, through the orchard, over the hill, and along the pike to the town. On coming out of the orchard, the men found the Confederates advancing in line of battle, about 300 yards to the left and rear of their late position. To the right, on the opposite side of the pike, was another line, the left of which extended nearly to the town ; this line was stationary and supported by artillery. In passing out, both these lines and the artillery delivered an enfilading fire, causing more loss than at any time during the day. The 6th Wisconsin, facing to the rear, with its right to the bank, moved steadily back to the city, almost directly towards the Confederate lines, which, having disposed of the 11th Corps, were now swinging round to surround the remnant of the 1st Corps.

THE PANIC IN THE TOWN.

The 11th Corps entered the town first, closely pursued by Hays and Hoke, who reached the edge of the village while the rear-guard of the 1st Corps was still disputing Hill's advance on Seminary Hill. Chaplain William H. Locke, in his "Story of the Regiment," plainly describes the situation in these words:

The Lutheran Church was crowded with our wounded. We were going in and out among these, when the broken and flying battalions of the 11th Corps came streaming in from the right. It was a sight never to be forgotten. Crowding through the streets and up the alleys and over fences, in utter ignorance of whither they were going, every moment increased the confusion and dismay. To add to the terror, the enemy gained possession of the town, and, firing rapidly into our retreating ranks, shot and shell mingled their horrid sounds with the groans of the dying. But that retreat was not all confusion. The same noble corps that had maintained its ground on the left fell back in solid phalanx. Shoulder to shoulder they marched, rank after rank halting to fire upon the advancing foe, and then closing up again with daring coolness.

Any attempt to make a stand in this bewildered and frantic mob was attended with the greatest difficulty and peril, yet many fragments of both corps did their level best to breast the storm and repulse the graybacks.

Amidst all this excitement the 17th Connecticut deployed in the streets, firing several rounds before it was compelled to fall back ; the 119th New York made a plucky stand at the foot of Washington Street, holding the enemy in check a little while and then retreating in good order to the hill. A section of Dilger's battery unlimbered near the Diamond, assisting the 119th by firing canister into the faces of the pursuers. Colonel Dawes, of the 7th Wisconsin, says that the crowd was frightful and the men almost prostrated with over-exertion and the great heat, while the Confederate sharpshooters occupied the streets on the left, their line of battle almost encircling the city. The 76th New York lost eight or ten men by falling bricks and rifle-shots, and Colonel Dana, of the 143d, claims that his command was the last organized body to pass through, all the time under a destructive fire, reaching the hill between five and six o'clock.

RALLYING ON CEMETERY HILL.

General Hancock, with orders from General Meade to take command, left Taneytown, thirteen miles distant, at 1.10 P.M., arriving on the hill about three o'clock. The stragglers, camp followers, and slightly wounded men from both corps were hunting the hill as a place of refuge before this hour, and as Hancock arrived the stream of stragglers and fighting men was setting strongly in this direction. Everybody appeared to feel that the retreat was at an end and that this position was the rallying-point, and as the begrimed and weary men came up the road they were quickly reformed and marched to the right or left to meet the expected attack. The many

cannon shotted and in position, with the cannoneers standing calmly
by, together with the firm front presented by Steinwehr's troops,
had a happy effect by assuring the worn-out soldiers that help was
at hand.

The cavalry division was in good form on the plain near the Emmittsburg road, the same ground over which Pickett's division
charged on the 3d.   Hancock says,—

The position was already partially occupied on my arrival by direction of
General Howard.   Some difficulty was experienced in forming the troops of the
11th Corps, but by vigorous efforts a sufficiently formidable line was established
to deter the enemy from any serious assault.   The enemy pushed forward a line
of battle for a short distance east of the Baltimore pike, but it was easily checked
by our artillery fire.   As soon as the line of battle was shown by the enemy,
Wadsworth's division and a battery were placed on the eminence just across the
pike.   The rest of the 1st Corps was on the right and left of the Taneytown
road and connected with the left of the 11th Corps, which occupied that part of
the cemetery to the right and left of the Baltimore pike.   Williams's division, of
the 12th Corps, arrived as these arrangements were being completed, and was
established to the right and rear of Wadsworth's.   Geary's division, of the 12th
Corps, subsequently arriving, I ordered it to the high ground near Round Top
Mountain.   The head of the 3d Corps appeared shortly afterwards (between five
and six P.M.) on the Emmittsburg road.

About dark, Hancock, considering the position perfectly safe,
turned the command over to Slocum and returned to Taneytown
to report to General Meade.   The above is Hancock's concise and
impartial report of the situation, and the reports of the subordinate
officers trend in the same direction.

Howard states,—

At 4.30 the column reached the hill, the enemy pressing hard.   He made a
single attempt to turn our right, but his line was instantly broken by Wiedrich's
battery.

Doubleday reports,—

All the troops passed tranquilly on, although the enemy was firing into them
from the side streets, and all reformed promptly on their arrival at Cemetery Hill,
and in a very short time were again ready for service.

Robinson's division formed line on the left, facing the Emmittsburg road, Baxter building temporary breastworks at the bloody

CAPTAIN EDWARD L. GILLIGAN,
Company F.

LIEUTENANT ALBERT BOOZ,
Company E.

CAPTAIN CHRISTIAN S. CARMACK,
Company E.

HENRY S. BOOZ,
Company E.

JOHN DE HAVEN,
Company E.

angle, this command being relieved on the 2d by the Philadelphia Brigade. Colonel Wainwright posted the batteries to command the approaches from the town in case the enemy should attempt to follow. The "Cannoneer" says, "It may have been about five o'clock when we got fairly into our new position on Cemetery Hill."

The batteries unlimbered in the following order: Captain Hall, with three serviceable guns, on the left of the cemetery, near the Taneytown road. In the cemetery, in the order named, were Wheeler, with five guns; Dilger, with six guns; and Wilkeson, with six guns. In the pike, near the cemetery gate, Stewart's four guns were posted; north of the Baltimore pike came Wiedrich, with four guns. Cooper, with four guns; Reynolds, with five guns; and Stevens, with six guns, were in position on the extreme right, to sweep the eastern face of the hill with a cross-fire. At this hour Heckman was on the road in reserve. The above shows forty-three serviceable guns ready to play on the enemy if he should advance. Several pieces had been disabled, one from Wheeler's battery being left dismounted on the field and two of Heckman's captured.

While forming on the hill, several important detachments arrived to strengthen the depleted ranks of the infantry, among them being the 7th Indiana, most of the 58th New York, 75th Ohio, and other details that had been on detached duty; in all, probably nearly 1000 men. There were undoubtedly more than 6000 soldiers in line close to the cemetery, ready to defend this position to the last, and it is preposterous to imagine that the few tired and fought-out brigades of Confederates who were on hand at any time before six o'clock could have made an impression on this well-defended position; it was well for them that no serious attempt was made. True, these men were scorched by the heat, tired, and thirsty, but they were in no worse condition than their pursuers, and if Early had attacked the position he would have found the old 1st Corps at the new stand and ready for business. His lines would have been raked by the numerous cannon and riddled by the bullets of the men of the sphere and crescent.

AN ANALYSIS OF THE UNION STRENGTH AND LOSS, JULY 1, 1863.

A brief glance at the losses furnishes an interesting study. The following statistics are taken from the official reports, histories, and inscriptions on the battle-field memorials. This data applies to the battle of July 1 only.

1st Corps.	Strength.	Loss.
Head-quarters	25	5
Iron Brigade	1806	1050
Cutler's brigade	1636	900
Paul's brigade	1370	950
Baxter's brigade	1394	575
Biddle's brigade	1396	750
Stone's brigade	1312	750
Artillery brigade	619	83
Total	9558	5063

The 7th Indiana is omitted in the above, it not having participated in the battle of the first day.

11th Corps.	Strength.	Loss.
Head-quarters	25	4
Gilsa's brigade	1119	300
Ames's brigade	1246	550
Coster's brigade	1356	450
Amsberg's brigade	1990	700
Kryzanowski's brigade	1392	575
Artillery brigade	645	50
Total	7773	2629

Smith's brigade is not included in the above, and but two companies of the 58th New York and 160 men of the 75th Ohio, the remainder being on a scout. The 41st New York was also absent on detached duty, and did not participate in the fight on the 1st.

Buford's Cavalry Division.	Strength.	Loss.
Gamble's brigade	1550	99
Devin's brigade	1500	28
Calef's battery	100	12
Total	3150	139

Summary.	Strength.	Loss.
1st Corps	9,558	5063
11th Corps	7,773	2629
Cavalry division	3,150	139
Total	20,481	7831

These figures indicate that the Union force engaged on July 1, not including guards and detailed men, was less than 20,000, but this is greatly in excess of the reports of the officers then in command. General Doubleday reports that the 1st Corps consisted of about 8200 men when it entered the battle, Robinson says that his division went in with less than 2500, and Baxter states that his brigade had a few less than 1200. Schurz gives the strength of his two divisions as hardly over 6000 effectives, and Howard says that the two corps numbered less than 18,000.

The losses of the first day are in some cases approximated, but a careful search of the official reports enables us to give close figures.

CONFEDERATE STRENGTH AND LOSS, JULY 1, 1863.

The task of accurately stating the Confederate loss is more difficult, but the figures given are in most cases official.

	Strength.	Loss.
Heth's division	7,448	2475
Pender's division	6,455	1100
Rodes's division	8,135	2525
Early's division	4,800	586
Artillery, nineteen batteries	2,280	92
17th Virginia and White's cavalry	700	. .
Head-quarters	200	. .
Total	30,018	6778

Smith's brigade is not included in Early's strength, it not having been actively engaged.

Of the 5063 men lost by the 1st Corps on July 1, about 3000 were killed and wounded, and of the 11th Corps (2629), 1500 can be accounted for in the same way, thus making a total loss of 4500 killed and wounded in both corps.

Of the Confederate loss, some 4300 were killed and wounded,

the remainder being captured, mostly by the 1st Corps. The loss of the Johnnies fighting the 1st Corps was about 5800, those pitted against the 11th Corps about 800, the remainder being posted to the credit of Buford's carbineers.

The 9000 men of the 1st Corps received the attack of Heth's, Pender's, and all of Rodes's division except Doles's brigade,—in all, upward of 17,000 men ; while the 7500 men in the 11th Corps withstood Early's division, Doles's brigade of Rodes's division, and part of O'Neal's,—about 7000 strong. In this calculation the artillery is not mentioned, but it should be understood that it was actively engaged all the time.

Some of the Confederate troops, although under fire and losing men, are not reckoned in this statement, as they did not actually exchange rifle-shots with their adversaries.

The historian is aware that the above figures materially differ from other statements given by careful speakers and writers on this subject, but the detailed facts are here, and the reader can readily judge as to their accuracy.

A PARTING SHOT.

So ended the first day at Gettysburg, and though a hopeless contest for the Union side at any hour after one o'clock, it was fought with a vigor and spirit that have always elicited admiration from the impartial observer.

Colonel Swallow writes,—

All bear testimony to the gallant manner in which Reynolds's corps behaved. Even at three o'clock, when the order was issued for a general advance of the whole Confederate line, Reynolds's veterans, although falling back before the Confederates, still to a great extent preserved that soldierly bearing in defeat that contrasted strangely with the terror and demoralization that had taken possession of their companions. In speaking of the first day's battle, therefore, the conduct of Reynolds's corps must not be confounded with the divisions of Schurz and Barlow. Had these two divisions been placed directly in the rear of Reynolds, instead of scattering them all around the northern part of the town, and had they stood up to Reynolds's corps like brave men, they might possibly have accomplished something great.

That writer appears to have a prejudice against the 11th Corps. General Schurz attempted to make the identical movement suggested by him, but circumstances then unknown foiled the plan. Some of the regiments composing that corps *did* go to pieces early in the action, but there were undoubtedly as good regiments in this corps as in any other in the army, and an analysis of the losses of some of them, notably the 75th Pennsylvania, 154th New York, and 107th Ohio, will confirm this statement. The entire line was raked by a terrific tempest of shot and shell from six batteries, sweeping every foot of ground with a fire that would have shaken any body of troops so posted. They did the best they could in a bad position, and made a gallant fight against a skilful opponent possessing an immense advantage in everything necessary to success. Take it all in all, the men on this ensanguined field, both Union and Confederate, fought with a courage unsurpassed on any battle-field during the terrible war of the Rebellion.

SOME OFFICIAL FIGURES ON GETTYSBURG.

The strength of the contesting armies at Gettysburg has been the subject of much dispute, and the following figures, covering the entire battle are given for general information.

The returns of the Army of the Potomac, June 30, 1863, show present for duty, equipped :

	Infantry.	Artillery.	Cavalry.
1st Corps	9,403	619	. .
2d Corps	12,363	551	. .
3d Corps	11,247	677	. .
5th Corps	11,954	555	. .
6th Corps	14,516	1,039	. .
11th Corps	9,197	644	. .
12th Corps	8,193	396	. .
Cavalry Corps	. .	. .	14,973
Artillery Reserve	335	2,211	. .
Cavalry on corps duty	. .	. .	258
Total	77,208	6,692	15,231

This gives a total strength of 99,131 ; but all these were not actively engaged in the battle, Huey's brigade of cavalry being with the trains, and of the 6th Corps, Wheaton's division was the only infantry seriously engaged. To obtain the actual number of com-

batants, deduct about fifteen per cent. for teamsters, hospital attendants, musicians, and men on detailed duty.

The field return of the Army of the Potomac for July 4, 1863, is
as follows:

	Strength.
1st Corps	5,430
2d Corps	6,924
3d Corps	6,130
5th Corps	9,553
6th Corps	12,832
11th Corps	5,513
12th Corps	9,757
Total	56,139

This does not include the cavalry and reserve artillery, but it does
include some re-enforcements received since July 1, among them
Stannard's Vermonters, assigned to the 1st Corps, and Lockwood's
Marylanders, to the 12th Corps.

LOSSES OF THE ARMY OF THE POTOMAC.

General Headquarters	4
1st Corps	6,059
2d Corps	4,369
3d Corps	4,211
5th Corps	2,187
6th Corps	242
11th Corps	3,801
12th Corps	1,082
Cavalry Corps	852
Artillery Reserve	242
Total	23,049

It is more difficult to obtain correct figures for the Southern side,
some of their officers apparently misrepresenting the Confederate
strength for the purpose of carrying out their favorite theory that
they were simply overwhelmed by numbers.

The returns for June 30, 1863, are missing, but for May 31 the
figures show:

Total present	88,754
Present for duty	68,352

Their army received heavy accessions after this date and before cross-ing the Potomac, many who had been wounded returning to their commands, and also conscripts and some regiments that had been on detached duty, these re-enforcements undoubtedly swelling the present for duty to 80,000, and it is fair to say that the above figures represent the force with which Lee fought the battle of Gettysburg. While he had every infantry regiment engaged, two entire divisions of the Army of the Potomac, comprising some 8000 or 9000 good soldiers, did not fire a musket during the battle.

The next return of Lee's army is at Bunker Hill, July 20, 1863, and shows the total present only, the cavalry not being reported.

1st Corps, Longstreet	16,041
2d Corps, Ewell	16,436
3d Corps, Hill	12,198
Artillery	5,487
Cavalry, no report	..
Total	50,162

Adding 10,000 for the cavalry, would make a total present of about 60,000, including the detachments that joined the main force on the retreat.

The Confederate loss is officially reported as follows:

1st Corps, Longstreet	7,539
2d Corps, Ewell	5,937
3d Corps, Hill	6,735
Stuart's cavalry	240
Total	20,451

A study of the above tables will show that the reported Con-federate loss is upward of 10,000 short of the true figures.

CHAPTER XVIII.

ON the 6th of July the pursuit of Lee's army was taken up by Robinson's division, and the vicinity of Emmittsburg was reached at nightfall, the chase being continued on the 7th in a terrific rain-storm which soaked the soldiers to the skin and rendered the roads almost impassable, the men's shoes being filled with dirt as they tramped along in the mud, wading through brooks and rivulets which had overflowed their banks until they appeared like good sized rivers; but the boys were in excellent spirits, willing to endure any amount of hardship if Lee's army could be at last bagged. Captain Whitesides led the regiment in the chase.

On the 8th the regiment marched through Emmittsburg, Milltown, and Lewistown, encamping near the Hamburg Mountains, and the next day, continuing the tramp through the rain and mud, passed through Middletown, and halted to throw up intrenchments. The march was resumed on the 10th, passing through Boonsborough, and on halting we again threw up breastworks, but on the 12th abandoned the works and marched to near Funkstown, where we rested in sight of the enemy. On the 13th the regiment moved out on the skirmish line to feel the enemy's position, but the following morning it was discovered that the rebels had crossed the river, so we marched to Williamsport and rested for the night. On the 15th we were ordered back, and passing through Funkstown and Keedysville, halted for the night near a little hamlet called Smoke-town, the following day marching through Burkettsville and halting near Berlin, close to the Potomac. Dr. Hayes, our assistant surgeon, had been transferred to the 9th New York on the 10th, and Dr. Rawlins was sent for temporary duty to the 90th on the 16th.

Since July 4 it had stormed almost every day, and the men were in a sorry condition ; but they patiently trudged along in the mire, on short rations, scantily clothed, bivouacking on the wet ground at night or standing picket in the rain and darkness,—all without a murmur, except from the old growlers, who would grumble anyhow.

On July 17 the morning report gave the strength of the regiment as 176. Of these, twenty-one were on extra duty, sick, music, etc., leaving about 150 for active service ; total present and absent 378.

On July 18 the Potomac was crossed, our apology for a band treating us to " Dixie" as the sacred soil was again invaded ; the march was continued to Waterford, and on the 19th to Hampton, over the same route taken in November, 1862. On the 22d marched down the valley west of the Bull Run Mountains, halting beyond Warrenton on the 23d.

To fill up the depleted ranks, on July 26 the following detail was made to bring up conscripts : Captain Richards, Lieutenants Nunneville and Hanlon, Sergeants J. R. Jones and J. Hartman, Corporals G. W. Armstrong and Gideon Moyer, and Privates H. Arnold and William Strickland. The ranks were further weakened on August 11 and 12, when William Hoffman, A. J. Schreffler, Joel Reifsnyder, Frank Charles, C. Winn, and J. Weiser were sent to the hospital.

The conscripts failed to materialize, but a few old soldiers rejoined the regiment, among them Frank Murphy, on July 30; John D. Vautier, on August 12 ; Captain Patterson, Lieutenant Levan, and John Sanders, on the 14th ; and A. J. Schreffler, F. Charles, and Edward Young, on August 24. On this date 168 men of all grades were reported present ; Captain Patterson in command.

On the 1st of August the Rappahannock was crossed at the railroad, the hills on the south side being occupied and fortified by a substantial line of rifle-pits, the enemy's pickets about two miles distant. On August 15 all the troops recrossed the river except the 6th New York Sharp-shooters, 90th and 88th Pennsylvania, who passed a pleasant time, the duty being easy, rations good, washing and bathing in the river very convenient, and the drilling not onerous.

Being the outpost of the army, the regiment was thrown into a ferment of excitement on August 19 by an excited cavalryman dashing into camp at a John Gilpin pace and reporting the enemy advancing in three lines. Every effort was promptly made to repel this attack, the 12th Massachusetts—a reliable regiment—coming over the river on the double-quick and with our boys manning the rifle pits, eagerly watching the woods in front for the coming foe ; but they came not, except in the mind of the demoralized messenger, and in a few hours peace again reigned in camp, the New Englanders returning to their quarters and the men of the 88th and 90th to trading camp yarns and kindred amusements.

On the night of September 7 one of the sentinels was surprised to see a soldier—Neptune-like—emerge from the river, his garments dripping with water. He proclaimed himself a deserter from the 28th Massachusetts, supposing we were part of the Confederate army, and the guards on the reserve, without enlightening him, pumped him of all the information he possessed. Next morning, when he saw the stars and stripes overhead, he realized his position and begged to be let off, but was sent to his regiment under guard. What became of the knave we never knew.

News of the capture of Morris Island and the bombardment of Charleston was promulgated by official orders on the 10th of September, the soldiers receiving the tidings with hearty satisfaction. On September 12 large bodies of cavalry massed on the opposite bank, crossing the river early on the 13th and going for the Confederate troopers hot-footed. The first charges could be plainly seen from the hill, and when the enemy had been forced back, the rumbling of cannon, the wounded in the ambulances, together with the captured guns and many prisoners going to the rear, indicated the nature of the sport that the boots and saddles were having at Culpeper. The 2d Corps also crossed the river and marched towards the firing.

The paymaster came to camp on the 15th, and after the boys had received their "dingbats," they struck tents and, crossing the river, rejoined the brigade. At four o'clock on the morning of the 16th the river was recrossed, the division marching under a scorching sun some twelve miles to the vicinity of Stevensville, encamping here until the 20th, when the tents were pitched near Stony or Pony Mountain, at which place the division—4000 strong—was drilled by General Robinson.

While on the march to this camp the regiment halted late one afternoon, preparatory to bivouacking for the night. A fence of nice dry rails, probably the only one remaining in this section, enclosed the lot, and as soon as arms were stacked each man went for a fence-rail for firewood ; but as they were triumphantly toting the rails towards the stacks, it was discovered by some one on the brigade staff that the regiment was not in its proper position, and the officer in command—Captain Patterson—gave the order to fall in. Here was a dilemma for the men. They did not want to lose their rails and they must obey the order ; so every man shouldering his rail, fell into line, marching over to another field a short distance farther on. The spectacle was ludicrous in the extreme, the more so as a rabbit ran along the line, evading capture as he bounded through the companies ; but the climax was reached when Captain Patterson tried to right dress the line after halting ; then the rails were so much of a burden to the men and the sight was so grotesque that Patterson lost his temper, and riding along the line, peremptorily ordered every man to "chuck them darned rails away," which order the soldiers obeyed very reluctantly. Then the line was promptly dressed and the rails recaptured as soon as ranks were broken.

On September 24 the brigade advanced to the Rapidan, relieving a portion of the Red Star Division of the 12th Corps, which had been ordered to the West, where the men hoped to find fresher pastures and more glory than this blighted region afforded, and our boys wished them God-speed.

The rebels were at this point in plain view and easy range over the river, but as they occupied a commanding position, our pickets were obliged to be very civil, and were careful not to make any threatening demonstration, so living in quietness with our quondam neighbors across the river, there being a tacit agreement not to fire without cause. All the movements of the rebels could be observed from our position, not being more than one hundred yards distant.

We were relieved from picket on September 26 by the 3d Division. When the relief column came in view it appeared like the advance of our army, and caused great commotion in the camp of the enemy, mounted men dashing around, the infantry falling in, and the cannoneers standing to their guns; but as the relief dropped its men at the different posts, the suspicions of the Johnnies were allayed, and they settled down again to peace and quietness. On the 28th the general was sounded because of a rapid firing heard down by the river, but the excitement subsided when it became known that it was only the rebel pickets emptying their rifles. In the evenings their bands could be heard, the favorite tunes being "Dixie," "Bonnie Blue Flag," and "My Maryland;" and so these balmy days passed, we being just near enough to the enemy to give zest to the routine of camp life.

On October 2 a deserter from the 90th regiment was shot by a detail from the 12th Massachusetts, a very sad sight as the rifles were discharged and the life-blood spouted from the poor fellow's breast as he fell back upon his coffin. Many who would have faced a battery unflinchingly could not bear to look at this sickening sight. Scarcely had the report of the rifles been heard when all along the line the regiments broke into column, and, exposed to the fury of a storm which suddenly burst upon them, marched swiftly away from the ghastly scene.

Another incident of a different nature occurred on October 4, when some teamsters attempted to confiscate a crop of corn in a field near the river; but the owner of the corn, in command of a Confederate battery posted on the southern bank, vetoed the proceeding by shelling the foragers. The shots were not well ranged, but they answered the purpose: the teamsters suddenly changed their minds; they didn't want that corn; and the way they dusted out of range was a caution. They stopped for neither corn-stacks, fences, nor anything else that impeded their flight, but made the liveliest imaginable tracks to the rear.

In the mean time the strength of the battalion exhibited but slight improvement. On August 31, 177 men were present with the colors, and a month later but 180 answered roll-call. On October 31, however, the number had grown to 221. About the last of August, Sergeant Clemens, Joel Reifsnyder, Wesley Hoffman, Charles Nette, and James Warren returned from hospital, and Harvey Myers was sent away sick. On September 13, Daniel Hagan and Hugh Mc-Mullin were detailed for duty with the supply train, and on the 19th,

George W. Duey was sent to the hospital, James Peoples returning from the same on the 27th.

On October 7 and 8 the hearts of all were gladdened by the return of a batch of our boys who had been captured at Gettysburg and entertained by the Johnnies until recently. Genial James Hague led the crowd, followed by G. W. Green, Sergeant Shirey, John Beaumont, D. Trexler, Samuel English, Henry Wortz, Isaac Krewson, William A. Boyd, John Hart, Willie Hand, and a few days later by Neal Devine and John S. Campbell.

The regiment continued in this vicinity until October 9, when at ten o'clock at night marching orders were received, and the column moved off silently at two o'clock the next morning, keeping under cover, and going in a northeasterly direction some four or five miles before halting. In the regiment there were always a few knowing ones who by some sign or other could generally guess the destination of the brigade; but this movement was a mystery to all, the wise ones looking in vain for a pointer from head-quarters, the wagon-train, or any other means usually employed to keep posted as to future movements. At nightfall numerous camp-fires were kindled at the edge of the woods for the purpose of deceiving the enemy, then the road was taken, the troops halting near Pony Mountain in the "wee sma' hours." Before day-dawn orders to move were again given, but the march was delayed until nine o'clock, when the column got in motion, passing through Stevensburg and fording the chilly waters of the Rappahannock at Kelly's Ford in the afternoon. Here the tired soldiers bivouacked for the night, while the cavalry were having a spirited engagement near Pony Mountain, the sound of the cannon being distinctly heard. The brigade remained at the ford during the 12th, but at midnight the men were aroused, and, proceeding to Warrenton Junction, formed line of battle to protect the immense wagon-train parked there. The position had hardly been taken when the bugle sounded "Forward, march," head of column pulling out at once for Bristoe, which was reached at nightfall, the command having marched not less than thirty miles by the sinuous route taken.

At daybreak on the 14th the bugle sounded "Fall in," and the march was directed across the country to Centreville, with skirmish-

ers out, rumor stating that Lee had the same objective.   The works
at Centreville were entered about noon, and in the afternoon the
smoke of the battle at Bristoe between Warren and Hill was seen
over the tree-tops.

On October 15 the regiment picketed Cub Run.   The view of the
country from Centreville Heights showed it to be heavily wooded
as far as the Bull Run range, and it was said to be inhabited by many
wild animals, the pickets of the regiment being saluted during
the night by the shrill yowls of wild-cats or other strange beasts in
the tree-tops.   The 16th Maine relieved the regiment on the 16th.

On October 19 the division marched through Bull Run battle-
field and halted near the burned town of Haymarket.   Here arms
were stacked, and while the men were cooking coffee, a band of
Confederate cavalry made a fierce onslaught on the battery a hundred yards or so to the front, filling the air with the rebel yell and
overrunning the batterymen ; but the latter rallied, and before the
regiment could go to the rescue they had sent the Johnnies dusting
to the Gap, pelting them with a shotted salute as they scurried away.
The troops lay on their arms all night, and the next morning the
88th and 11th Regiments advanced through Thoroughfare Gap and,
finding no enemy, encamped on the west side.   Here Lieutenant
Robert B. Beath left the regiment to accept a captaincy in the 6th
United States Colored Infantry, subsequently seeing hard service
and losing a leg in action before Richmond ; Lieutenant George E.
Wagner also accepted the same rank in the 8th Regiment.   Thus the
regiment lost the companionship of these two excellent officers, to
the regret of the entire command.   While at this place several more
of the Gettysburg captives returned to the regiment, among them
Peter D. Shearer, George W. Leader, Mayberry Dautrich, William
Fisher, C. D. Good, Reuben Sanders, and Charles Marple, all being
received with open arms and feasted on hardtack and coffee.

On October 23, 206 men were present, commanded by Captain
Patterson.   On October 24 the brigade marched to Bristoe, encamping on the battle field where Warren defeated Hill, the ground being
well filled with Confederate graves, mostly North Carolinians.   Re-
constructed the railroad until November 5, when camp " busted up,"
the division going to Catlett's, and on the 6th to Kelly's Ford to attack

the enemy, said to be in force there. While on the road the woods took fire, enveloping the country in a pall of smoke. The enemy had either been all captured or had skedaddled from the Rappahannock, so the division forded the river and struck for Brandy Station. On the road many prisoners were met, and judging from the sound of the cannon, the boys were having a frolic down near Culpeper, but Robinson's division had no share in it.

On November 9 we left the station with the bibulous name, crossed the Rappahannock, camped at Bealeton, and earned our wages by again working on the railroad.

Captain J. S. Steeple assumed command of the regiment on the 15th, and Nathan S. Auble, William Truett, Daniel W. Ney, Hugh Rutherford, John F. Keller, and several others returned, making 230 present; aggregate present and absent, 396. The command remained in this camp about two weeks, rebuilding the railroad and doing a minimum quantity of drilling, with the usual Sunday inspection, which day was further utilized by Chaplain Clothier in preaching some earnest sermons to the men, who were sadly in need of the good chaplain's wholesome advice.

On November 26 pulled up stakes, crossed the Rappahannock, thence over the Rapidan at Gold-Mine Ford, bound on what is known as the Mine Run campaign. Early next morning the advance was resumed through the thick woods, brush, and briers of this wilderness until night, when a halt was called near the turnpike.

On Saturday morning, November 28, line of battle was formed and we advanced through the interlacing brambles and thickets to a tavern (presumably Robertson's), where we ran against the claimants of this part of the country, strongly intrenched behind Mine Run and ready for a quarrel. The regiment was thrown out as skirmishers over an open field, under a heavy artillery fire, to the banks of the run, and the men, throwing up rifle-pits, lay low, looking at the ugly intrenchments on the other side, manned by long lines of graybacks with bristling bayonets and many cannon waiting to give the boys in blue a shotted salute. All of Sunday was spent by the Union generals in trying to find a vulnerable point in the Confederate line, and by the men in dread at the thought of the proposed assault under so many adverse conditions. Meade's quarters were near by, and the inquisitive ones went there for information, one well-known but illiterate soldier of the regiment affirming that he heard the general tell one of his staff that "we were to charge the enemy's works and not receive a shot until we were over their intrenchments." He insisted that his version of the order was correct in every particular, notwithstanding the hurrah his story created.

The brigade changed position on the 30th to the right of the pike, orders having been promulgated that the Pennsylvania Reserves would form the storming line, with Robinson in support. Knapsacks were unslung and every preparation made for the assault ; but as the boys looked across the ravine at the lines of strong works on the opposite bank, they were not very sanguine of getting back, and pinning bits of paper on the inside of their blouses, on which were written the name and regiment, for identity in case of death, they waited for the orders to forward the colors.

Early on the succeeding morning the Union artillery opened a fierce fire upon the Confederates, for the purpose of unmasking their cannon ; but the rebels responded very feebly, evidently reserving their fire for a period when it would be more effective. All hands now expected the bugles to sound the advance, but the charge was not made, and when night came the men rolled themselves in their blankets for protection from the chilling wind that swept through the leafless trees.

December 1 dawned clear and cold. At five o'clock the regiment marched silently to the picket line, strict orders having been issued against unnecessary noise and the men forbidden to kindle fires ; but, soldier-like, some of the boys crawled down the slope towards the enemy, and soon had a surreptitious fire doing excellent service in preparing breakfast. Meantime, two or three Confederate sharpshooters, perceiving their carelessness, were sneaking down to get a shot at them, when some pickets on the left shouted a warning and gave the Johnnies a salute from their rifles. At the alarm every coffee-cooler, quickly gathering up his "contraptions," scrambled up the hill to a place of safety.

The regiment occupied the skirmish line during the 1st, sometimes being exposed to a galling artillery fire from both sides, and at dark, after posting videttes well out, the men lay down for another night

CAPTAIN GEORGE B. RHOADS.
(Killed at White Oak Swamp.)

LIEUTENANT ATWOOD G. SINN.
(Killed at Petersburg.)

CAPTAIN J. PARKER MARTIN.

JAMES G. CLARK.

PHILIP SCHRINER,

of uneasy slumber; but about three o'clock next morning orders came to quietly withdraw. When the rear was reached it was discovered that the entire army had gone, so the regiment "hiked out" for the Rapidan, reaching Germanna Ford at daylight and halting about ten o'clock, on the road to Kelly's Ford. The surprise of the Confederates in the morning, when they found the Union line deserted and not a Yank within ten miles of them, may be imagined, but the boys unanimously voted that they were fooled this time, sure.

Having stayed so long in the wilderness, the men had consumed all their rations, having been compelled to contract their stomachs by eating persimmons, thus making their allowance of three days last six; but the fasting was patiently endured, except when a general officer rode by, at which time the entire line would lustily howl "Hardtack," oft repeated, much to the disgust of the officer, who, if he exhibited the least annoyance, would be saluted with such a chorus of yells as to be glad to escape with all possible speed.

The march was resumed on the 3d, many of the men being without a mouthful of food, except what was given them by their more provident comrades, who, in expectation of such a famine, had carefully husbanded their provender; but at noon the last cracker was eaten, with no prospect of a near supply, the country being entirely destitute of forage of any kind. The boys were in pretty hard lines now, and some of them said that they would never love another country if they were going to lose their coffee and lobscouse in this way; but the punsters would have their little jokes, remarking that Uncle Sam was going to give us all a farm when this cruel war was over.

168

HISTORY OF THE

CHAPTER XIX.

FROM MINE RUN TO THE WILDERNESS : DECEMBER 3, 1863, TO MAY 1,
1864.

WE reached Kelly's Ford a little after that traditional hour which
in better days was called dinner-time, and though the water was waist
deep, very swift, and cold as ice, the troops, in accordance with
orders, plunged into the river and waded to the north bank, finding
the quartermaster there waiting to distribute rations,—a most welcome surprise to the half-famished men. The bivouac fires were
soon kindled, the brigade remaining here all night ; on the morning of December 4 the bugle sounded " Fall in," and to the intense
disgust of all hands, the river was forded again to the south bank,
camp being formed in the woods a mile from the river. Here
another surprise awaited us in the shape of a ration of fresh bread,
the first the men had eaten for many months ; and though Uncle
Sam forgot the butter, he was voted a good fellow, the bread being
keenly relished by all.

An important arrival at this time was that "skinner" known as
the sutler, who came with loads of delicacies to which the men were
strangers ; and though he charged a dollar or more for his canned
goods, he speedily had purchasers for all he brought. Another and
better visitor came to camp in the person of Colonel Louis Wagner,
who, having been disabled by a severe wound received at Bull Run,
had been on detailed duty elsewhere ; but on December 16 he paid
the camp a welcome visit, bringing two beautiful new silk flags, a
present to the regiment, which were formally given to the command
at dress parade on the 18th, Major Alfred J. Sellers, of the 90th,
receiving them in behalf of the regiment. The flags represented the
national and State colors, two blue silk markers completing the set.

The brigade broke camp on December 24, going to Mitchell's
Station *via* Brandy Station and Culpeper, a circuitous route of about

twenty-five miles. The next day was Christmas,—a cold, cheerless day to the soldiers encamped in these desolate woods ; but a few of the men got boxes of eatables from home, some containing a liquid similar in name to that of the station on the other side of Culpeper.

On January 1, 1864, camp was moved about a mile nearer Cedar Mountain, Captain Steeple being in command of the regiment. The following report shows the strength of the regiment by companies, together with the names of the commanders:

Field and staff present 4
Company A.—Lieutenant Ninesteel 34
Company B.—Sergeant Swavely 30
Company C.—Lieutenant Walmsley 22
Company D.—Sergeant Hunter 15
Company E.—Sergeant Gilligan 18
Company F.—Captain Rhoads 17
Company G.—Lieutenant Gardiner 7
Company H.—Lieutenant Houder 25
Company I.—Lieutenant Nunneville 24
Company K.—Captain Patterson 24

Total present 220

Of these, twenty-three were sick or on detailed duty, leaving less than 200 with the colors. Total present and absent, 380. Conscripts required to fill the regiment, as per morning report, 628. The detail that went for these expectant soldiers in July was unsuccessful, the supply of conscripts at Camp Cadwalader having run short, so the boys said ; consequently, the regiment would have to wait for a fresh lot, and it proved a long wait.

On January 2 camp was removed to the top of the south spur of Cedar Mountain, a bleak spot, the timber being green and hard to burn and water very scarce ; a snow-storm on the 4th also added to the general discomfort. Very unexpectedly on the 5th the brigade marched to Culpeper, the regiment being quartered in the Baptist Church, and afterwards removing to a long brick warehouse opposite the dépôt ; the 90th Pennsylvania and 12th Massachusetts were also in town.

The question of re-enlistment for the war had been agitated for several days, the majority expressing a desire to see the war through

and to accept the furlough and bounty offered to all who were eligi-
ble. The 8th Illinois Cavalry, our sister regiment, passed through
on the 11th, bound home on veteran furlough, and this event revived
the re-enlistment fever until the regiment was remustered on January
28. The veterans now anxiously waited for orders to go home, but
were intensely disgusted at receiving marching orders on the 29th,
going into camp a mile or two west, on the Sperryville pike, only to
come back to town the next day. On February 4, 1864, Colonel
Coulter's 11th Regiment took the cars for home, and the boys of the
88th thought that surely the next day or two would bring orders for
them ; but on the 6th the army began a movement to the Rapidan,
large numbers of troops passing through Culpeper, most of them
wearing the diamond badge of the 3d Corps. The weather was
stormy, and as the mud-bespattered soldiers splashed through the
rain and mire they looked hard enough, and the prospect for the
veterans going home appeared very poor, furlough stock falling away
below par on the next day, when orders were issued to pack up and
be ready to march at the traditional moment's notice ; but, to the
great relief of everybody, the 3d Corps came marching back during
the afternoon.

At last the long-expected furlough for the re-enlisted came, and
on the 9th of February they left Culpeper on their way to greet
their families and to meet friends whom they had not seen for more
than two years, many of the soldiers not having been home since
October, 1861. The veterans who remained were sent to Colonel
Lyle's regiment, encamped on the Sperryville pike, until the battalion should return from furlough. There were quite a number in
this detachment, including Sergeants Swavely and Montgomery,
Privates Reuben Neider, Edward Ball, Charles H. Turner, Peter D.
Shearer, Charles S. Butler, Tobias Deemer, Isaac Brown, A. Waterman, H. C. Richardson, Harry Booz, William Campbell, G. Lukens,
B. Markley, Adam Hersh, Jacob Drexle, J. Reifsnyder, Frank Heller, Hugh Rutherford, James Perara, Edward Nunneville, Neal Devine, J. D. Vautier, and others, who were organized as an independent company of the 90th Regiment, Lieutenant Jewell being
assigned to command, and the boys dubbing the detachment Company Q.

In due time the regiment reached Philadelphia and was given a rousing reception by the citizens, while the squad with the 90th made themselves as comfortable as possible, erecting log huts and going into winter-quarters. Duty was light, and the boys passed a pleasant time knocking around camp in daytime and attending the meetings of the Christian Commission in the neighboring chapels at night, at which places many of the soldiers were converted, making a public profession of religion.

On March 22 ten inches of snow fell, but the warm sun that succeeded soon melted it. Struck tents on April 3 and marched to Mitchell's Station, occupying the abandoned camp of the 107th Pennsylvania, where the command remained until the 10th of April, when news came that the veterans were coming to the front again, putting on their war-paint, and the 88th having returned and all things being in readiness, the army would soon move; that the commanding general had been anxious to tackle the rebs for several days, but refused to budge a step until assured of the support of the 88th. This is what the boys of Company Q affirmed, but the veterans simply said that it was a lie.

The detachment had been with Colonel Lyle exactly two months. The veterans were found encamped on the Sperryville pike near Culpeper, and many happy greetings were exchanged after so long a separation. They told of the good times they had had at home, and nearly all of them had purchased new uniforms of fine cloth, artistically trimmed with braid and binding, presenting a sharp contrast on dress parade to the plain clothing furnished by Uncle Sam to those who did not go home; but after a few weeks' wear and consequent exposure to the rain and sun the contrast was even more striking, as the fancy uniforms lost color and shrunk from the original cuts, this time the difference being in favor of the men who remained in the field.

The furloughed men returned slowly; on April 12, at dress parade, less than one hundred men were in line, thirty-nine of these being from Company Q; but at length they all arrived, together with about sixty recruits who had been induced to join the regiment. Active preparations were now made for the spring campaign. The army was reorganized, the 1st Corps consolidating with the 5th, under

General Warren, the badge being a circle with Maltese cross within. Good progress was made in drilling, target practice, inspections, reviews, and so on, the regiment now numbering about three hundred men, commanded by Major Steeple; but many excellent officers and soldiers were still absent, among them Company B's commissioned officers and Captain Schell, of Company I, all having been captured at Gettysburg and still held as prisoners of war.

CHAPTER XX.

WITH GRANT IN THE WILDERNESS: MAY 1 TO 7, 1864.

SUNDAY, May 1, pleasant and quiet; preaching by Chaplain Clothier. Christian Commission delegates going home,—chapels closed; the calm before the storm. Boys all happy, though, because we are going to end the war right off. May 2, stormy, but clear again on the 3d, and the great southward movement has begun.

The 88th struck tents at eleven P.M. Detailed for wagon guard, and with the trains reached Brandy Station at daybreak; but if there was any brandy about other than the name, the officers had it all, the privates did not even smell it.

No halt was made at this place, but turning southward, the march was directed to the Rapidan; indeed, the entire country was filled with marching troops and moving trains, all bound south. On the 4th the march was continued towards the river; being compelled to cover the train, our progress was slow, and the men were constantly enveloped in a stifling cloud of dust that covered them from head to foot, causing them to resemble graybacks rather than honest bluecoats. As the sun was sinking behind the crimson western clouds the river-bank was reached, and, parking the train, the regiment bivouacked in the fields for the night.

The Rapidan was crossed on the morning of the 5th at Gold-Mine Ford, at which place many buildings and shafts indicated the location of the abandoned workings, and climbing the steep banks, we were on the edge of that dark region known as the Wilderness, not searching for gold, but for the Johnny Rebs, who, according to indications, would not be very hard to find. The regiment rested under the trees, an occasional report of a cannon or a rifle telling that the advance was feeling for the enemy; but about four o'clock, when the line again formed and the march was resumed, the sound

had increased to a long, steady roll of musketry with the deep bass
of the artillery rumbling through the trees ; this was the music of
the battle-field, the *diminuendo* and *crescendo* of the terrible refrain :

> The rattling musketry, the clashing blade,
> And ever and anon, in tones of thunder,
> The diapason of the cannonade.

The crackle of the rifles resounding through the gloom resembled
the noise made by swiftly rasping a stick along a paling fence, or
by packs of shooting-crackers exploding in a barrel, and as the men
listened to the ominous sounds that indicated the bloody work ahead,
every voice was stilled, nothing was heard in the ranks but the steady
tramp, tramp, or the incisive command, "Close up, men ; close
up."

At dusk a halt was ordered, and the command rested until three
o'clock A.M. of the 6th, when the march was resumed, the 1st Brigade being soon found.   It had been in action, and had lost heavily
in killed and wounded.   All day long the sun was scorching hot,
but the dense clouds of smoke and the trees somewhat obscured its
rays, affording a welcome protection to the men.   The brigade lay
in reserve on the ford road, listening to the sounds of battle coming
sometimes through the woods in front, again in intermittent spells
on the right or left ; but suddenly it burst with great fury on the
right, and the bugles pealing out "Fall in," the brigade quickly
reached the threatened point.   The enemy was soon repulsed, however, and, returning to near the first position, we constructed a slight
breastwork of logs and earth ; but later in the day, the firing increasing on the left, the column was hurried there only to find that
the enemy had been driven back, when we built more breastworks,
remaining here all night, ready for action.

The night passed, however, with nothing more serious than a
few false alarms, and at the first blush of dawn the men were up,
cooking their morning meal of coffee, hardtack, and toasted pork.
After breakfast a long line of low earthworks was thrown up along
the road and skirmishers sent into the woods to locate the enemy's
position ; but they had scarcely disappeared among the trees when
the Confederates made an attack a half-mile or more down the

road.   Our troops, kneeling in their low breastworks, at once
opened on the Johnnies as they emerged from the slashed timber,
the fire gradually running along the line until it reached the 88th.
Our men knew that there could be no enemy in front, as the detail of skirmishers had gone into the woods not ten minutes before,
and as the firing reached the regiment, some of the boys mounted
the logs and ordered it to cease, at the same time looking towards
the woods to see if the rebels were coming, but not a grayback was
in sight.   But though the Confederates did not appear, our skirmishers did, for the smoke had scarcely lifted before Clemens, Booz,
and the rest of them came tearing out of the woods, inquiring in
very vehement language as to the cause of this fire in their rear.   It
would be putting it very mildly to say that they were mad about it ;
they threatened to charge the regiment and clean the whole gang
out if it was repeated, and those on the left of the battalion who
had fired into the woods were soundly berated and warned to be
more careful in the future.

The skirmishers could not find any one to fight, so, calling them
in late in the afternoon, the column marched back to near the Lacey
house, being massed in the centre.   Dry wood was very scarce, but
a frame school-house standing by the road was quickly pulled to
pieces, and the men soon had their scanty suppers cooked and
eaten.

As the shades of evening fell, bodies of moving troops, with the
occasional flash of a cannon, could be seen several miles out in the
direction of the Catharpin road, and it was rumored that the enemy
was preparing for a retreat.   The questions of interest among the
men were whether the battle was over and what the next move
would be, back across the river or straight after the enemy; but
about nine o'clock at night, when the head of column pulled out,
headed south, the matter was settled : the campaign was to be
fought through to the end ; no more retreating, but a steady advance
to where the enemy should make a stand.   The column marched
quietly along towards Spottsylvania Court-House until the Brock
road was reached ; then, from some unknown cause, long and vexa-
tious delays occurred, comparatively little progress being made.
The column would start, march probably one hundred yards, then

halt, and just as the men were about to lie down, would start again, repeating this over and over; so the exhausting march continued for hours, being the most cruel and aggravating kind of a night march to which tired soldiers could be subjected. At such times the patience as well as the endurance of the men were tried to the utmost, and if it had not been for the good-natured fellows who gave a humorous turn to everything, they would have died of the blues. Stumbling and groping through the darkness, in the small hours, Sam Fusman's cheery voice was heard : " Halloo, Copey ; are you there?" and upon receiving a response, " Well, then, stay there." When every one was so tired that a bed of thorns would have been esteemed one of roses, " Fussy" edged towards " Copey" and inquired if he had ever heard Mr. Shakespeare's thrilling lines,—

> We'll all drink stone blind ;
> Johnny, fill up the bowl.

Copestick disputed the authorship; said he wrote that poetry himself, and that we should

> all be forgotten one hundred years hence,

and wanted to know

> What shall we do when the war breaks the country up
> And scatters the darkies all around ?

And with these scintillations of humor the weary march was continued through the dreary night.

CHAPTER XXI.

LAUREL HILL AND SPOTTSYLVANIA: MAY 8 TO 20, 1864.

About four o'clock on the morning of the 8th of May (Sunday) the head of column reached the cavalry, who were exchanging shots with the enemy a mile down the road. The regiment filed off the road to the right, resting for an hour among the embers and ashes of the burning woods, when the command to fall in was given, and just as daylight was breaking the column moved forward, passing the horses of the cavalry, then filing to the right and coming into line of battle. Every preparation was now made for a fight,—flags unfurled, guns loaded and primed, and at the command "Fix bayonets," the sharp click of the rattling steel ran down the line like a miniature volley of pistol-shots. When everything was ready the brigade bugle sounded the advance, and Captain Rhoads gave the order "Attention, 88th. Carry arms. Forward, guide centre, march," and at the order the battalion stepped briskly forward, shoulder to shoulder, in line with the rest of the brigade. The line soon ran into a high snake-fence, which was quickly demolished, and as the column emerged from the woods it received the fire of the enemy posted in the edge of another woods on a hill across the fields about two hundred yards distant, a swamp being in the middle of the intervening field. In grand array the blue line swept over the field with flags unfurled, and as the combatants approached each other the enemy fired more rapidly, knocking a man over here and there, but their cannon-shots flew wildly overhead.

When the soldiers reached the swamp, it was found to be impassable except by a narrow foot-path, and along this path Sergeant Clevinger dashed, followed by about twenty of the regiment, who, vaulting the fence and scaling the hill on the other side, gave the fleeing Southerners a few parting shots to accelerate their speed. The lines now reformed, the men congratulating each other on the easy victory and telling of the incidents and narrow escapes in the charge. One of the close calls noticed was that of Peter D. Shearer, who was fired at by a Confederate sharp-shooter, the ball skimming by Shearer's ear and burying itself in the blanket rolled on his knap-sack.

As soon as the regiments were in line the bugle sounded the advance, and the brigade again moved forward through the woods, over fences, and through a large clearing known as Alsop's farm. Here line of battle was formed brigade front, and, moving forward, we passed the farm buildings, then through a thick belt of timber, and came out in a large open field, the enemy being strongly posted behind works some three or four hundred yards on the opposite side.

The brigade, supporting some other troops, marched straight across the field, receiving the enemy's fire when about half way over, but this did not for a moment check its advance; in some places the works were scaled and the regimental colors planted on the captured line. But the advantage was all on the Confederate side; being sheltered, they were comparatively safe, while the Union bat-talions were raked by a severe artillery and musketry fire, the plain being strewn with the disabled, while many of the slightly wounded were streaming to the rear; still, the survivors stuck to their position and essayed by a rapid musketry fire to drive the enemy off. This unequal contest continued for some time, when the Confederates (Kershaw's and Humphrey's brigades) threw out a large force on our left flank. The first intimation that our men had of the presence of this force was when they received a cutting flank fire which enfiladed the line from left to right; then it was time to go, and every man that could get back did so without delay. It was a plucky advance and well maintained, but circumstances (and the Johnnies) compelled a retreat.

Upon reaching the friendly covert of the woods, the men halted to take breath, while a brass band struck up the inspiriting tune, "Hail Columbia;" but the soldiers kept right on to the rear, helped along wonderfully by a few rebel batteries which administered an extra dose of "Hail Columbia" as they retreated through the woods. In the fields around the farm-house the men stopped and reformed.

The loss of the regiment was about fifty, among the killed being Sergeant Eagle, George W. Rodgers, John Irwin, and Amos Fisher.

As the shades of night fell upon the scene, amid the smoke and battle-pall, the brigade quietly marched to the front again, passing in the twilight by the roadside a mortally-wounded soldier, with his head resting upon a comrade's knee, who was intently reading from a small book to his dying companion. It is needless to surmise, under the circumstances, what book it was.

Upon arriving at the front we took position in reserve, and the weary soldiers rested for the night. On the morning of May 9 the regiment changed position several times, at one point the Confederate wagon-train being in plain view a mile or two distant, travelling down the Catharpin road. The opposing lines were uncomfortably close, the bullets zipping and spinning around in a most unhealthy manner, and the soldiers erected numerous bullet-proofs from the old logs lying around.

In the afternoon the brigade advanced through the woods to the skirmish line, then held by the Bucktails. The enemy's works were about two hundred yards distant and very strongly built, but it wasn't healthy for a Johnny to show his head. Back somewhere they had a battery which had good range of our position, and their gunners kept up an interesting fire, much to our discomfort. They threw canister, and the charges whizzed directly over the heads of the men; luckily, however, the shots always struck a little too far front or to the rear, and then went buzzing like an angry swarm of hornets, and every man was sure that the next shot would settle his hash; but though there were many narrow escapes, no more harm was done than badly frightening the men as they crouched on the ground. After having been subjected to this harassing fire for some time the regiment was ordered back, and right gladly did the men leave the "bad lands," the Bucktails again taking possession and looking after their friends the graybacks.

About noon of the 10th the brigade was ordered to again assault these works, and accordingly advanced through the woods to the charge. The enemy had cut down all the trees in front of his position, felling them outward and trimming the branches, thus forming an impenetrable abatis that the Union soldiers could not enter; behind this tangle, stretched to the right and left, were elaborate fortifications several feet high, manned by Confederate riflemen, who poured a destructive fire upon the division as it uncovered from the woods. The advancing line went as far as the obstructions would allow, and opened a rapid but apparently ineffective fusillade upon the men back of the works, probably fifty or one hundred yards distant. This contest was maintained some fifteen or twenty minutes, when our commanders, seeing the impossibility of taking the works, ordered a retreat, which was promptly obeyed in good order and without a murmur of disapproval, except that the bodies of the killed were necessarily left where they fell. The loss of the regiment in this short but sanguinary duel was thirty-eight killed and wounded,—about one out of every four that went into the action.

As usual, the casualties included some of the bravest members of the regiment. Sergeants Charles A. Sines and James A. Devlin, Privates James Spear, John Simms, David C. Davis, John F. Goodheart, Joseph Myers, David G. Arnot, C. Nette, and William Raider were either killed or mortally wounded, and among the many others severely wounded were Sergeants Koch, Robert Herron, and C. Strohecker, Captain Bemesderfer, James Hague, Lieutenant Nichols, Joseph Burris, George W. Hain, George Bossler, Reuben Drexle, Samuel C. Fusman, James C. Richardson, John McKee, and Charles Burbridge.

As the men were coming slowly back through the woods, the 1st Division, wearing the red Maltese cross, was met marching up, going in to try their hands on the Confederate intrenchments; but they did not stay long, having accomplished just what we did,— namely, lost heavily in killed and wounded and then retired. In the afternoon heavy columns of troops wearing the lozenge or diamond badge of the old 3d Corps were massed in an open field in the rear, preparatory to a grand assault on the works which the old 1st Corps had failed to take. The rebels evidently suspected some movement on our part, for they opened a fierce cannonade, and, being within easy range of their batteries, they raked the ground with a howling tempest of flying projectiles, which whizzed, struck, and burst in such close proximity to the regiment that it seemed as if every man would be torn to pieces by the awful instruments of destruction falling *almost* everywhere, the exception being where the men were lying. Sometimes in this, as in similar cannonades, it was noticed that the cannon-balls would strike all around a body of men, but seldom among them. There were, of course, many exceptions to this rule,—as, for example, where a single shell had disabled many; but to a soldier lying on the ground the noise of one of these projectiles is more terrible than the damage usually warrants. The Union batteries quickly replied, and between the noise of the guns and the exploding shells the place received a shaking up such as these old woods had never before experienced and it is hoped never will in future.

While this infernal uproar continued, a huge black snake, awakened by the unearthly clatter, made his début among the men of the 88th; presumably, he came to see what all the racket was about. There was a grand scattering of the men, and it seemed for a little while that the snake would do what the rebs couldn't,—put the regiment to flight; but the boys rallied, and, charging his snakeship, soon impaled him on a sharp bayonet. In a field in the rear lay the 3d Corps, much exposed to this iron tempest, and, like us, the men sought protection by hugging the ground, though one fellow caused much merriment by hiding behind an empty barrel. A prominent figure was the color-bearer of one of the regiments, who, disdaining to lie down, stood erect with his flag in his hand. Presently, with a fiendish shriek, a shell struck the ground in front of the color-bearer and exploded, throwing up a cloud of dust and smoke and hiding him from view. We all thought the brave fellow had been blown to pieces; but soon the smoke rolled away, the dust settled, and "our flag was still there." Unharmed and erect as ever, the heroic standard-bearer stood as though on dress parade.

After the fierce cannonading had ceased this massed force moved into the woods on the right, but the troops had not been gone ten minutes, nor fired a hundred shots, when they came tumbling and scrambling back in the greatest confusion, a wild panic taking possession of the men and causing them to break to the rear without ceremony; but their officers soon rallied them and marched them away to the left.

Towards evening a cold rain began to fall, the first since the 2d of May, and the soldiers passed an uncomfortable night lying behind their breastworks, drenched to the skin.   After a miserable night the morning of the 11th dawned on the lads, who, with dripping garments and aching limbs, gathered around the tiny fires to boil their coffee, larger ones being forbidden for fear of drawing a hotter fire from the unfriendly Yahoos on the other side.   After breakfast, the men grubbed in the mud, strengthening the works until they were six or seven feet thick ; so the cheerless day passed quietly enough, except for an occasional shell or stray bullet that hummed through the trees.

At nightfall the men erected their shelters and packed in these frail tents spoon fashion, like sardines, the closer the warmer, while the rain fell in torrents, flooding most of the tents; but the unfortunates could do nothing but lie still in the water and think of the warm, dry beds at home.   About midnight the sullen boom of a cannon awoke the men, but none stirred except the disconsolate sentinels as they trudged through the mud ; nobody wanted to turn out unless it was imperative.   Soon another and another gun pealed in re-echoing chorus over the woods, the dying shrieks of the shells and the reports as they exploded far away being faintly heard.   Presently an answering shot from the Confederates came whistling overhead ; then all hands appeared satisfied and the firing ceased, much to the relief of the expectant men in the tents.

Daylight brought but scant comfort, the rain continuing, everybody being soaking wet, the trees dripping showers of water, while underfoot the ground was like dough, the situation trying the patience and patriotism of the strongest hearts ; but some of the boys made light of it, saying that there was a good time coming, only wait a little longer,—and they waited.   Things are never so bad but that they might be worse, and this was proved when the brigade was again ordered to assault the works, at the same time being informed of the capture of the rebel Johnson's division by the 2d Corps.   The line soon came in sight of the rebels and a steady fire was opened upon them, which was replied to with all the vigor characteristic of our ubiquitous Southern friends.   This unequal contest was continued about half an hour, after which the line of battle was withdrawn, nothing having been accomplished except to add more names to the long list of disabled.

The regiment lost fourteen men in this action, among the killed being Jonathan Wiser, and Joseph Sergeant, William Threapleton (Boocock), and Neal Devine, wounded,—all excellent soldiers. The next day (13th) was stormy, and in the afternoon most of the regiment were sent on the skirmish line, being compelled to lie low among the festering and bloated bodies of many Union soldiers who had fallen in the assaults on the enemy's elaborate intrenchments. About midnight most of the pickets were relieved, but some were overlooked, and in the morning were gobbled by the enemy. After coming off picket we took up the march in the mud and darkness to the left; but it was the hardest kind of work to make progress through this plastic sea of mire and misery, though at dawn the attenuated column was on the Fredericksburg road, but not in condition to risk an attack with good prospect of success. Spent all of the 14th near this road, building breastworks and dodging the shells of the Washington Artillery, which was on hand ready to entertain us, though its performance was not appreciated.

Rained again on the 15th; rain is becoming monotonous. On this day a number of veterans returned, including Captain Whitesides and James G. Clark. On the 17th the sun appeared from behind a bank of clouds, the first clear day in a week. On the 18th edged up towards the enemy, and on that day and the next were on the skirmish line, then were relieved and sent to the rear with Birney's division to meet an attack by Ewell's corps on the Fredericksburg road; but the "Heavies" had attended to their case and given Ewell such a drubbing that he was glad to get away.

After the disastrous engagements of May 8, 10, etc., the losses of the 2d Division were found to be so heavy that the command was broken up, Baxter's brigade, commanded by Colonel Coulter, being assigned to Crawford's 3d Division. This change entitled the men to wear a blue Maltese cross (emblem of the 3d Division, 5th Corps) within a white circle, the old insignia of the 2d Division, 1st Corps.

CHAPTER XXII.

ON May 21 we abandoned the extensive earthworks in front of
Spottsylvania and marched to Guinea Station in a vain attempt to
force Lee to attack away from his defences. Crossed the Mattapony
and bivouacked until Sunday morning, the 22d, when the brigade
formed line of battle and pushed out westward towards the roads
the Southern army was moving over, driving the mounted Confederates off; but after going two or three miles, fell back and rejoined
the division, and encamped on the Bowling Green road.   Up at
five o'clock on the 23d, and having no rations, marched to Jericho
Ford, crossing the North Anna River at that place and resting
on the south bank.   The soldiers had rehearsed the Bible story of
the man going down to Jericho and falling among thieves, and as
they jested and waited for the commissary to show up, they little
anticipated the fun that was coming.

Suddenly the Confederates opened a terrific cannonade upon the
unsuspecting divisions quietly bivouacking on the river-bank.   It
has been stated that eight Confederate cannon were used in this impromptu reception, but there wasn't a man in Crawford's division
or the Pennsylvania Reserves on that hill but was fully convinced
that at least a hundred cannon were belching their howling shot
upon those storm-swept hills.   The missiles screamed, shrieked,
fluttered, whistled, and spitefully plunged with terrific force all
around, over, before, behind, and everywhere else among the
crouching soldiers; no place appeared to be secure from their devil-
ish course, except the insignificant spots where the soldiers lay; for,
strange to relate, though the Confederate cannoneers had accurate
range of the position, planting their shots right among the troops,
yet but little damage was done, except among the stragglers and

coffee-coolers in the rear, who got the benefit of all the shots that went bounding in that direction; the most harm done was in stampeding many valuable horses belonging to the staff officers, some of which were never recovered. In the heterogeneous mass on the river-bank, behind a friendly cliff, was Jim Warren, who had toted a choice cut of confiscated mutton all day without opportunity for cooking it. He was making the most of the halt by boiling the meat when the bombardment opened, one of the first shells demolishing fire and pot alike and sending the mutton to kingdom come. The next projectile quickly following was a frantic camp-follower with an old army mule rigged port, starboard, and fore and aft with pots, kettles, blankets, and so on, who wildly leaped off the cliff, hoofs and all, followed by a terror-stricken rabble, who certainly found "Jordan am a hard road to trabbel," and who, not particular about the order of their going, did not stop until the river separated them from their enemies. In the ranks there was no panic, the men merely lying low till the fury of the tempest was spent. The movement consisted of an attack by Wilcox's and Heth's divisions with the expectation of driving Warren into the river, but, in army slang, they had "bit off more than they could chew," and were badly punished for their venture. At twilight the brigade marched to re-enforce Cutler, then back again, and by way of recreation the men dug dirt all night and carried ammunition and rations.

The regiment went on the skirmish line on May 24, staying there until late in the afternoon, when the line moved to the left. Next day the regiment was pushed out again and kept up a lively, though probably harmless, fire against the opposing line in the woods, about two hundred yards distant. On the night of May 26 this wing of the army folded its tents and silently recrossed the river, leaving the disputed ground to the Johnnies, who appeared to want it more than we did. Head of column was directed through a well-cultivated country to the Pamunkey, which we crossed at noon on the 28th, and, halting, built some more earthworks, just to keep our hands in.

About ten o'clock on May 30 the brigade marched down the south bank of Totopotomoy Creek and lay in line of battle, while a large regiment of German "Heavies" was pushed to the front.

After this command had formed, a rebel regiment charged it, and though the men stood for a little while, soon the whole line broke and came back in the greatest confusion, and when the boys jeered them, the poor fellows appeared to feel their disgrace, and explained how "Goompany L" had broken first; then they all had to run. The 88th was then deployed out towards the Johnnies, but they retired. In a short time, however, a large force of the enemy, preceded by skirmishers, again came towards our regiment, which quickly formed a strong skirmish line along the edge of the woods, while the enemy had to come across the open fields. The boys opened a severe fire upon the advancing graybacks, who soon halted and lay down for a while, and then retired. This attack had scarcely been repulsed, when large bodies of Confederates were observed moving through the woods on the opposite side of the field, their purpose evidently being to assault the line of the Pennsylvania Reserves on the right. There appeared to be three lines as they moved past our flank, and the boys opened a rapid fire which undoubtedly made it very hot for them. When they reached the Reserves they struck a snag, and the Pennsylvanians objecting to their presence in that quarter, they soon came streaming back in great disorder, again receiving the fire of our skirmishers.

The regiment remained on the skirmish line near Bethesda Church until the morning of May 31, when the whole line was advanced about half a mile. Near by were two neat farm houses, and at the time that our troops first occupied this ground two safeguards had been posted to protect the property; but when the enemy drove the line back, these guards were unable to escape, or perhaps supposed that their duty would shield them. However that may have been, the occupants of the houses had turned them out and the rebels had shot them both; their lifeless bodies were found lying in the yard. The sight of these men, killed while in the discharge of a benevolent duty, greatly incensed the soldiers, and going through the houses, they smashed the furniture, took the provisions, and broke up house-keeping generally, in spite of the piteous appeals of the owners.

CHAPTER XXIII.

FROM COLD HARBOR TO PETERSBURG: JUNE 1 TO 16, 1864.

JUNE came in hot, dry, and dusty: the sun scorching hot, the country dry, and the roads dusty. The Army of the Potomac was in the woods and thickets around Cold Harbor, within two hours' march of the Confederate capital, gradually feeling its way towards the enemy.

At nine A.M on the 1st the brigade cautiously advanced towards Richmond, the batteries shelling the woods in front; in reply, the Confederate cannon opened a quick fire, their projectiles tearing through the trees over the swaying lines of men, as they very carefully pushed towards the enemy's position. Upon passing through a thick strip of timber their lines were in plain view, not a thousand yards distant, heavy columns of infantry moving in rear of their breastworks towards our left. About noon the Confederate skirmishers made a break for the regiment, but were easily repulsed, and at three o'clock the brigade advanced again, stopping every few hundred yards to throw up breastworks.

The mortality of battle and the sickness incident to so continuous and severe a campaign had told fearfully on the ranks of the regiment, scarcely 150 men being present. Every day some comrades fell in battle, little noted by the world, but greatly missed by their companions as well as by the loved ones at home, and yet the handful of survivors—a mere fragment of a regiment—marched and fought, wondering who next would fill a soldier's grave or be carried to the hospital disabled and incapacitated from making a living in the future.

On June 2 we built more works, with traverses for protection from cross-fire; the enemy's artillery taking the line in flank and his sharp-shooters in front, made it dangerous to raise the head higher than the works. A member of the 11th Pennsylvania, while jesting

with some of our boys, incautiously looked over the cap log, when
a rifle-ball pierced his brain and he fell back dead.   Orders to move
were expected at any moment, and not wishing to leave the body
lying there, his comrades dug a shallow trench and buried him, and
within a half-hour were sitting on his grave, speculating as to who
would be the next to fall.   The boys left the dead soldier, not alone
in his glory, for there were hundreds of new-made graves in the trail
of the army, occupied by the boys in blue,—

> Lying so silent by night and by day,
> Sleeping the years of their manhood away.

June 3, 1864, was a beautiful day, one that would have been much
enjoyed if our Southern friends had let us alone ; but they were most
disagreeable people, and consequently made our lives very unhappy,
pitching cannon-balls at us in the most reckless manner.*   John
Keller said that they ought to be arrested, and volunteered to send
Jim Hague, John Williams, and Boocock over to bring them in ; but
the proposition was vetoed, though Charley McKnight said he would
lead the gang.

Next morning the 90th Regiment was ordered to occupy a strip
of woods a couple of hundred yards to the front; it accordingly
moved out, battalion front, in fine style, under a sharp fire, and
succeeded in taking the position.   Then Colonel Tilden, of the

— —

* During one of these intermittent ball matches at Cold Harbor the writer received an ugly gash in the hand from a fragment of shell, and had all the glory
there is in bleeding for one's country without much physical harm, as probably
his feelings were hurt more than his hand. If he has not done so before, he
desires to apologize now to the too-confiding comrades who generously intrusted
him with about a score of canteens to fill with pure water, and who lost them
in his rapid change of base to the friendly shelter of the breastworks, after the
shell overtook him. If there is any blame to be scored against anybody for this
loss, he wants it chalked to the account of the bad man on the other side of the
line who sent the shell, and not against him. He probably forgot to gratefully
thank his messmates for their sympathetic advice to "keep a stiff upper lip," and
other like comforting expressions which were possibly not rightly appreciated at
the time. At any rate, these thanks can go with the regrets for the tins, and will
probably square the account.

JOHN HART,
Company I.

JOHN D. VAUTIER,
Company I.
Historian.

CAPTAIN WILLIAM J. HARKISHEIMER,
Company I.
Major U. S. Vols.

JOHN W. SICKELS,
Company K.

SAMUEL MARTIN,
Company K.

COMPANIES I AND K.

16th Maine, was ordered to advance his pickets, and at the head of the line led them on and triumphantly occupied a new line close to the enemy's position.

On June 5 we marched from Bethesda Church to Cold Harbor, being placed in reserve behind the 18th Corps, and remaining here until the 11th, when the brigade moved to near Bottom Bridge, on the Chickahominy. Crossed that stream and formed line of battle at White Oak Swamp on the 13th, at which place the enemy made a fierce attack, but was shaken off at all points. While under this fire the regiment suffered an irreparable loss in the death of its leader, Captain George B. Rhoads, who was killed by a solid shot or shell. He was one of the bravest officers in the service, greatly beloved, and his untimely death was regretted by every man in the regiment. He doubtless had a presentiment of his fate, as for some days prior to his death he often read his Bible and gently rebuked any one using profane language in his presence. When Comrades Wallace and Street raised his bleeding body, they found his Testament in his pocket. With sad hearts the boys dug a shallow trench, and tenderly laid to rest the mortal remains of as brave a soldier as ever followed the colors through this terrible war.   •

> No useless coffin enclosed his breast,
>   Nor in sheet nor in shroud we wound him;
> But he lay, like a warrior taking his rest,
>   With his martial cloak around him.

On June 7 our old comrades composing the 9th New York bid the brigade farewell and left for the quieter and more congenial scenes in Gotham, their three years' service having expired. The 9th (83d of the line) was an exceptionally good regiment, and had a record for reliability second to none. It entered the campaign on May 4 with 515 men, and had lost 257 killed and wounded, 98 going home under command of Colonel Chalmers and the recruits being transferred to the 97th. Colonel Moesch was killed in the Wilderness and buried under the supervision of Chaplain Roe. In 1887, Captain George A. Hussey, the historian of the 9th, had his body removed and reinterred at Fredericksburg, his memory being perpetuated by an elegant and appropriate monument erected by his

comrades. When his remains were disinterred there were found in
the grave one pair of boots in pieces, some fragments of cloth, the
buttons from his uniform, and the bullet that killed him, which had
been placed under his head. Truly, "Ashes to ashes, dust to dust."

With the action at White Oak Swamp ended this stage of the
campaign, the army now being transferred to the vicinity of Petersburg. During the forty days from the 5th of May to the close of
the campaign on the Chickahominy the stubborn, steady, and sanguinary character of the fighting had been unprecedented in the
history of this country. In that time Grant had lost in killed,
wounded, and missing upward of 54,000 of his bravest soldiers,
and Lee over 32,000. Such havoc is appalling, and it has often
been remarked that this loss was useless, that the army might have
been safely and speedily conveyed south of the James without the
sacrifice of a single life. The writer wishes to express his humble
opinion on this point, being satisfied that it is worth as much as any
other, and if the reader does not like it he can form one of his own ;
that opinion is, that General Grant pursued the correct and only
route and adopted the surest means of ending the rebellion. Richmond was not the true objective of the Union army. So long as
Lee's army remained intact, the fall of Richmond, important as it
was, would not have ended the war. That army, therefore, was the
true objective, and if it could be destroyed or its power of resistance seriously impaired by heavy and continuous hammering, the
solution of this difficult problem would be easily reached. Of
course the frightful loss of life is sad to contemplate, and no one
feels that more keenly than the soldier who marched and fought in
this dreadful contest, and who mournfully buried so many gallant
comrades wherever the lines were formed. But war means mangled
bodies and gaping wounds, ruined homesteads and blighted house-
holds, hospitals filled with the sick and wounded ; nevertheless, it
had to be fought out ; the bitter cup had to be drained even to the
very dregs, and then the fratricidal contest ceased. When General
Grant assumed command he bent all his energies to the destruction
of Lee's army, and he fought it out on that line, though it took
all summer and winter, too.

So much for the overland campaign.

CHAPTER XXIV.

PETERSBURG TO THE WELDON RAILROAD: JUNE 16 TO AUGUST
23, 1864.

LEFT White Oak Swamp on the night of June 13, marched all
night, and encamped near Charles City Court-House, remaining
here until daylight of the 16th, when we marched to the James
River, and at two P.M. boarded the steamer John Brooks and crossed
the river. Fell in and marched all night, halting at three A.M.
After a very brief rest and an abbreviated breakfast, again fell in and
took position supporting the 2d Corps, but in the night moved back
out of range.

On the morning of the 18th the division moved to the front to
assault the Confederate fortifications. Advanced through an orchard,
over the railroad, took a hill within 200 yards of the enemy, and
then made a grand swoop for his main line,—all this under a fire that
thinned the ranks at every step ; but the line on our flank not marching as fast as the regiment, the charge, like a breaking wave, spent
its force, and the men, disdaining to run, dropped behind a slight
wattling fence and opened on the rebs. Still, the command was to
forward : " Forward Baxter's brigade ;" but the experienced eyes of
the veterans had taken the measure of those frowning forts, and,
knowing that it was a hopeless job, not a man moved.

At this time, John Ewing, the color-bearer, seeing the men holding back, charged up to within a few yards of the works with his
flag, and called the regiment to him. The boys, encouraged by
this noble example, rallied up to the colors, only to be driven back
with severe loss. Returning to the fence, the men opened on the
enemy, and so effective was the fire that it was extremely unhealthy
for a Johnny to show his head. In one of their cannon a swab had
been left by a Confederate gunner ; but they were not allowed to
remove it, and after several attempts, they fired the swab into our

line. Presently the rebels began to strengthen their works, and our marksmen practised on their shovels, hands, backs, or anything that offered a shot, one poor Johnny getting a Minié in his back from Harry Booz's rifle that caused the dust to fly from his coat.   ◦

There were quite a number of expert marksmen in the regiment at this time, notably Harry Booz, John Wallace, Peter Shearer, Reuben Neider, George Armstrong, Morris Robbins, Harvey Myers, Mortimer Wisham, Frank Charles, Jonathan Wenzell, Charles Butler, William Fisher, and, in fact, almost every man was a good shot. But this was a sad day's work for the regiment, among the killed being Lieutenant Sinn, John Beaumont, Pierson Miller, Henry Roth, and Henry Rhoads ; while the wounded included James G. Clark, John Ewing, James Seifert, and Sergeant McChaliker.

Harry Booz vividly describes the above-mentioned movements as follows :

We started on the march from Turkey Bend about four P.M. and continued until about eight A.M. of the 18th, then cooked breakfast near some negro troops ; soon advanced in line of battle, the rebs falling back. Once we lay in line several minutes, the bullets whistling and the shells flying overhead, one bursting directly over us in the top of an oak-tree. I heard something dropping from one limb to another : it was the butt of a shell, about a pound in weight, and it fell on the ankle of one of our boys, who jumped up and danced around for a while, holding his ankle, thinking he was shot. Presently a shell burst directly over the back of a man next me and paralyzed him completely, there being no sign of life in him as they carried him back. That explosion seemed to lift me clear off the ground and partly stunned me ; my hearing has never been good since. We soon advanced across an open field, our battery lining with us, one gun at a time, firing as fast as they could. We halted in that field and lay close for fifteen or twenty minutes, bullets and shells flying everywhere, Montgomery saying that they would hurt some one yet with their carelessness. We soon got orders to go for the railroad cut, and John Campbell and I were the first in, the cut being some fifteen or eighteen feet deep, a road bridge over it where we went in. When we were all there we got orders to double-quick to a little stream by a hill-side, a meadow with high grass intervening, the place being probably 200 yards from the railroad. Campbell and I had the advance, and when we got there we were amused to see the boys coming through the knee-high grass and tumbling in and over a concealed ditch some four or five feet wide. There was a steep hill thirty-five or forty feet high running north and south, and the stream was just at the foot of it. I climbed to the top, and, looking across a cornfield (corn five or six inches high), saw that the reb skirmishers had carried piles of rails, about a wagon-load in each place and about twenty yards apart, facing us, and beyond that about 175 yards was their main line, with a battery facing us.

After quite a while an aide instructed our commander to keep his men well in hand for a general charge at six o'clock. Roll was called, and Ninesteel said that there were just sixty men with the colors. I heard the order coming down from the right to fall in, but I just climbed to the top of that hill and sat there looking back at the line forming. I made up my mind that we couldn't go into that line of works, but I was going to make the best time for a rail-pile, anyhow, and if the line came up I would go along with them.

When the line got the order to "Forward," I started, and when our bayonets cleared the hill I was half-way over. When the Johnnies saw our line of battle they opened a vicious fire, the air hissing with screaming shot and shell; but I flopped down behind my pre-empted pile of rails, soon being joined by Gilligan and Campbell.

In looking back at our advancing line, coming up with a hurrah, it was horrible to see the men falling by dozens, Montgomery going down, a grape-shot hitting his blanket; the next day we counted thirty-two holes in it. But the sergeant wasn't the man to stay down; he was up at once. George Smith, of A, was hit in the leg. I heard it strike him and watched to see where he was wounded. He took off his equipments and went to the rear.

In looking back, I saw something fly in the air; I took it to be cotton; but a piece of brain the size of a thimble fell on my arm, a shell having struck one of the men in the face, and it was the scattered brains I saw. A part of the brain struck one of our boys in the eye, knocking him senseless. He returned to the regiment two or three weeks afterwards, a circle three and a half inches in diameter over one discolored eye.

About the time Smith was hit, the two boys, Devine and Ewing, came along with the colors. All this had happened while the two boys were coming from where the line had started. They passed on just to our right. Campbell remarked, "Just look at those boys; they will lose the colors; I can't stand this; I'm going, too," and away he went, followed by Gilligan and myself. They had reached a worm-fence sixty-five or seventy yards from the fort containing the four-gun battery. The fence was in a depression just a little lower than the field, fifty yards back, and running parallel with the reb line, some rag-weed and poison-ivy growing along it. Their line was on higher ground, and we silenced their battery at once. They tried to load, but it was no use; we would fire at their hands and arms and put a veto on their work. One piece had a rammer in, which they tried several times to remove; but we were superintending that, and at dark it was there yet, but they removed it in the night. For a while they did some peeping over the works; but we, having the sky for a background, could see a bird at that distance, so we let go every time a head appeared, aiming to hit the slope a foot or so in front of the eyes, and the head would disappear awful quick. Night soon

13

closed down, clear but no moon, and we supplied ourselves with ammunition and strengthened our line, the neighbors up the hill doing the same work; but the shooting was kept up all night, no one getting much rest.

About eleven P.M., Lieutenant Lawrence came to us and asked if we knew what dark object that was moving about fifty yards in our front. We had not noticed anything, but could see it plainly when pointed out. We went out about twenty yards to ascertain its identity, but could not make it out, when Lawrence said he would fire at it anyhow, which he did, making an excellent shot in the darkness, and hit a cow that was grazing there, which bellowed fearfully and raised such a racket that the enemy thought we were charging them, for their whole line opened a hot fire at once, but they generally overshot us. An hour or so later I was watching for a shot, when farther to my right I saw the flash of a reb gun that appeared to be higher than the others, as though he were standing on the rifle-pits. I took a quick aim at his flash and caught him somewhere, for he yelled lustily for a bit. Directly we noticed some excitement among our boys, and found that the reb's bullet had struck one of the Beaumont brothers in the forehead, killing him instantly.

We were tired and hungry, and before daylight we went back to the stream to cook coffee, and happened to get on the ground occupied by the 21st Pennsylvania Cavalry, who were fighting dismounted. They had received rations and had left lots of pieces of crackers in the boxes, and as we had coffee, we were feasting again. On my way back I found a patent carbine with plenty of ammunition, and used this weapon while we remained in this position, my shoulders being very sore from the concussion from my Enfield.

Through the day the rebs tried several plans to build peep-holes, so they could draw a bead on us. They first got a small camp-kettle with the bottom out, laid it on the works, then with a shovel threw earth around it. We let them amuse themselves a while, and when they got it built, we sent kettle and dirt to kingdom come with a few well-directed shots; but they tried it again with some stiff sods ; set them on edge five or six inches apart, leaning the tops together, covering all with earth. We had so much fun with the pot that we let them finish this, then opened on it, every shot apparently moving a shovelful of dirt, until the hopes of the graybacks for a peep-hole were knocked into a cocked hat.

Towards the middle of the day William John Finley was standing looking over our works, when a reb fired at him from away off to our left, striking him in the shoulder. Then I kept a sharp lookout for reciprocity on William John's account, and soon one of them carelessly exposed his back, and when he worked up far enough I let him have it, and Reuben Neider said there was one reb short. So Finley was promptly avenged.

About three P.M. the 9th Corps relieved us. There was a spring near us, the drain winding back across the cornfield, and through this slight ravine they came in and we went out, but in some places we were in sight of the Johns and had to run the gauntlet of their fire, three of the boys being wounded coming out. We found the main line had built works just back of the cut, our regiment on the left of the brigade.

There was an ice-house in our front, sunk in the ground, and though it was dangerous work, our boys would have their ice-water, balls or not. On the afternoon of the second day a ration of whiskey and quinine was issued, and some of the 90th getting too much, got fighting on the higher ground, where they mauled each other, the bullets meanwhile whistling all around them. Presently one got the other down and began kicking him, when the kicker got a ball in his leg, breaking the leg and breaking up the fight.

The next morning we moved to the left and went to the front, but at night moved again, the next day going to the Jerusalem plank road. There had been considerable fighting here, and as we marched up we came to the arms of a whole brigade that had been captured, they having grounded arms, and they lay there in line of battle farther than we could see. I had the small of the stock of my rifle nearly cut through by a ball on the 8th of May, and as I had fired 212 rounds while we were at the front, it had gotten very weak, so I exchanged my old gun for a good one. . . . This is my story of Petersburg, from memory, and I think you will find it substantially correct. Our boys were true blue; twenty-eight got to the fence, all of the 88th. All the boys I have mentioned were daisies and had true grit, so were Joe Burris and Wes. Martin and Henry Lloyd and scores more whom I could name.

The above is Booz's version of the operations on June 18, 19, and 20, 1864, and those who knew Harry will credit every word of it. The historian desires to say here that there were many splendid soldiers in the regiment, but he has omitted to mention a number of heroic actions that came under his own observation for the reason that hundreds of good soldiers who were just as brave would have had an injustice done them, because, unfortunately, the writer did not witness their soldierly conduct. In this battle the boys realized, as they had often done before, what a "soft thing" the Johnnies had on us, they fighting under cover of their stout earthworks, our boys with no other protection than the blue blouses that covered their stout and loyal hearts. Each man fired on an average nearly 200 rounds, but it is reasonable to suppose that most of these were wasted.

Threw up breastworks, and on the afternoon of Sunday, the 19th, were relieved and retired in line behind the railroad. Lay here doing picket duty until the 24th, when we resumed the march under a heavy shelling, halting near the Jerusalem plank road.

On June 25 the 12th Massachusetts left for home, time having expired. Good-by, boys; there was no better regiment branded U. S. than the 12th. From May 5 to June 25—fifty days—it had been under fire forty-one times and lost 172 men. Only eighty-five men left with the colors. What a gory, glorious record !

On the 25th in reserve, on picket at night, and remained there until the 27th, making a treaty with our friends the enemy, not to fire on "you-uns, if you-uns won't fire on we-uns."

Friday, July 1, very hot, water scarce; regiment engaged all day and night building works on the right of the Jerusalem plank road, continuing in this place for several weeks, meantime celebrating the Glorious Fourth with flying colors and enjoying an extra ration of good things issued by the Sanitary Commission. On the 7th the regiment moved to the right of the brigade; lively firing; several men wounded. On the 12th the brigade moved to the rear, the regiment deploying along the works and filling its place; the brigade returned on the 15th, when we were assigned the job of building Fort Crawford and some contiguous breastworks.

On July 22 the major of the 107th Pennsylvania took temporary command of the 88th, and on the 26th he treated the boys to a dress parade,—a rare thing in these days,—but no rations. It is needless to say that the men would have been more thankful for the rations.

On July 29 only one shell fell in camp, this being so remarkable as to cause mention in Sergeant McKnight's diary. The 13th Massachusetts, another gallant regiment that had been closely identified with our brigade, went home on the 14th, its three years' arduous service having expired. Good-by, boys.

> If you get there before we do,
> Look out for us, we're coming, too.

On Saturday, July 30, 1864, the regiment was up at two A.M., and drawing forty rounds extra ammunition, took the place of the 94th New York in Fort Crawford, while the division was massed in the rear, to assist in the mine explosion. The sad story of that abortive assault need not be retold here, except to say that credit for the defeat should be again ascribed to General John Barleycorn.

The early days of August were times of feverish and wearing expectancy to the boys, who were in line nearly every morning at three o'clock, waiting for something terrible to turn up; so the wilting days passed, sometimes on picket, sometimes in camp, until the middle of the month, the best thing happening in the interim being the visit of the paymaster on the 11th, who gladdened the boys' hearts with two months' pay.

On August 18 the cavalry and the 5th Corps struck for the Weldon Railroad, reaching the Yellow Tavern about ten A.M. The 1st Division was engaged in destroying the railroad, while our division, deploying on the right of the road, pressed the enemy through the woods a half-mile towards Petersburg. Then, under a heavy rain and a lively fire, both extremely uncomfortable circumstances, we lay in line of battle all night, expecting an assault.

On the 19th, Crawford's division again advanced through the thick woods, after being relieved about seven A.M., and built a line of breastworks, repeating this pastime until three light lines had been thrown up. Meantime, the Confederates were not idle; massing their troops at a weak point in the Union line, they burst through, while Crawford's men, in the dense woods, all unconscious of peril on the flanks and rear, repelled every attempt of the enemy to drive our line by an assault in front. The first intimation that the men had of the enemy being in their rear was the unexpected appearance of a squad of Confederates, led by a hatless and excited officer, coming directly through the woods from a direction that every man in the 88th was fully convinced was the rear. They were immediately halted and ordered to surrender, but decidedly objected, explaining that we were the ones to surrender, as they had us surrounded; this story was not credited, and, taking the officer's sword, Sergeant John Wallace, with an escort, proceeded with the prisoners back through the woods, when they ran into a moving column of the enemy, and were in turn captured and run Dixieward without further ceremony. To make matters worse, the Union artillery posted near the Yellow Tavern, seeing the Confederates in our rear, opened fire directly upon the woods, and between this fire and that of the enemy it appeared as if Crawford's division would be wiped out,—a veritable case of between the devil and the deep sea; but the Confederates, sweeping across our rear, quickly disappeared, capturing in their erratic course a large number of the 5th Corps who were so unlucky as to be in their way.

Among our men captured were John Wallace, Harry Durfer, William Hutchinson, Jacob Drexle, Joseph Hock, Henry Arnold, William Carey, Morris Robbins, James Miller, Frank Swavely, Charles Yerger, Isaac Eyrich, William D. Clemens, Reuben Neider, Enoch Shaw, Ben Goodheart, and John and Lewis Waterman,—in all, about thirty; of these, the last eight died in captivity. Clemens and Neider were especially well known to all the regiment on account of their tall figures and soldierly appearance, and they, with thousands of others, were starved to death. In the stockade, Neider shared the scanty blanket belonging to Robbins, and on the morning of December 28, when Morris awoke, Neider was dead in his arms.

After getting out of the Wilderness, the brigade reformed and pushed in again, when Captain Jacob Houder, a most estimable and gallant officer, commanding the regiment, was struck in the head by a musket ball and instantly killed. Houder was a favorite young officer who had been identified with the regiment and had won his shoulder-straps by hard service. Coming so soon after the death of the lamented Rhoads, the men felt the loss of this officer keenly, and very mournfully another lowly grave was fashioned, the boys tenderly laying their fallen chief in his narrow bed.

> Slowly and sadly we laid him down,
> From the field of his fame fresh and gory.
> We carved not a line, we raised not a stone,
> But we left him alone with his glory.

That all the brigade was not captured was due to the skill of Colonel Wheelock and the valuable services of Captain S. H. Martin, Private Threapleton (Boocock), and others of the 88th, who, at the request of the colonel, reconnoitred the woods and located the position of the enemy.

The 5th Corps now connected with the 9th Corps, and, throwing up works, planted itself firmly across the road in a manner that said we have come to stay. On account of the incessant rains since

the 13th, the condition of the roads was frightful, the wagons stall-
ing and the soldiers sticking in the mire ; but the boys understood
the value of substantial defences, and during the 20th were diligently
employed in strengthening the lines, and it was well for us that we
did so, for on the 21st—Sunday—Lee sent Hill's corps with instructions to drive Warren off. Hill concentrated thirty cannon on our
left and opened a wicked fire, following with an assault by his infantry, which was easily repulsed ; then he moved farther to the left,
intending to strike the line in left and rear, and launched his battalions to the attack ; but they were repulsed everywhere with heavy
loss, including many prisoners and colors.

The Union line at this point was somewhat in the form of a horse-
shoe, the position assigned to the regiment being on the right ; consequently, when the enemy opened fire it took the men in the back,
and for protection they were compelled to take position outside of
the breastworks. Through all this fearful hurricane of shot and
shell General Warren rode as leisurely and calmly as if nothing was
the matter, while the shells were knocking the stacked muskets sky-
high, tearing off legs and arms, and smashing the bodies of the unfortunate victims into unrecognizable masses of blood, flesh, and
bones. After this bloody repulse Lee gave it up, having lost about
3000 men ; the loss of the 5th Corps was about 4500, over 3000
being taken prisoners, the 88th having thirty-two killed, wounded,
and captured.

The loss of some of the regiments in the division is here given,
mostly in prisoners :

16th Maine 152
104th New York 146
39th Massachusetts 293
90th Pennsylvania 121
107th Pennsylvania 152

The next few days were spent in building more works, cleaning
camp, cleansing uniforms, and tidying up generally, and on August
23 fresh bread was issued ; nobody could remember when the last
had been received.

CHAPTER XXV.

SIEGE OF PETERSBURG : AUGUST 24, 1864, TO MARCH 27, 1865.

ON August 25, 1864, the soldiers were called to arms at three
A.M., and after some delay, head of column was directed towards
Petersburg and passed through the thickets where the recent battles
had been fought, the trees and saplings being much scarred by the
balls of the contestants. A column of the enemy was reported
coming down the road, and line of battle was formed ; but the Confederates not appearing, the column countermarched, passing the
Yellow or Globe Tavern and marching about a mile towards Ream's
Station, where heavy firing was heard, then halted and threw up
earthworks ; it was hard labor handling this soggy earth. Next day
a treat, in the shape of whiskey and quinine, potatoes, onions, and
fresh bread, was issued ; we then moved from the works and went
into camp. Details were made daily to build Fort Wadsworth and
some other heavy earthworks.

The regiment now had about 150 present, but as the time of many
who had first enlisted would soon expire, the command was shortly
to be still further reduced in numbers.

The first of those to go home who had not re-enlisted was from
Company A, on August 23, and other squads quickly followed from
time to time as their terms of service expired. The following list
gives the names of those who were mustered out during the fall,
though not all were present with the regiment, some being absent
sick or wounded and others on detailed duty :

Company A.—Sergeants George Shirey and Gabriel Hill; Privates Aaron
Bechtle, Daniel Clouser, James Fagan, Henry Haywood, Henry Himmelright,
D. Hagan, G. W. Hoffman, M. Hughston, W. M. Johnson, Levi Miller, Edward
Miller, William Miller, Isaac Kelchner, L. Roland, C. A. Roland, C. Strohecker,
John Wooden, and John Zeiber.

Company B.—Sergeant Zach. Swavely ; Corporals Charles S. Butler, Isaac J.

Brown, and Aaron Guenther; Musician Edward Ball; Privates Daniel Beidler, Jacob Behm, George W. Boger, Joseph C. Clement, Tobias Deemer, H. Greimes, Joel Reifsnyder, William Reiff, Henry D. Reiff, Peter D. Shearer, Charles H. Turner, Jonathan Wentzell, and Samuel Wesley.

Company C.—Sergeants J. N. Hanson, C. B. Keil, and John W. Waters; Corporals Henry C. Richardson, Neal Boyd, James W. Colen, and J. Pugh; Privates W. Buckings, James Hague, P. Hinkle, J. McDowell, M. Pinyard, and Peter Wilfong.

Company D.—Sergeant William Coppes; Corporal George W. Armstrong; Privates Michael Ruth, John Sanders, and C. Wilday.

Company E.—Sergeants William Montgomery and John R. Jones; Privates Henry S. Booz and Henry Lloyd.

Company F.—Privates James G. Clark, A. Hersh, Frederick Restine, and William H. Scott.

Company H.—Privates Emanuel Able, John Albright, William Bixenstine, Henry Bosler, Harrison Eddinger, J. K. Gorman, F. Heller, and William Spicker.

Company I.—Corporal Hugh Rutherford, Privates Edward D. Nunneville, James Perara, and John D. Vautier.

Company K.—Corporal Gideon Moyer; Privates William P. Clark, Michael Conover, and Joseph W. Hanaman.

After these old war-dogs had gone the battalion was but a skeleton, a shadow of its former strength ; but the soldiers that remained were veterans both in name and service, as true as tempered steel.

The division broke camp on September 2, and, preceded by the cavalry, pushed out to the left through the woods, thickets, swamps, jungles, and briers for which this part of the country is famous. The column thridded the unknown wilderness very carefully, and as the long line wound its sinuous way through forest and clearing, every man was as silent as the grave, communing with his own thoughts and wondering what fate had in store for him. But after marching a mile or two the order was given to about-face and go back to camp; then every tongue was loosed, and the procession that a little while before was as silent as a funeral broke out in noisy jest and cheerful talk. It seemed as though the men were glad that they were alive.

On the 5th of September, while cutting timber, a tree fell on Corporal Hoffman, of Company A, inflicting mortal injuries, and on the following day Patrick Clickett, of Company K, was injured by a similar accident, but recovered. Another movement to Poplar

Grove Church was made on September 15, the Confederates being pressed back some three or four miles, when the division returned to camp.

On September 16 moved camp to near the left fort, behind the breastworks, and remained in the vicinity of Fort Dushane for several days, doing fatigue and picket duty and eating Uncle Samuel's rations when the quartermaster was kind enough to remember us. Some of our officers were never appreciated by the men, the quartermaster being in this list; sometimes they were condemned very unjustly. But the boys must have something to growl about and somebody to growl at, and the quartermaster filled the bill as well as any other officer; the men certainly gave him "bally-hoo" on many and various occasions.

On September 27 the monotony of camp life was broken by the accidental explosion of a caisson while a battery was on drill, killing one and wounding seven men. The same day a flag-pole 130 feet high was raised at Fort Dushane, so named after an officer who had been killed in action on this ground. On the 29th the monotony was further disturbed by a reconnoissance of the brigade towards Ream's Station, but the command returned in the evening; nobody hurt, though under fire.

After the departure of the three years' men affairs in camp were very quiet, with the exception of an occasional expedition in the general direction of the South Side Railroad; on one of these trips the enemy was encountered at Preble's farm, but Adjutant Detre (in command) brought the regiment safely back to Fort Dushane.

In November 200 conscripts joined the regiment, being the first important addition of recruits since the command had been in service. This accession brought promotion to many deserving soldiers who had been debarred advancement because the regiment had been so weak in numbers, many privates attaining non-commissioned rank and the following changes being made in the higher grades:

Company A.—Lieutenant Ninesteel to captain, Lieutenant Kram to first lieutenant, Sergeant Koch to lieutenant.
Company C.—Sergeant Thwait to captain, Sergeant Herron to lieutenant.
Company D.—Sergeant Hunter to lieutenant.

Company E.—Lieutenant Gilligan to captain, Sergeant D. J. Lehman to lieutenant.

Company F.—Lieutenant Clevinger to captain.

Company G.—Lieutenant Gardiner to captain, Sergeant Bright to lieutenant.

Company H.—Lieutenant Lawrence to captain, Sergeant McChaliker to lieutenant.

Company I.—Lieutenant Copestick to captain.

Company K.—Lieutenant Martin to captain, Sergeant McKnight to lieutenant.

On December 7 the division marched down to the North Carolina border, on what is known as the apple-jack raid, each man having six days' rations of food and unlimited rations of rain and mud, for it stormed almost every day while on the raid. The Johnnies were scattered and the railroad thoroughly destroyed as far as the Mulherrin River; then the mud-bespattered column halted and, meeting strong opposition, concluded to return. While coming back a force of cavalry acted as rear-guard, the 88th and 11th Pennsylvania, 97th New York, and 39th Massachusetts being thrown out as flankers. Presently the Confederate troopers following the column made a furious and unexpected charge upon the Union horsemen bringing up the rear, driving them in confusion up the road towards brigade head-quarters. The field and staff of the 88th were interested spectators of this rout, as the combatants came yelling and tearing along the muddy road, the buttermilk hunters having a fine time cutting and slashing at the Union troopers, and letting themselves out on the rebel yell to the full capacity of their healthy lungs. This humiliating scene thoroughly disgusted Adjutant Gilligan, and directing Dr. Shoemaker and the rest of the staff to seek protection at brigade head-quarters, he determined to stop the stampede. Drawing his sword, he rode boldly down to the fleeing mob, calling upon the Union troopers to halt and rally, but his appeal had no effect upon them. The confusion was so great, and our cavalry were in such haste to get the aid of the infantry, that they passed the lieutenant, and before he realized the situation he was in the midst of the Confederates, nearly every one of whom cut and lunged at him in the most spiteful manner. Gilligan was dazed at this kind of reception, but by parrying the vicious thrusts he managed to save his skin, until an unkempt and unwashed grayback rode within a few

feet of him and, presenting a navy revolver, ordered him to surrender. This the lieutenant did, but the Confederates were so intent
on the fun they were having that they all chased off after our horsemen, leaving the captive alone in the road. They had not proceeded far before they received the fire of the infantry; then the
whole squad came tearing back, the Union troopers now in pursuit.
Gilligan saw them coming, and hoping to save himself from being
taken south, he slipped off his horse and lay flat in the mire in the
road. When the Johnnies reached him they had no time to stop,
and though they tried to sabre him as he lay in the mire, he escaped
without a scratch, being, however, completely covered with mud.
The boys had seen him captured, and when he rode into the lines
again, encased with mud from head to foot, he was received with
shouts of welcome and laughter at the unique appearance he presented. This was Gilligan's first and last attempt to rally cavalrymen; he had enough and he knew it. To punish the pursuing
squadrons a trap was laid for them, our infantry lying in ambush on
the flanks, while the cavalry again allowed themselves to be chased
along the road. The Confederate troopers took the bait, hook and
all, and when the infantry rose and delivered a telling fire into their
ranks at short range, what was left of them kept at a respectful distance during the remainder of the march, and the rear was not again
molested.

The division returned to camp on December 14, many of the men
with apple-jack in their canteens; hence the name given the raid.
After the apple-jack raid the command settled down in winter-quarters, any extensive movement in this alluvial country being impossible, and only the usual hyemal work was done, enlivened by an
occasional foray into the disputed territory when the weather per-
mitted, Captain Lawrence being in command.

On December 17 details cut logs for winter-quarters, and on
Christmas-eve the new huts were occupied. There were no stock-
ings hung, nor any Santa Claus in that camp, nor turkey fixings that
Christmas, the only luxury enjoyed being the dispensing with all
drills in honor of the day.

January 1, 1865, dawned pleasant and quiet; on the 5th a detail
with twelve wagons went four miles beyond the lines for boards to

complete the quarters. It is needless to remark that in such business the 88th was eminently successful. On February 5, by way of diversion, the brigade marched down the Weldon Railroad, destroying *en route* all property that gave comfort and shelter to the enemy, and lay in line of battle all night. Candor compels the statement that the term "lay" is a misnomer, as the boys had to walk around all night to keep from freezing, fires being prohibited.

On the 6th marched across Hatcher's Run and bivouacked till noon, then formed line and pushed on towards the Boydton road, Baxter, with the 97th New York, 16th Maine, and 39th Massachusetts, in the first line, and the 11th and 88th Pennsylvania in the second. In this order they ran against Pegram's division and a lively scrap ensued, Pegram being killed; but Mahone's Confederate division flanking Crawford's right, the whole division was forced back with loss. The woods were so dense that it was impossible to see far, and, remembering their rough experience in a similar position on the Weldon Railroad in August, the men were very reluctant about advancing in such a thicket, unless assured of prompt support. Ayers's division was assigned a position on the right of Crawford, but before his troops could get into line the enemy advanced, and the scattering shots of the skirmishers, followed by the long, steady ripple of line firing, announced that the battle had opened on the right, and taking Ayers before he could fully form to receive their onset, the Confederates broke his line, sending some of his troops back in disorder. The giving way of Ayers involved Crawford, the fire of the enemy quickly opening through the woods, and Baxter and the rest were forced back to near the run; but here the men rallied, and when the exultant Johnnies came dashing through the woods they received so severe a fire that they were brought to a stand very quickly. The Confederates then drew off, and the 5th Corps bivouacked for the night in this position, in the mud and rain,—a most cheerless and miserable one, the men being scarcely able to keep from freezing to death.

The troops were up early on the morning of the 7th; in truth, they were up all night, and a more disagreeable time it would be hard to conceive. Under the circumstances, to have lain down and slept would have resulted in death.

After a not very exhilarating feast on hardtack, hog fat, and
water, the muskets were put in order, line of battle formed, and
we got to work to earn the day's wages.   The line pushed through
the woods and bogs, the rain freezing as it fell and coating everything—trees, brush, soldiers, and ground—with a sheet of ice.   The
men were chilled to the bone, but there was no help for it, so the
line painfully and slowly swept on.   Now, it happened that the rebs
were anxious to learn what these lost children of the 5th Corps
wanted in this debatable land, and about the time that the Union
line advanced, the divisions of Pegram, Mahone, and Evans also
moved forward, the result being a sharp fight in the woods, the
Johnnies being pressed back to their works.   Here Baxter remained
close up to the enemy's line until the 10th, when the 2d Corps
occupied the line permanently, the 5th returning to camp.

The loss of the 5th Corps and the cavalry in this movement was
officially given as 1165 killed and wounded and 154 missing.   The
loss in the 88th was partially reported as follows : Killed, C. McNulty,
James Phillips, James Yoder, H. Jaques, E. Phillips, F. Monroe, J.
Bryner, M. Volkir.   Among the wounded were Captain Martin,
Frank Charles, August Kissinger, William A. Boyd, and Mortimer
Wisham.

This was the initial battle of the recruits who had lately joined
the regiment, and it may be said to their credit that they acquitted
themselves very well, being undoubtedly influenced by the personal
example of the veterans, all of whom behaved with signal bravery,
Sergeant William A. Sands, of Company G, being especially mentioned and honored with a furlough, which, in view of the stirring
events quickly following, he declined.

After this little episode the boys remained in camp attending to
business, when there was any, until the 25th of March, when pan-
demonium broke loose on the right, caused by Gordon's irruption
on our lines at Fort Steadman, and our division was pulled out of
camp and marched in the direction of Meade's head-quarters, to
take part in the fray, if needed.   But Hartranft's Pennsylvanians
settled Gordon's hash, and our boys moved to near Fort Dushane,
where they were reviewed by President Lincoln and lots of lesser
stars : major-generals were so thick in these days as to cease to cause

CAPTAIN CHARLES McKNIGHT.

LIEUTENANT ROBERT L. CARNS.

CAPTAIN SYLVESTER H. MARTIN.

SERGEANT JOSEPH SERGEANT.

CORPORAL WILLIAM B. THREAPLETON.

COMPANY K.

remark. During the first year of the war, if a general of any grade came along the boys thought it the orthodox thing to get up as big a hurrah as possible, and the generals relished it; but nowadays "Old Grant" or "Pop Meade" passed by with scarcely a salute, they appearing to enjoy this quietness just as much as the smaller commanders did the hubbub in other days. General Warren was always with his men : in the front where the missiles were thickest, building works, or wherever else the soldiers were stationed, there Warren could be found.

CHAPTER XXVI.

THE LAST CAMPAIGN.

ON March 29, 1865, the bugles sounded for the final pack-up, and soon the camps were deserted, though many of the incredulous ones, bearing in mind the numerous former abortive movements, confidently predicted a speedy return ; but the column pulled out towards the Boydton road, and the soldiers never saw those camps again.   ˎ

The line of march was along the Halifax road parallel to the Weldon Railroad, beyond the breastworks turning sharply westward and crossing Rowanty Creek at Monk's Neck Bridge and road, then north on the Quaker road, finally reaching Boydton plank road near the junction of the two roads, where the corps halted and intrenched. The weather, probably to maintain its past record during like movements, went back on the boys again, a heavy rain drenching them to the skin and presaging another unsuccessful attempt on this flank ; but on the morning of Friday, the 31st, it cleared nicely, though the country was a vast swamp, the only hard ground apparently being the ridge upon which the enemy was securely posted. About noon a general advance was made against the Southern works along the White Oak road, defended by the brigades of Hunton, Wise, McGowan, and Gracie ; but the assault was repelled, the enemy advancing and, flanking Crawford and Ayres, forced them back upon Griffin, where the broken battalions reformed. Later in the afternoon another advance was ordered, the men going in with confidence and spirit, striking the Confederate line near the road, and by a gallant charge carrying the works, capturing many flags and prisoners. This action is generally known as the battle of White Oak road or Gravelly Run. Several of the regiment were wounded in this spirited fight, among them Captain Gilligan, Jacob Shuster, Thomas H. Anderson, and John S. Campbell.

News now came that Sheridan, with his cavalry, was hard pressed by Pickett's infantry at Dinwiddie, and that the 5th Corps must go to the rescue; so late at night the march was made to Sheridan's assistance, and the morning of April 1 found the 5th Corps pushing through the fields, concentrating near Gravelly Run, close to Crump's farm.   Early in the afternoon the column marched to Gravelly Run Church and massed, preparatory to a united advance upon Pickett at Five Forks, Warren to smash his left and the cavalry to break his front.   Behind his works, Pickett, with the brigades of Corse, Terry, Steuart, Ransom, and Wallace and the cavalry divisions of Munford, Lee, and Rosser,—in all, upward of 13,000 veteran Confederate soldiers,—confidently waited for Warren's attack.   The 5th Corps was about 12,000 strong, the cavalry mustering several thousand more, and when this force moved to the attack it bore all opposition before it.   The 88th, with Baxter's brigade, deflected somewhat to the right, striking the graybacks well to their left and rear, and though they made a plucky stand, nothing could resist the impetuous rush of Crawford's troops, who, bursting through, captured men by the thousands, together with colors and whole batteries.   The victory was complete; Pickett's brigades were dispersed, those who escaped the infantry being chased by the cavalry, and not a battery or regiment maintained its organization.   After the men had yelled themselves hoarse over the victory, the corps moved back towards Gravelly Run Church and rested for the night, and there wasn't a man in that jubilant camp but felt he had grown a foot taller since sunrise.

The Union loss was about 1000; of these, 634 were from the 5th Corps, over 300 being from Crawford's division.   The enemy lost nearly 6000 in prisoners alone, the 5th Corps capturing about 3300, with eleven colors and one entire battery.   The loss in our regiment included some who had served in every campaign and participated in every battle, only to die in this our last general engagement of the Rebellion.   A partial list is as follows: killed, Captain Koch, Lieutenant Lehman, and David Whitaker; wounded, Lieutenants Wade and Ney, and Charles Small.

Sunday, April 2, 1865, dawned calm and peaceful, but there was no rest for the weary; the corps marched towards Petersburg, then

countermarched to Hatcher's Run, crossed and went to the famous
South Side Railroad, then, facing towards Petersburg again and bearing to the left, halted at night north of Sutherland Station on the
Namozine road, and after a skirmish, bivouacked at eleven P.M., all
the men very tired.

The absence of General Warren had been noted, but it was not
generally known until late on the 2d that he had been relieved by
General Sheridan.   General Warren had endeared himself to his
command, was universally respected as a brave, careful, and ener-
getic commander, and his removal was regarded as an act of injustice to a man who was always at the front among his men, regardless
of his own comfort or safety.

On April 3 the corps, under General Griffin, was astir bright and
early, but Lee had evacuated Petersburg and was breaking away for
the mountains, evidently hunting the last ditch ; so the column was
started in hot pursuit, halting at ten o'clock P.M. at Deep Creek ; up
again at day-dawn on the 4th, on the trail of the Confederate army,
and passing many discouraged stragglers, most of whom were fast
losing faith in the Confederacy.   Remained at Jetersville on the
5th, in line of battle, but Lee slipped by ; then about faced and
went to Paineville, then to Legontown, and halted for the night.
On the 7th marched to Prince Edwards, on the 8th to Prospect
Station, thence to Appomattox, which was reached on the morning
of the 9th, after an exhausting march.

The 5th and 24th Corps, with Sheridan's troopers, were now
planted across Lee's line of retreat, while the 2d and 6th Corps
came driving up in his rear.   On the 9th he made a determined
effort to break through what he supposed to be the Union cavalry,
but when he discovered the infantry in line of battle, he saw that
further resistance was useless, and surrendered the Army of Northern
Virginia to its old foe, the Army of the Potomac.   When the formal
announcement of the surrender was made the soldiers were wild
with joy.   Towards their late foes only the kindest actions were
manifested, and when it was known that Lee's ragged veterans were
starving, the Union soldiers willingly shared their scanty rations with
them.   To the 5th Corps was assigned the duty of executing the
conditions of the capitulation, and the regiment remained here

until April 15, then marched back to Wilson's Station, under command of Captain Aaron Bright. While here the regiment received several hundred conscripts, but it seemed like a new organization, as less than one hundred of the original members were now with it.

In recognition of long and faithful service, many of the veterans were promoted to commissioned officers during the spring, the roster of the regiment in June, 1865, being as follows :

Colonel, LOUIS WAGNER.

Lieutenant-Colonel, EDMUND A. MASS.

Major, AARON BRIGHT, JR.

Adjutant, ISAIAH MCINTIRE.

Quartermaster, ALBERT C. WESTER.

Surgeons, JOHN WINDSOR RAWLINS, M. B. McALEAR.

Quartermaster Sergeant, ELIAS D. KERST.

Commissary Sergeant, GEORGE T. DONALDSON.

Hospital Steward, FRANK K. MURPHY.

Principal Musician, JOHN F. KELLER.

Company A.—Captain, D. W. Ney ; Lieutenants, G. H. Reiff, Joseph H. Kline.

Company B.—Captain, Albert Nagle ; Lieutenants, A. H. Moyer, L. K. Mohn.

Company C.—Captain, Robert Thwait ; Lieutenants, Robert Herron, Jonathan E. Rogers.

Company D.—Captain, James P. Meade ; Lieutenants, John Ewing, M. Wisham.

Company E.—Captain, E. L. Gilligan ; Lieutenants, J. S. Campbell, Joseph Burris.

Company F.—Captain, R. B. Clevinger ; Lieutenants, Matthew Myers, H. S. Wade.

Company G.—Captain, William Huber ; Lieutenants, C. R. Soder, William Truett.

Company H.—Captain, J. H. Lawrence ; Lieutenants, Jefferson Good, John Witmoyer.

Company I.—Captain, H. J. Copestick ; Lieutenants, H. D. Evans, J. K. Shelcup.

Company K.—Captain, Charles McKnight ; Lieutenants, D. Linsenbigler, C. C. Lambert.

Early in May the march (for the last time) was taken for Washington and home ! Passed through Richmond on the 6th, thence in successive stages past Hanover Court-House, across the Pamunkey, Mattapony, through Bowling Green, over the Rappahannock to near Fairfax, and encamped near Alexandria. On May 24 passed in grand review before the President, returning to camp in the evening. Less than 100 of the men who left Philadelphia with the regiment marched in this grand parade. Nearly 200 filled soldiers' graves, hundreds were discharged disabled for life, and many more occupied cots in the hospitals, wrecks of humanity, maimed and helpless, dependents upon the bounty of their families for daily bread. But those men of iron and pluck who fought the long war through deserve greater praise and more extended mention than can be given here.

The regiment remained in camp until June 30, 1865, when the men were formally released as soldiers of Uncle Sam. The regiment was then sent to Philadelphia, encamping at Camp Cadwalader, and, upon the completion of the respective rolls, the soldiers were sent to their homes, most of the conscripts living in Western Pennsylvania.

And now the author's task is done. He has tried to write a fair and correct history without fear or favor. Much that is interesting has been omitted; all has been condensed. Doubtless, if another edition is issued a much better book will be produced. If the historian has succeeded in pleasing his comrades, he will feel abundantly rewarded for years of labor spent on this work; if he has failed, he promises not to do so again.

CHAPTER XXVII.

SOME STRAY SHOTS.

WHILE the Confederate army near Richmond was during the last weeks of the war in desperate straits, owing to insufficient means for providing for the soldiers, yet Lee had at this time more men under his command than at the beginning of Grant's campaign. According to Confederate reports, there were present, including local and independent commands, 78,780 ; present for duty, 64,786. Doubtless, in March, 1865, Lee's strength amounted to upward of 70,000 troops of all arms.

Appended is a statement of the losses of the rebel army in the final death-struggle :

Fort Steadman, March 25, 1865	4,500
White Oak road and Dinwiddie, March 31	1,500
Five Forks, April 1	6,000
Petersburg, April 2	3,500
Richmond, April 2 and 3	1,000
Sailor's Creek, April 6	7,000
Minor engagements	3,000
Stragglers picked up	2,500
Surrendered April 9	28,356
Total	57,356

In addition to the above, the country was swarming with thousands of demoralized stragglers who never surrendered, while the cavalry, which on February 20 reported 9437 present, surrendered only 1559 men, the remainder escaping and scattering to their homes.

The returns of the Confederate Army of Northern Virginia for almost the entire war are appended. They make an interesting study, not only as showing the strength present at various battles, but also the demoralization of this army towards the close of the war.

Date.	Present and Absent.	Total Present.	Present for Duty.
February 28, 1862	84,225	56,396	47,617
July 20, 1862	137,030	94,686	69,559
September 30, 1862	139,143	62,713	52,609
March 31, 1863	109,839	73,379	60,298
May 31, 1863	133,689	88,754	68,352
July 31, 1863	117,602	53,611	41,135
November 20, 1863	96,576	56,088	48,269
April 10, 1864	97,576	61,218	52,626
June 30, 1864	92,685	62,571	51,863
July 10, 1864	135,805	68,844	57,097
November 30, 1864	181,826	87,860	69,290
February 28, 1865	160,411	73,349	59,094

The foregoing table indicates that after the seven days' campaign upward of 43,000 men were absent; after Antietam, 76,000; after Gettysburg, 63,000; in July, before Petersburg, 66,000; in November, 93,000; and during the last weeks of the siege upward of 87,000 were absent from various causes. We may further learn from this table, taking into consideration those killed and the many who were discharged in consequence of disabling wounds and disease, that the Army of Northern Virginia aggregated during the war upward of 400,000 soldiers.

The following percentage is from the "Medical History of the War:"

Out of about every 65 men, one man was killed in action.
Out of about every 56 men, one man died of wounds.
Out of about every 13 men, one man died of disease.
Out of about every 9 men, one man died in the service.
Out of about every 15 men, one man was captured or missing.
Out of about every 10 men, one man was wounded.
Out of about every 7 men captured, one man died in captivity.

The following table of the losses of our old brigade, as constituted at various times, is from the Official Records. It will be noticed that there are two more in the mortality of the 88th than this History gives. All the other regiments had a much larger enrolment than the 88th, hence their greater loss:

	Killed and died of Wounds.	Died of Disease.	Total Deaths.	Total Enrolment.
11th Pennsylvania	236	181	417	2052
97th New York	181	157	338	2105
12th Massachusetts	193	83	276	1535
9th New York State Militia .	164	97	261	2278
94th New York	110	137	247	. .
90th Pennsylvania	103	127	230	. .
88th Pennsylvania	109	72	181	1213
13th Massachusetts	121	40	161	1439

LOSSES BY STATES.

The percentage, by States, of men killed in battle follows.

Pennsylvania stands highest, with 7.1
Vermont is second, with 6.8
New Hampshire is third, with 6.5
Maine is fourth, with 6.4
Massachusetts is fifth, with 6.2

On the Southern side accurate figures are not obtainable, but the States follow in this order : North Carolina, South Carolina, Mississippi, etc.

Occupations.—Forty-eight per cent. of the soldiers were farmers ; twenty-four per cent., mechanics ; sixteen per cent., laborers ; five per cent., commercial men ; three per cent., professional men ; and four per cent., miscellaneous.

Nationality.—Over seventy-five per cent. of the soldiers were native Americans, and of the half million foreigners, 175,000 were Germans, 150,000 Irish, 50,000 English, 50,000 from British North America, and 75,000 from all other nations.

THE REGIMENTAL ASSOCIATION.

The survivors of the regiment met at No. 402 Walnut Street, Philadelphia, on July 23, 1874, and effected a permanent organization, which has been continued until the present time. An annual reunion of all the surviving soldiers of the regiment was appointed for August 9 of each year, but this date was subsequently changed to October 5, the anniversary of the departure of the regiment from Philadelphia in 1861. The gatherings are appointed to be held

alternately at Philadelphia and Reading, but this has been changed
to suit the occasion, several meetings having been held at Gettysburg, one at Fortress Monroe in 1885, and one in 1892 at Alexandria, Virginia. On this last occasion the grave of every deceased
member of the 88th Regiment in the Alexandria and Arlington
National Cemeteries was suitably decorated with the national emblem.

REGIMENTAL COLORS.

In the early part of the Association's life the Reading contingent,
through the exertions of Comrades Boone and Witmoyer, assisted by
Mrs. Boone and Artist Philip Igle, procured an elegant banner for the
organization, which was proudly carried at the head of the old regiment in public displays for years; but the banner, like the old soldiers, after years of good service, became faded and worn. In order
to give the veterans something new and bright to follow, Mrs. John
D. Vautier conceived the idea of procuring a flag for them without
their knowledge, and, calling on Mrs. Frank K. Murphy, Mrs. G.
W. Boger, Mrs. E. A. Mass, Mrs. R. B. Beath, and Mrs. John T.
Williams, these ladies constituted themselves a committee on flags,
and went to work with a will to see what they could do for the old
boys. They called in the aid of Mrs. G. P. McLean, Mrs. James
Hague, Mrs. C. Hunter, Mrs. J. T. Wentzell, Mrs. W. W. Stretch,
Mrs. S. H. Martin, Mrs. C. W. Clothier, Mrs. H. Copestick, Mrs.
W. Coppes, Mrs. E. L. Gilligan, Mrs. T. W. Dunham, Mrs. W. H.
Harkisheimer, Mrs. T. Albright, Mrs. J. C. Rutherford, Mrs. J. C.
Clement, Mrs. W. B. Threapleton, Mrs. J. G. Clark, Mrs. S. G.
Boone, and others. These ladies pushed the affair so vigorously
that they collected enough to buy two handsome silk flags, costing
$125, which they presented to the surprised members, whom they
had inveigled, under some false pretence, into the hall of Post 5, on
October 2, 1890. It is needless to say that the boys were very
proud of their flags, and freely forgave their wives and sweethearts
for their duplicity.

GETTYSBURG MONUMENTS.

In 1868 the United States government dedicated the beautiful
monument in the National Cemetery to the memory of the heroic

REUNION AT READING, OCTOBER, 1890.

dead who on this field gave their all to their country. This example has been followed by the organizations engaged in the battle, thus appropriately perpetuating the sacred and patriotic memories of the place. The Veteran Association of the 88th Regiment was among the first to follow this fitting example, erecting three granite tablets, designating the positions of the regiment in the three days' contest. They were formally dedicated on August 27, 1883, the orator being General George W. Gile, who delivered an eloquent and impressive oration that was attentively listened to by a large gathering of the survivors of the regiment, who came to Gettysburg for the purpose. The oration was reported in full in some of the daily papers, and was universally accepted as a masterly and scholarly address on this interesting subject.

Subsequently the State of Pennsylvania appropriated $1500 for a suitable memorial for each command engaged in the battle, and to this sum the survivors of the 88th Regiment added $1500, making $3000 in all; with this amount a magnificent granite monument—the handsomest and most unique on the field—was erected and unveiled before the regiment on September 11, 1889. Colonel George E. Wagner delivered the dedicatory address, an exceedingly well prepared sketch of the regiment's share in the fight, which was heartily received by the assembled veterans and their friends, and subsequently published in full by the State in " Pennsylvania at Gettysburg."

INSCRIPTION ON THE MONUMENT.

[*Front.*]
88TH P. V.
[*Rear.*]
88TH PENNA. INFANTRY.
2D BRIGADE, 2D DIVISION, 1ST CORPS.
[*Right.*]

About noon July 1, 1863, the regiment was in line along the Mummasburg road, 200 yards S. E. of this monument. Later it changed direction and formed here, charged forward and captured two battle-flags and a number of prisoners. At four P.M. the division was overpowered and forced through the town. July 2 the regiment was in position facing the Emmittsburg road, and on July 3 at Ziegler's Grove, as indicated by markers. Number engaged 296; killed and mortally wounded 7, wounded 52, captured or missing 51.

[*Left.*]

Recruited in Philadelphia and Reading.   Mustered in September, 1861.   Re-enlisted January, 1864.   Mustered out June 30, 1865.

ENGAGEMENTS.

Cedar Mountain.	Fredericksburg.	North Anna.	Dabney's Mills.
Rappahannock Station.	Chancellorsville.	Totopotomoy.	Boydton Road.
Thoroughfare Gap.	Gettysburg.	Bethesda Church.	Five Forks.
Second Bull Run.	Mine Run.	Cold Harbor.	Appomattox.
Chantilly.	Wilderness.	Petersburg.	
Antietam.	Spottsylvania.	Weldon Railroad.	

REGIMENTAL MONUMENT AT GETTYSBURG.

CHAPTER XXVIII.

CAPTURE, CONFINEMENT, AND ESCAPE. BY SAMUEL G. BOONE, OF COMPANY B.

WITH the lapse of more than thirty years since the great battle of Gettysburg, many of the minor details have faded from memory, and although the brave struggle and final defeat of the gallant old 88th on July 1, 1863, is still fresh in my memory, I will confine myself in this sketch to the details of my capture, march back to Dixie under rebel guard, confinement in rebel prisons, final escape from Columbia, South Carolina, and return to "God's country;" but in doing so must rely almost wholly upon memory, as my book of "mems" was burned during the destruction of Columbia by fire, February 17, 1865.

With the foregoing by way of introduction, I will begin with *my* experiences in our charge on Iverson's brigade of North Carolina troops on July 1, 1863.

When the command "Charge!" came, a long line of steel swept across the field in our front and into the very ranks of the enemy. Previous to this I saw white flags affixed to bayonets waving in token of surrender. This was a strange sight to me and one that I had never seen before, although I had participated in all the engagements with the regiment up to this time. Under our withering fire they could not rise, but took shelter in a gully or ditch. When we were within a few paces of their line they lay down their arms, rose, and held up their hands. One poor fellow came towards me still grasping his musket, which I ordered him to drop and go to the rear as fast as possible, and as he passed me I struck him on the back with the side of my sword-blade, which act I have often regretted, for in looking after him I noticed blood trickling down underneath his canteen ; he had been shot.

This was the 23d North Carolina Regiment upon which the 88th charged, and their battle-flag fell into our hands. A part of the lance attachment I had in my possession up to the destruction of Columbia, South Carolina.

We captured nearly all the troops in our front, and those whom we did not capture again took up arms against us when from the Mummasburg road on our right flank came an enfilading fire which wrought terrible execution among their troops as well as among ours, and retreat became a necessity. About five hundred men, wounded and dead, lay strewn all over the field as we retreated, very much disorganized, in the direction of Gettysburg, the only avenue of escape left to us.

I reached Gettysburg in safety, but the enemy already had possession of the eastern part of the town. At one place a brave fellow crossed the street amid a perfect shower of bullets from Baltimore Street on our left, and thinking this my opportunity, I followed before the rebs had time to reload and also crossed in safety. I continued my retreat to the southern suburbs of the town, and seeing our retreating troops coming into Baltimore Street, concluded that I was safe, and could have reached them in a few minutes had not fate decreed otherwise. Turning to my left to get into Baltimore Street, I ran through a garden and along a house, but cautiously approached the street, with the intention of looking to my left to see that the way was clear before running out, and the instant I put my head beyond the building line I came face to face with one of the most desperate soldiers in the rebel army,—a Louisiana Tiger!

For an instant both stood transfixed. Neither knew which was the victor or vanquished, but it required only a few seconds to decide, as he was evidently prepared to fire into our retreating troops when we met, having his musket full cocked and at a ready. I had no side-arms except my sword, and this in the scabbard. Terror was depicted on his countenance; but quick to notice that I was unprepared to defend myself, he jumped away far enough to bring his piece to bear on me, and quick as a flash levelled it at my breast and at the same instant very excitedly ordered, " Surrender !" and there being no other alternative, I was compelled to submit.

A group of my captor's companions were close at hand when I was ordered to surrender. Stepping towards my captor to show that I did not intend to resist, I raised my right hand and quickly, and no doubt excitedly, said, " You've got the best of me." He next ordered, " Give me that sword." I had partly turned to my left to go to the rear, and as I took hold of my belt-plate to unbuckle it, he thought I was reaching for a pistol, and became more excited than ever, jumped back, and levelled his piece at me again and asked, " Have you got any pistols about you ?" This, I think, was the most critical moment of my life. Turning full face towards him to show what I was doing, he again demanded, " Now give me that sword," and, throwing the sword, belt and all, on the pavement against the house, I said, " I won't *give* it to you; if you want it, you must pick it up." This was the sword used on one of their own men but a short time before; now I, in turn, was ordered to " go to the rear." What a change in the tide of battle !

I did not value my life much among these wild, unrestrained rebels who were yelling, " Go in, Tigers !" and in a minute after my capture was in the middle of the street, when a Tiger came towards me and asked, " What kind of a watch have you got thar ?" and when I answered that it was only an old silver watch, he said, " Oh, keep it," and in almost the same breath asked, " Whose troops are them comin' in out thar ?" Our troops were so thickly covered with dust that he did not know them from theirs, and in order to delay his firing, I told him they were their own; but doubting the truthfulness of my answer, with a terrible curse, he took aim and fired. This was the first shot fired at this point, but the window-frame over the spot where I threw my sword is perforated with bullet-holes, and the battered walls, scarred trees, and riddled fences attest the severity of the fight between our fleeing troops and the Tigers to this day.

I attempted to outflank my captors at the first opening I came to, and which appeared to be a street running eastward, but ended up against a fence about fifty

FRANK K. MURPHY,
Hospital Steward.

PETER D. SHEARER,
Company B.

LIEUTENANT-COLONEL EDMUND A. MASS.

JOHN SIMMS,
Company F.

CORPORAL THOMAS H. ANDERSON,
Company J.

or one hundred yards from Baltimore Street. I ran to this fence and attempted to clear it, but balanced on the top rail in such a manner that for a moment I could get neither backward nor forward, and while in this position a rebel on the extreme right of a long line of skirmishers, and about fifty yards from me, sang out, in clear, slow, measured words, "Git—back—thar,—git—back," and was in the act of taking a right-oblique aim at me, when with a great effort I succeeded in falling on the side of the fence from which I came. Running back to Baltimore Street, I ran into the main body, who marched me to the rear of their lines, where, to my great surprise, I met Captain Mass and Lieutenant Grant, of my company, Captain Schell, of Company I, and many enlisted men of the 88th and hundreds of others, but not one of whom had got so near liberty as myself.

We were moved on the same evening to a point on Willoughby Run, now known as the Katalysine Spring, where we remained until the commencement of the retreat on July 4.

Space will not allow a description that would do justice to the trials and fatiguing marches of about 4000 Union prisoners, in torrents of rain, for more than a week after our departure from Gettysburg, goaded on at the point of the bayonet; our departure from Monterey Springs before breakfast on the morning of the 5th, with the shells from Kilpatrick's artillery exploding near us; our hopes of rescue, which continued until the Potomac lay between us and our army, when all hopes of recapture were abandoned, and after a hard march of nearly two hundred miles, reached Staunton, Virginia, on the 18th, and Richmond by rail the same evening, being escorted to the infamous Libby Prison. On entering Libby, seeing the prisoners ahead of me being searched, I buried my watch in a loaf of bread, and the bread passed inspection.

In the famous tunnel escapade of February 8, 1864, when 109 officers "leaked out," I was in line and only a few feet from the hole when the alarm was raised that the officials were coming, and a rush was made for our respective quarters up-stairs.

Without the knowledge of the prison authorities, a few of us passed out on the roof of the building through the hatchway one evening to get the fresh air. I ventured up the roof to the flag-staff, caught hold of the halyards, and looked up at the rebel flag, wishing to capture it and bring it safely north, and while thus meditating, my comrades suddenly darted down the hole. I was not shot at, but a guard was afterwards stationed on the James River side, with instructions to shoot any one on the roof.

About 1100 commissioned officers bid adieu to Libby on May 7, 1864, and were taken to Danville, Virginia, where we remained but a few days, going from thence to Macon, Georgia, where I contracted chills and fever, and, notwithstanding my illness, was selected as one of 600 officers, sent to Charleston, South Carolina, and placed in the jail yard under fire of our own siege batteries around Charleston Harbor. My affliction began to tell on me, and I asked for shelter, when I was assigned to one of the gloomiest cells in the building, the mouldy stench being anything but conducive to health.

Although in imminent danger of death, the booming of our heavy sea-coast guns and the bursting of their snells among us was sweet music to our ears. The thought of once more being so near our lines buoyed up our drooping spirits, and cheerfulness once more took the place of despondency as the prospects of an early exchange seemed brighter. At night we could see a flash of light from the neighborhood of the "swamp angel" against the horizon far down the bay, and then a streak of fire similar to that of a meteor ascending towards the zenith until it appeared like a great comet, coming nearer and nearer, and when its force was finally spent, would descend with an unearthly, roaring, hissing sound, sometimes exploding half a mile up in the air or among the buildings, setting the city on fire and spreading consternation among the inhabitants thereof.

From Charleston we were removed to Camp Sorghum, near Columbia, South Carolina, where escapes were more frequent; but the prisoners were hunted down with blood-hounds and almost invariably returned to camp. One day a couple of the Southern chivalry, equipped with hunters' horns, etc., returned an escaped prisoner, when a brace of hounds, highly valued, strayed into our camp and were despatched in short order. Their dead bodies were found by a searching party hastily buried in a hole out of which we dug clay to plaster our huts; but the authorities not being able to single out the guilty parties, as a punishment to all, tied the dead dogs in the brook outside the guard line and above the point at which we obtained our water for cooking purposes.

On December 12, 1864, we were removed from Camp Sorghum to the grounds of the State Insane Asylum in Columbia, and from this place, on February 17 following, I made good my escape, which was the happiest day of my life.

On February 14, 1865, we received orders to be in readiness to move at five A.M. next morning, no one knew where. Having learned that Sherman was coming, before five A.M. on the 15th thirteen of us hid away under the roof of a two-story frame building used as a hospital for our sick, ten more under the porch roof, and many more in subterranean hiding-places all over the grounds. Next morning all the prisoners who could be found were marched outside the stockade, but many were missing. Search was made, and perhaps all were found except we who were concealed in the building. A searching party of guards was sent all over the grounds to hunt up the missing, and fired the barracks in which was the entrance of an unfinished tunnel and out of which they took fifteen prisoners. Had the flames communicated with our building, escape would have been impossible, as there was no outlet through the roof. The guards came upstairs, and I found a crack through which I watched the enemy below. One guard, after thrusting his bayonet into the heaps of hay and straw lying around, came directly underneath me, and, looking up, wondered—addressing himself to his companions —"if there could be any Yanks hiding overhead;" at the same moment I was looking him square in the eye, with scarcely four feet between our faces,—in fact, could almost feel his breath,—and, strange to say, was not discovered.

During the two nights of our concealment quite a number ventured out to reconnoitre, and were shot at as they made their escape over the stockade wall, whilst a few returned with the information that the stockade was still guarded.

After evading the vigilance of the enemy, in constant dread of having the old building fired under us, and suffering untold hunger and thirst for nearly three days and two nights in midwinter, in the cold, dark loft, the hour of our deliverance came. About noon on the 17th the four who were left—the other nine having escaped during the last two nights—were deliberating what course to pursue should our army be repulsed, for we had heard musketry, and shells were exploding near us in the morning, when suddenly we heard great cheering, and presumed it came from the rebels and that our army had been repulsed. We had just decided to attempt an escape that night and to follow up the army, when we heard heavy footsteps ascending the stairs and coming direct to where we had sawed the ends off several boards,—with an ordinary table-knife, the back of which had been filed into a saw,—through the opening of which we crept to our place of concealment, and instantly the short boards which we had replaced flew against the roof, just grazing my face. Being nearest the opening, I looked down, and, to my utter astonishment, saw a soldier in blue uniform with musket clubbed, looking up, who, with a frown, ordered, "Come down!" As I was the first one discovered, I acted as spokesman, and asked, "Well, tell me, are you a Confederate or Union soldier?" With a smile, he answered, "Why, we are Billy's boys," and with one glad bound of joy we fairly sprang from our gloomy abode of suffering, from captivity to liberty, and alighted among our friends, once more under the protection of the glorious stars and stripes. Instead of Sherman suffering defeat, the city had surrendered to him, and these were the advance troops, who were directed to our hiding-place by one of my companions who made his escape over the stockade wall the night before.

Directing my course towards our troops, I witnessed the grand *entrée* of our victorious army into the fallen and *doomed* city, for on that very night the city was laid in ashes. During the conflagration a Captain Smith, also an escaped officer, and myself were sitting on the steps of a large building, when the provost guard came along and the lieutenant in charge pointed towards us with his sword, saying, "Those two men in there," when we were put under arrest on suspicion of being rebs; our blue uniforms having long since worn out, we were obliged to substitute gray, which gave us a seedy, rebel-like appearance. The provost marshal being on horseback close by, we requested to speak to him, and after informing him that we were escaped Union officers, he said, "Lieutenant, release these officers at once."

On the 18th, with many other escaped prisoners, I reported to General Sherman, who provided us with passes, and who felt confident that he would recapture those who had been removed to Charlotte, North Carolina; but his hopes were never realized, as they were soon after exchanged.

Travelling along with the army, unassigned, and subsisting upon what I could forage, I often barely escaped violence from our own troops on account of my rebel-like appearance. Riding along a body of infantry one day on a horse that I had got out of a corral, a man shouted, "Shoot the rebel!" I wheeled around, rode up to him, told him who I was, and before we parted had his coat on my back, not because he thought he had the best of the trade, but because of his kindly feelings and sympathy for me. This, I think, was about the last time I was called a rebel.

Upon another occasion, while riding along unarmed in advance of the army, with foragers,—Sherman's "Bummers,"—after crossing a creek swollen by the recent rains, we were turned upon by the rear-guard of the rebel army and driven back, with the loss of several wounded. I left my horse and took to the thickets in the swamp, knowing that cavalry could not pursue me. The advance of our army now made its appearance on the opposite bank, hastily constructed a trestle, pushed forward a section of artillery, sent over a detachment of infantry, and advanced in line of battle, and, strange to say, recovered my horse after the line had advanced beyond the point where I left him. This was the last hostile affair of the Rebellion in which I was an actor.

We reached Fayetteville, North Carolina, on March 11, and during that night I had my horse stolen while lying asleep in front of him; the knot of the hitching strap was still fast to the scrub oak to which I had tied him, the thief having cut the strap to save time. Fortunately, I needed no horse on the morrow, as I obtained passage on the steam-tug Davidson next day, which left Fayetteville for Wilmington, North Carolina, with detailed information of Sherman's movements. Nothing occurred during the passage, except a night alarm at a very narrow point of the river,—Cape Fear,—at which place we were challenged by a body of Federal cavalry pickets, and, from the excited manner of the challenging party, I feared we would receive a volley from the land forces.

At Wilmington I took passage on an old vessel named J. S. Green, and after a perilous voyage arrived safely at Fortress Monroe, thence to Baltimore and to Washington, where I was recorded as an escaped prisoner of war, and after some trouble in having my name taken up on the rolls of my regiment, from which I had been dropped, probably because I was not present at the expiration of my three years' service to be mustered as a veteran, I received an order to join my regiment, with permission to delay thirty days.

I returned home after an absence of nearly three and a half years, languishing nearly half that time in loathsome rebel prisons, but only to recruit my health. Being far from well, I returned to Washington and awaited the arrival of my regiment, then on its way with the army to Washington, and upon joining it was informed that the war was ended, and I was mustered out May 16, 1865, having served over eight months longer than my term of three years,—nearly four in all, including my term of three months' service.

Weary and tired of the clash and clang of arms, I longed for retirement to the peaceful pursuits of life and the bosom of friends, hoping nevermore to be called upon to take up arms in defence of our glorious banner, under whose folds the oppressed of the earth may find refuge and protection so long as it is honored and respected.

LIEUTENANT JONATHAN E. ROGERS.

CORPORAL JAMES W. COLIN.

LIEUTENANT HARRY HUDSON.
(Killed August 18, 1862.)

SERGEANT JOHN B. DONAHOE.

SAMUEL BINNS.

COMPANY C.

CHAPTER XXIX.

ECHOES FROM THE BATTLE-FIELD.

EXTRACTS FROM LETTERS WRITTEN BY CHARLES McKNIGHT, OF COMPANY K.

CAMP NEAR THE CHICKAHOMINY, June 8, 1864.

FRIEND STEPHEN STEVENS,—I promised to write you an account of the first battle of this campaign, but had no idea it would be so long a one. . . . Our regiment broke camp on the night of May 3; on wagon-guard to the Rapidan, which we crossed on the 5th and marched to the front.

We joined our brigade on the Wilderness battle-field, just as it came out of the fight. We had no severe fighting there, but kept our hands in in building breast-works. On the night of the 7th we marched for Spottsylvania Court-House, our brigade on the advance. We marched all night, and about four o'clock Sunday morning (8th) found the enemy. We deployed in line and charged over an open field, the rebs being posted in the woods beyond with a battery and mounted in-fantry. We gave a yell and charged on the double-quick, and after a half-hour's fight the rebs gave way. Followed them about two miles, when we found them in force behind breastworks.

We now had something to do, our whole division being brought up, our brigade in the front and the other two in the second line. We charged across an open field under a heavy musketry and artillery fire and got within twenty yards of their works, when they opened on us a flank fire which drove both wings back, leaving the centre exposed,—our regiment being in the centre,—and drove us into a road which ran to the rear. We fell back to the woods where we had formed for the charge, but the rebs had us started and, pressing hard, drove us about a mile and a half, when the 3d Division—the Pennsylvania Reserves—came to our relief and drove them all the way back to their works, the battle continuing long after dark. Our regiment lost about fifty men. It was a hard Sunday on us, and General Robinson was wounded while leading a charge.

On the 9th we were attached to Crawford's division, and on the 10th charged the works in the woods in our front. We went in about ten o'clock, and when we got within sight of their works we saw it was no use to charge them, for even if no rebs were behind them we could hardly have climbed over, so we did not charge, while the staff officers who did not have to charge ordered us on; but we are old soldiers; if we had been recruits we would have gone in and got whipped.

15

We halted there about five hours, then two brigades of the 2d Corps came to charge these works and we were to follow; but they did worse than we, for when they saw the works they broke and fell back. Then we fell back after being in seven hours and losing forty men. On the 11th we were quiet, but on the 12th were ordered into the woods again. We went in, but it was the same as before; did not charge, but lost fifteen men. I had the colors, and was hit in the head by a grape-shot while lying on my face, but it only stunned me. After the 12th we had only skirmishing and picket firing until the 23d, when we crossed the North Anna River, and after our corps was all over the rebs tried to drive us into the river. I tell you the shells flew thick and fast, but it was no use, and when they found that we would not fall back they gave it up.

On the 22d the brigade was on a scout, our regiment being out as flankers, until we reached the Richmond telegraph road, where we concealed ourselves to see who would pass, as we were in the rear of the rebel army. I was near the road, behind a tree, when I heard horses coming up the road, and soon a fine-looking man, unarmed, on a good horse, came in sight. He appeared to be an officer, and did not see us, but seemed suspicious, for when he got within twenty-five yards he stood up in his stirrups and looked around, when I jumped up without much noise, but he saw me. I called " Halt !" and I thought he was about to dismount, but, turning, he put spurs to his horse and dashed down the road, when I let go, not intending to hit him, and as I fired about twenty-five of our men let fly at him; but it is not easy to shoot a bird on the wing, and after he got down the road we could hear the rattle of horses' feet as his men joined him in the flight. We all broke into a laugh ; but we were too sure of our game, hence all missed him.

On the 24th we were on picket, and on the 25th had a hot time on the skirmish line, losing three men. On the 30th had three hours' fighting on the skirmish line, losing five men, and have been under fire every day except yesterday and to-day, losing one man on the 3d of June. We are now in camp, but our stay is uncertain, the lines being within 300 yards of each other.

Many men whose time has expired are going home. The 9th New York left the brigade last night; it only took about fifty men away out of 1200 it once mustered. A regiment of colored troops has just passed ; they looked well and seem to make good soldiers. Last night one company passed, and it being as large as our regiment, some one asked where their colors were. "Oh, ho!" said one of the blacks, " I thought dar was color enough along." . . . On the 5th of May we had twenty-one privates for duty in our company, now we have ten, besides one sergeant and one corporal wounded; half our men gone in one month. . . .

. . . We have fought seventeen battles since this campaign began, on May 5, 1864. . . . All night of June 17 we pressed the rebels back, and at daylight had taken two lines of works. Then we advanced through a woods into a wheatfield, when they opened on us with artillery and made us hug the ground until the word came, " Forward!" when we went across a field and into an orchard, where the Minié-balls whistled around us, but we had to take it all in fun. We were then ordered to the railroad cut, and away we went on a run, the rebs dosing us with canister and musket-balls, but nothing could stop us.

We formed on the railroad, and presently were ordered forward again, over two fields, across two ditches, to the slope of a hill about 200 yards from the reb works; so again we started, every man for himself, and by the time they had fired three rounds of canister I was safe under the hill. I tell you a man can run when it's for a place of safety.

We were in a thick woods, and I lay down to cool off, lying here a couple of hours, when we were ordered to walk right over the enemy's works, a thing easier said than done. Well, we fixed bayonets and charged out of the woods with a yell, but after going about fifty yards, I looked around and could only see our regiment in the opening, and in about a minute I did not see one of our men standing, the field was covered with them, and all who were not down were running back to the woods, and as I knew it was useless to remain there, I turned and ran into the woods also, where I found nearly all our officers and many of our men, besides all the rest of the brigade, their commanders calling to them to go to the support of the 88th, but it was no use.

I felt ashamed of myself, and getting up, asked who would go out. A man of my company and myself went and saw the colors with about eight or ten men out near the rebel works, and amidst a shower of balls we safely reached them. We were now under the shelter of a hill where the enemy's artillery could not reach us, and only seventy-five yards from their works. We called to the rest of the boys who were back that we were safe, and they came out one at a time, until we had fifty men. The Johnnies tried to load their cannon, but every man who was plucky enough to try it was shot. One gun had a swab in it, and there it remained until we left the place. We had only one man killed and two wounded while there, but lost about twenty-five in getting there. While in that position we fired 250 rounds to a man. Our brigade had given us up for lost, until we went back on the 19th. . . .

CAMP NEAR WELDON R. R., September 4, 1864.

. . . On the 18th of August we marched to this place, called Yellow Tavern. The 1st Division was destroying the railroad, and we deployed on the right of the road, the 2d Division on our left, and advanced into the woods in line of battle by battalions in mass. After going about half a mile the 2d Division became engaged, and the brigade on our left came back, the men saying that they had run into a trap and were surrounded. The woods were so dense that a person could not see more than twenty yards, and everything was mixed up. For my part, I was disgusted with the way things were; there were about 2000 men, with nobody to direct them, moving about in the woods, expecting an attack every minute, the bullets even then flying around us; but at last Crawford sent for our regiment to support the pickets on the right. So after running around in the wet and mud two hours, we were put on the skirmish line, remaining there until the morning of the 19th.

Upon rejoining our brigade we found the men building breastworks, and taking our place in line, we took a hand at the same work; but some one found that they were not in the right place, so we moved and fooled around for two hours, and got to work again, but before they were finished the rebels charged our left and right, gobbling our thin line on the right, and, bursting through, came on yelling like demons, while at the same time they charged our left, carrying the works and forcing all the 1st Brigade down on our line. There was no firing on our regimental front just then, but the enemy swooped down the works to our right and left, capturing lots of the men and placing us in a most uncomfortable and bewildering position. A line forming in our rear gave us a volley, causing us to jump on the other side of our breastworks; but the rebs were as much perplexed as we were, some of them coming into our line, thinking they were going to their rear. Our men and theirs were so mixed up in the woods that we dare not fire, and I suppose the rebs did not fire for the same reason; but our battery let fly a dose of shot and shell right into us, thinking there were none but Johnnies in the woods. Oh, it was a pretty kettle of fish; but Colonel Wheelock, our brigadier, called to fix bayonets and follow him. He said as soon as he gave the word to fire and charge, and we went out on the double-quick, our cannon raking our line, but we could not stop. When we reached the opening a Union line of battle was ready to fire on us, but we rushed out and shook "Old Glory" at them, and the next minute we were safe again. We rejoined our brigade and soon charged into the woods, recapturing all our works and resting there all night. This happened on Friday, August 19, and our regimental commander, Captain Houder, was killed, four wounded, and about twenty-five missing.

On Sunday, the 21st, the rebs charged our works, but were repulsed with awful slaughter. Taking it all in all, I think the Dixieites will not own this railroad very soon; that Grant has a mortgage on it which must be satisfied before he will surrender it. Excuse my writing; it is tiresome to write on a board, holding it on my knee.

Your brother in Christ,
CHARLIE McKNIGHT.

Oh, whether we live or whether we fall
By sabre-cut or by rifle-ball,
The hearts of the free can never forget,
My country, my country will remember us yet.

REUNION AT PHILADELPHIA, OCTOBER 4, 1844.

88TH PENNSYLVANIA VOLUNTEERS,

AUGUST 9, 1861, TO JUNE 30, 1865.

THIS record of personal service has been carefully prepared, so that every member of the regiment may here have an accurate outline of his service. So far as possible, the dates are from the individual discharge papers; in other cases, from Bates's "History" and from company registers.

In the latter part of 1864 a number of conscripts and substitutes were assigned to the regiment, most of them remaining until the close of the war, and proving good soldiers. They are not placed with the volunteers, but follow immediately below. After the surrender, while the regiment was in the vicinity of Petersburg, marching towards home, another large body of conscripts was received and assigned to the various companies. The names of these men are given; but, as the war was over, it is not considered that they had any share in making the glorious and honored record of the regiment, consequently their names bring up the rear.

A number of abbreviations are necessarily used in the record, the most important being as follows: Brig.-Gen. for Brigadier-General, Col. for Colonel, Lt.-Col. for Lieutenant-Colonel, Maj. for Major, Capt. for Captain, Lt. for Lieutenant, Sgt. for Sergeant, Corp. for Corporal, m. o. for mustered out, V. R. Corps for Veteran Reserve Corps, exp. of term for expiration of term of service, not must. for not mustered, Cem. for Cemetery, Hosp. for Hospital, and disch. for discharged.

Field and Staff.

Rank.	Mustered In.	Record.
Colonels.		
George P. McLean.	Oct. 3, '61	Acting Military Governor of Alexandria, Dec., '61, and Jan., '62; resigned Dec. 1, '62.
George W. Gile.	Sep. 18, '61	From Maj. to Lt.-Col., Sep. 1, '62; Col., Jan. 24, '63; disch. Mar. 2, '63, for wounds rec'd at Antietam; Brevet Brig.-Gen., May 6, '65.
Louis Wagner.	Aug. 11, '61	From Capt. Co. D to Lt.-Col., Dec. 1, '62; Col., Mar. 3, '63; in command Camp Wm. Penn, Philadelphia, 1864–65; wounded in right leg and prisoner at Bull Run, Aug. 30, '62; Brevet Brig.-Gen., Mar. 13, '65; disch. June 6, '65.
Lieutenant-Colonels.		
Joseph A. McLean.	Sep. 16, '61	Killed at Bull Run, Aug. 30, '62.
Edmund A. Mass.	Sep. 12, '61	From Capt. Co. B, June 16, '65; wounded and captured at Gettysburg, July 1, '63; prisoner until Mar., '64; m. o. with Reg.
Majors.		
David A. Griffith.	Sep. 14, '61	From Capt. Co. H, Sep. 1, '62; wounded by shell at Rappahannock, Aug. 23, '62; resigned Dec. 31, '62.
J. S. Steeple.	Sep. 10, '61	From Capt. Co. C., Feb. 17, '64; disch. June 15, '64, for wounds rec'd at Antietam.
Benezet F. Foust.	Sep. 10, '61	From Adj. to Capt. Co. A; to Maj., Dec. 31, '62; wounded at Gettysburg, July 1, '63; to V. R. Corps, as Lt.-Col., Nov. 6, '63; Brevet Brig.-Gen., Mar. 13, '65.
Aaron Bright, Jr.	Sep. 13, '61	From Capt. Co. G, June 6, '65; disch. July 10, '65.
Adjutants.		
Cyrus S. Detre.	Oct. 1, '61	From 1st Sgt. Co. K, Dec. 4, '62; disch. Dec. 4, '64, in field near Petersburg, exp. of term.
Charles H. Kartsher.	Aug. 31, '61	From Sgt. Co. D, Nov. 24, '62; not must.; killed at Fredericksburg, Dec. 13, '62.
Isaiah McIntire.	Feb. 23, '64	From Priv. Co. E to Sgt.-Maj., Nov. 1, '64; Adj., June 26, '65; wounded at Spottsylvania, May 12, '64; m. o. with Reg.

Rank.	Mustered In.	Record.
Quartermasters.		
Daniel D. Jones.	Sep. 10, '61	To Assistant Quartermaster U. S. Vols., July 17, '62.
Albert C. Wester.	Sep. 2, '61	From Quartermaster Sgt., Oct. 14, '62; absent on detached service at m. o.
Surgeons.		
J. H. Seltzer.	Sep. 16, '61	Resigned July 22, '62.
G. H. Mitchell.	Sep. 9, '61	From Assistant Surgeon, Aug. 15, '62; disch. Nov. 24, '62.
John W. Rawlins.	July 15, '62	From Assistant Surgeon 116th P. V., Feb. 3, '63; m. o. with Reg., June 30, '65.
David Kennedy.	. . . . . .	Assigned temporarily to the Reg., '62.
Assistant Surgeons.		
Jos. H. Hayes.	Aug. 4, '62	To Surgeon 90th P. V., Dec. 28, 63.
Jos. T. Shoemaker.	Aug. 20, '62	To Surgeon 56th P. V., Mar. 25, '65.
M. B. McAlear.	Apr. 22, '65	M. o. with Reg., June 30, '65.
Chaplain.		
Rev. Chas. W. Clothier.	Oct. 3, '61	Disch. Oct. 3, '64, exp. of term.
Sergeant-Majors.		
John J. Levi.	Sep. 10, '61	From Priv. Co. D; disch. Dec. 22, '62.
Samuel G Boone.	Sep. 12, '61	To 2d Lt. Co. B, Mar. 1, '63.
Geo. M. Donnelly.	Sep. 24, '61	To 1st Lt. Co. D, Mar. 7, '65.
Richard L. Street.	Sep. 5, '61	To Co. F, Nov. 1, '64.
Quartermaster Sergeants.		
Elias D. Kerst.	Aug. 30, '61	From Corp. Co. H, Feb. 28, '65; m. o. with Reg.
John Perry.	Sep. 14, '61	Transf. to V. R. Corps.
Harry O'Neil.	Aug. 29, '61	To 1st Lt. Co. I, Jan. 2, '65.
Commissary Sergeants.		
Jacob S. Kram.	Aug. 23, '61	From Priv. Co. E, Oct. 4, '61, to 2d Lt. Co. A, Jan. 1, '63.
Geo. T. Donaldson.	Oct. 22, '61	From Corp. Co. E; m. o. with Reg.
Hospital Steward.		
Francis K. Murphy.	Oct. 21, '61	From Priv. Co. E; m. o. with Reg.
Principal Musicians.		
Jno. F. Keller.	Jan. 1, '62	From musician Co. I, Feb. 28, '65; m. o. with Reg.
Albert F. Hardy.	Aug. 31, '61	From musician Co. D, May 30, '65; m. o. with Reg.
William Sands.	Sep. 12, '61	To 1st Sgt. Co. G, Jan. 31, '65.

Regimental Band.

Mustered In.

Leader.		
E. Ermentrout.	Aug. 30, '61	

Musicians.		
Byerly, Blasius.	Aug. 30, '61	
Boyden, Wm. A.	Sep. 13, '61	
Breedy, Jno.	Aug. 30, '61	
Clay, Jos. J.	Aug. 30. '61	
Eben, Wm. C.	Aug. 30, '61	
Gehart, Aug.	Aug. 30, '61	
Hill, Jas. Y.	Sep. 20, '61	
Hoch, Albert.	Aug. 30, '61	
Hoch, Thos.	Aug. 30, '61	Discharged by General Orders, June 21, 1862.
Krug, Casper.	Aug. 30, '61	
Miller, Christ.	Aug. 30, '61	
Moser, Julius.	Aug. 30, '61	
Rinehart, J. B.	Sep. 20, '61	
Robinson, J. R.	Aug. 30, '61	
Snyder, J. B.	Aug. 30, '61	
Sanders, Jas. D.	Aug. 30, '61	
Sehl, Stephen.	Aug. 30, '61	
Turner, S. W.	Aug. 30, '61	
Warner, J. S.	Aug. 30, '61	
Windbigler, C. B.	Aug. 30, '61	

Company A, Recruited in Berks County.

Rank.	Mustered In.	Record.
Captains.		
Geo. W. Knabb.	Aug. 23, '61	Resigned on account of paralysis, July 28, '62.
B. F. Foust.	Sep. 10, '61	From Adj., Nov. 28, 1862, to Maj., Dec. 31, '62.
Henry Whitesides.	Aug. 23, '61	From Sgt. to 1st Lt., Nov. 23, '62; Capt., July 1, '63; wounded at Antietam; disch. Sep. 1, '64, exp. of term.
Thos. J. Koch.	Aug. 23, '61	From Sgt. to 1st. Lt., Nov. 24, '64; Capt., Jan. 6, '65; wounded at Spottsylvania, May 12, '64; killed at Five Forks, April 1, '65.
Jacob D. Ninesteel.	Aug. 23, '61	From Sgt., Co. E, to 2d Lt., Dec. 22, '62; 1st Lt., Mar. 16, '63; Capt., Oct. 4, '64; not must.; wounded at Fredericksburg and Gettysburg; disch. Dec. 3, '64, exp. of term.

Rank.	Mustered In.	Record.
Captains.		
Daniel W. Ney.	Aug. 23, '61	From Sgt. to 1st Lt., Mar. 17, '65; Capt., June 14, '65; not must.; wounded at Chancellorsville, May 4, '63; Gettysburg, July 4, '63; and at Five Forks, April 1,'65; m.o. with Co.
First Lieutenants.		
Fred. R. Fritz.	Aug. 29, '61	Resigned Nov. 23, 1862.
Jacob S. Kram.	Aug. 23, '61	From Com. Sgt. to 2d Lt., Jan. 1, '63; 1st Lt. Oct. 4, '64; not must.; disch. Nov. 22, '64, exp. of term.
Geo. H. Reiff.	Aug. 31, '61	From Sgt. to 1st Lt., June 14, '65; not must.; disch. June 30, '65.
Second Lieutenants.		
Albert H. Seyfert.	Aug. 23, '61	Resigned Oct. 9, '62.
Jos. H. Kline.	Aug. 23, '61	From Sgt. to 2d Lt., June 14, '65; not must.; disch. July 10, '65.
Sergeants.		
George Shirey.	Aug. 23, '61	To 1st Sgt., July 22, '62; captured at Gettysburg; disch. Aug. 23, '64, exp. of term.
Jacob P. Becker.	Aug. 23, '61	To 1st Sgt., May 1, '65; prisoner from May 24 to Nov. 24, '64; wounded at Gettysburg; disch. June 12, '65.
And. J. Schreffler.	Aug. 23, '61	To Sgt., June 1, '65; m. o. with Co.
Geo. Beaumont.	Aug. 23, '61	To Sgt., June 1, '65; wounded at Fredericksburg, Gettysburg, and Laurel Hill; m. o. with Co.
Jno. S. Kennedy.	Aug. 23, '61	From Priv. to Sgt.; disch. May 10, '62.
Thos. Kinsley.	Aug. 23, '61	From Priv. to Sgt.; disch. Dec. 17, '62.
Gabriel Hill.	Aug. 23, '61	To Sgt., Mar. 1, '63; disch. Aug. 23, '64, exp. of term.
Joseph Hoch.	Sep. 10, '61	To Sgt., May 1, '65; prisoner from Aug. 19 to Dec. 3, '64; disch. June 12, '65.
Conrad Strahle.	Aug. 23, '61	Wounded at Antietam; transf. to V. R. Corps, Nov. 15,'63.
David Whitaker.	Aug. 23, '61	Captured at Gettysburg; died April 20, '65, of wounds rec'd at Five Forks; buried in Nat. Cem., Arlington, grave 10,482.
Corporals.		
John Whitaker.	Aug. 23, '61	From Priv. to Corp.; m. o. with Co.
Wm. Heller.	Aug. 23, '61	To Corp., June 15,'65; wounded at Spottsylvania, May 12, '64; m. o. with Co.
Russel Miller.	Aug. 23, '61	From Priv. to Corp.; disch. June 21,'64.
Emerson Kline.	Aug. 23, '61	Wounded and prisoner at Bull Run; disch. June 9, '63.
Henry Drum.	Feb. 22, '64	To Corp., June 15, '65; wounded at White Oak Swamp, June 13, '64; m. o. with Co.

Rank.	Mustered In.	Record.
Corporals.		
David Davis.	Aug. 23, '61	From Priv., Dec. 1, '64; disch. June 10, '65.
Wm. P. Fisher.	Aug. 23, '61	From Priv., June 1, '65; prisoner at Gettysburg, and from Aug. 19 to Dec. 17, '64; disch. June 12, '65.
Jeremiah Boyer.	Aug. 23, '61	Died Oct. 13, '62, of wounds rec'd at Antietam; buried in Military Asylum Cem., Washington.
J. Wesley Hoffman.	Aug. 23, '61	Captured at Gettysburg; wounded at Laurel Hill, May 8, '64; killed by falling tree, Sep. 5, '64.
Chas. Matthews.	Feb. 24, '64	To Corp., June 15, '65; m. o. with Co.
Isaac Madison.	Feb. 28, '64	From Priv., May 20, '65; prisoner from May 24 to Nov. 20, '64; disch. June 12, '65.
Musicians.		
Wm. L. Hawk.	Aug. 23, '61	Captured at Gettysburg; wounded June 27, '64; m. o. with Co.
Jno. F. Nagle.	Aug. 22, '61	Disch. July 1, '62.
Manoah Metz.	Oct. 4, '61	Wounded at Antietam, also on June 24, '64; disch. May 28, '65.
Privates.		
Arnold, Henry.	Aug. 23, '61	Wounded at Gettysburg; prisoner from Aug. 19, '64, to March 1, '65; disch. June 21, '65.
Arrington, F.	Dec. 6, '61	Deserted April 11, '62.
Adams, G.	Aug. 23, '61	Deserted June 18, '63.
Buckley, F.	Aug. 23, '61	Disch. on writ of *habeas corpus*, Sep. 5, '61.
Bishop, Henry.	Aug. 23, '61	Disch. April 1, '63, for wounds rec'd at Fredericksburg
Bechtel, Aaron.	Aug. 23, '61	Disch. Aug. 23, '64, exp. of term.
Beaumont, Wm.	Aug. 23, '61	Killed at Gettysburg, July 1, '63; buried in Nat. Cem., Gettysburg, grave 73.
Beaumont, Jno.	Aug. 23, '61	Captured at Gettysburg, July 1, '63; killed at Petersburg, June 18, '64; buried in Poplar Grove Cem., grave 27.
Becker, Chas.	Aug. 23, '61	Deserted May 1, '63.
Cresswell, I. C.	Aug. 23, '61	Disch. June 20, '62.
Clouser, Danl.	Aug. 23, '61	Disch. Aug. 23, '64, exp. of term.
Clingman, Geo. W.	Mar. 4, '64	Disch. for wounds rec'd at Laurel Hill, May 8, '64.
Dautrich, Alfred.	Aug. 23, '61	Wounded and prisoner at Bull Run; to Co. H, Feb. 6, '64.
Dautrich, Mayberry.	Aug. 23, '61	Captured at Gettysburg; to Co. H, Feb. 6, '64.

Rank.	Mustered In.	Record.
Privates.		
Drexel, R.	Aug. 23, '61	To Co. II, Feb. 6, '64.
Dell, M.	Aug. 23, '61	Deserted June 18, '62.
Eppinger, Jno.	Aug. 23, '61	Died at Alexandria, Nov. 17, '61.
Eyrich, Isaac.	Aug. 23, '61	Captured Aug. 19, '64; died at Salisbury, Feb. 8, '65.
Fagan, Jas.	Aug. 23, '61	Prisoner at Gettysburg; disch. Aug. 23, '64, exp. of term.
Fisher, Amos.	Feb. 22, '64	Killed at Spottsylvania, May 10, '64.
Fox, H. T.	Aug. 23, '61	Deserted Dec. 13, '63.
Grim, Jno. A.	Aug. 23, '61	Disch. Dec. 27, '62.
Hoffman, Ross.	Feb. 24, '64	Wounded at Laurel Hill, May 8, '64; absent in hosp. at m. o.
Howard, David.	Aug. 23, '61	Absent sick at m. o.
Hagan, Barnet.	Aug. 23, '61	Wounded and prisoner at Bull Run; disch. Aug. 23, '64, exp. of term.
Haberacker, Wm.	Aug. 23, '61	Disch. Oct. 24, '62.
Haywood, Henry.	Aug. 23, '61	Disch. Aug. 23, '64, exp. of term.
Himmelright, Henry.	Aug. 23, '61	Disch. Aug. 23, '64, exp. of term.
Hagan, Daniel.	Sep. 3, '61	Disch. Sep. 3, '64, exp. of term.
Hoffman, Geo. W.	Aug. 23, '61	Wounded at Spottsylvania, May 10, '64; disch. Aug. 23, '64, exp. of term.
Hughston, Mel.	Aug. 27, '61	Wounded at Laurel Hill, May 8, '64; disch. Nov. 21, '64, exp. of term.
Hughes, J. J.	Feb. 24, '64	Wounded at Laurel Hill, May 8, '64; disch. June 14, '65.
Henninger, Jno. H.	Aug. 23, '61	Died at Frederick, Oct. 7, '62, of wounds rec'd at Antietam; buried in Charles Evans Cem., Reading.
Hoffman, Wm. G.	Aug. 23, '61	Captured at Bull Run; killed at Fredericksburg.
Hawk, Albert.	Aug. 23, '61	Wounded and prisoner at Bull Run; captured Oct. 10, '63; died at Salisbury, Mar. 23, '64.
Haller, Ebenezer.	Sep. 9, '61	Captured Aug. 19, '64; died at Salisbury, Dec. 20, '64.
Hetrick, J.	Sep. 3, '61	No record.
Hoffman, W. J.	Sep. 9, '61	Deserted July 21, '63.
Johnson, Wm. M.	Aug. 23, '61	Wounded and prisoner at Bull Run; disch. Aug. 23, '64, exp. of term.
Keen, Albert.	Aug. 27, '61	Wounded at Spottsylvania, May 12, '64; disch. June 21, '65.
Kelley, John.	Aug. 23, '61	Disch. Feb. 27, '63.
Kelchner, I. C.	Aug. 23, '61	Disch. Aug 23, '64, exp. of term.
Morrow, Wm.	Feb. 24, '64	Wounded at Spottsylvania, May 10, '64; m. o. with Co.
Miller, Levi.	Aug. 23, '61	Disch. Aug. 23, '64, exp. of term.
Miller, Edw.	Aug. 23, '61	Wounded at Fredericksburg; disch. Aug. 23, '64, exp. of term.

Rank.	Mustered In.	Record.
Privates.		
Miller, Wm.	Aug. 23, '61	Disch. Aug. 23, '64, exp. of term.
Mohr, Daniel.	Aug. 23, '61	Wounded at Antietam; transf. to 2d U. S. Art., Nov. 14, '62.
Milhoff, Charles.	Aug. 23, '61	Killed at Antietam; buried in Nat. Cem., grave 74.
Miller, V.	Aug. 31, '61	Deserted April 11, '62.
McAvoy, J.	Aug. 23, '61	Deserted Sep. 28, '62.
Naugle, M.	Aug. 23, '61	Deserted Aug. 30, '62.
Oliphant, Jos.	Aug. 23, '61	Transf. to 15th Reg. U. S. Inf., June, '63.
Platz, Franklin.	Sep. 10, '61	Wounded at Laurel Hill, May 8, '64; transf. to V. R. Corps; disch. July 27, '65.
Peiffer, Levi J.	Aug. 31, '61	Died at Philadelphia, Dec. 10, '63.
Pugh, Wm.	Aug. 23, '61	Died at City Point, Aug. 1, '64.
Roland, Lucian.	Aug. 23, '61	Disch. Aug. 23, '64, exp. of term.
Roland Chas. A.	Aug. 23, '61	Wounded at Laurel Hill, May 8, '64; disch. Aug. 23, '64, exp. of term.
Reedy, Wm.	Aug. 23, '61	Wounded at Laurel Hill, May 8, '64; disch. May 3, '65.
Reilley, H.	Aug. 31, '61	Transf. to V. R. Corps, Aug., '63.
Roland, H.	Aug. 23, '61	Deserted Sep. 23, '62.
Reed, J.	Aug. 27, '61	Deserted Nov. 23, 62.
Sanders, Chas.	Aug. 23, '61	Captured Oct. 10, '63, and died in captivity.
Snyder, Wm.	Aug. 23, '61	Wounded and prisoner at Bull Run; disch. Oct. 9, '62.
Strohecker, Cyrus.	Aug. 23, '61	Wounded at Spottsylvania, May 10, '64; disch. Aug. 23, '64, exp. of term.
Swoyer, L.	Aug. 23, '61	Transf. to 2d U. S. Art., Jan. 23, '62.
Smith, Geo.	Aug. 23, '61	Died at Alexandria, Dec. 12, '62; buried in Nat. Cem., grave 141.
Smith, Henry.	Aug. 23, '61	Killed at Petersburg, June 18, '64.
Schaeffer, H. M.	Aug. 23, '61	Deserted, but returned to duty.
Trout, Daniel.	Feb. 22, '64	Disch. May 13, '65.
Wise, Albert G.	Sep. 16, '61	M. o. with Co., June 30, '65.
Wynn, Chas.	Aug. 23, '61	Wounded at Antietam; m. o. with Co.
Wharton, Jas.	Aug. 23, '61	Captured at Gettysburg; disch. Feb. 4, '65.
Wootten, Jno.	Aug. 23, '61	Wounded on Weldon R.R.; disch. Sep. 27, '64, exp. of term.
Wallace, Jno. M.	Aug. 23, '61	To Co. G, Feb. 6, '64.
Yerger, E. S.	Aug. 23, '61	To Co. G, Feb. 6, '64.
Yoder, Jeff.	Aug. 23, '61	Died at Alexandria, Dec. 12, '62.
Young, Edwd.	Aug. 24, '61	Captured at Gettysburg, July 1, '63; died at Culpeper, Feb. 1, '64; buried in Alexandria Cem., grave 1357.
Zeiber, Jno.	Sep. 3, '61	Wounded at Antietam; disch. Nov. 30, '64, exp. of term.

Company A, Recruits.

Rank.	Mustered In.	Record.
Corporals.		
W. J. Hutchinson.	Sep. 24, '64	Drafted; disch. June 10, '65.
L. Briggs.	Sep. 25, '64	Substitute; disch. June 10, '65.
J. Harris.	Sep. 25, '64	Substitute; disch. June 10, '65.
Privates.		
Altimon, S. R.	Sep. 25, '64	Substitute; disch. June 10, '65.
Bell, Alex.	Sep. 25, '64	Drafted; wounded at Hatcher's Run, Feb. 6, '65.
Boston, E.	Sep. 25, '64	Substitute; disch. June 3, '65.
Dyer, G.	Sep. 25, '64	Substitute; disch. June 10, '65.
Grant, J.	Sep. 24, '64	Substitute; disch. June 14, '65.
Green, J.	Sep. 24, '64	To 107th P. V., Dec. 1, '64.
Hilliard, O.	Sep. 5, '64	Drafted; disch. June 10, '65.
Hilliard, I.	Sep. 5, '64	Substitute; disch. June 10, '65.
Hatlon, J.	Sep. 5, '64	Substitute; disch. June 10, '65.
Harp, J. P.	Sep. 24, '64	Substitute; disch. June 5, '65.
Hoffman, W. H.	Sep. 24, '64	To 107th P. V., Dec. 1, '64.
Jesse, J.	Sep. 24, '64	Drafted; disch. June 10, '65.
Kieffer, Val.	Mar. 11, '65	Drafted; died June 2, '65; grave 3191, Alexandria Cem.
Leaves, J.	Sep. 24, '64	Substitute; m. o. with Co.
Martin. W.	Sep. 24, '64	Drafted; disch. June 20, '65.
Martin, R.	Sep. 24, '64	Drafted; disch. June 10, '65.
Pryor, T.	Sep. 24, '64	Drafted; disch. June 10, '65.
Phillips, Jas.	Sep. 24, '64	Drafted; killed at Hatcher's Run, Feb. 7, '65.
Ross, G.	Sep 24, '64	Substitute; m. o. with Co.
Sullivan, J.	Sep. 24, '64	Substitute; disch. June 10, '65.
Stevenson, B.	Sep. 24, '64	Substitute; disch. June 13, '65.
Waid, J.	Sep. 25, '64	Drafted; disch. June 13, '65.
Wilson, H.	Sep. 27, '64	Drafted; in hosp. at m. o.

Company B, Recruited in Berks County.

Rank.	Mustered In.	Record.
Captains.		
Henry A. Myers.	Sep. 18, '61	Resigned Nov. 1, '62.
E. A. Mass.	Sep. 12, '61	From 1st Lt., Jan. 7, '63; Lt.-Col., June 16, '65.
Albert Nagle.	Sep. 12, '61	From 1st Sgt. to 1st Lt., June 17, '65; Capt., —— '65; not must.; m. o. with Co., June 30, '65.

Rank.	Mustered In.	Record.
First Lieutenants.		
Geo. B. Rhoads.	Sep. 18, '61	From 2d Lt., Nov. 1, '62, to Capt. Co. F., April 10, '63.
Geo. W. Grant.	Sep. 12, '61	From Sgt. to 2d Lt., Nov. 1, '62; 1st Lt., April 10, '63; prisoner at Gettysburg, July 1, '63; disch. April 25, '65.
Aaron H. Moyer.	Sep. 12, '61	From Sgt. to 1st Lt., Mar. 3, '65; not must.; m. o. with Co.
Second Lieutenants.		
Samuel G. Boone.	Sep. 12, '61	From Sgt. to Sgt.-Maj.; to 2d Lt., Mar. 1, '63; captured at Gettysburg, July 1, '63; prisoner at Richmond, Danville, Macon, Charleston, and Columbia; escaped to Sherman's army, Feb. 17, '65; disch. May 17, '65.
Laf. K. Mohn.	Sep. 12, '61	From Sgt. to 2d Lt., Mar. 3, '65; not must.; wounded June 18, '64; m. o. with Co.
Sergeants.		
Rich'd Bell.	Sep. 6, '61	From Priv.; m. o. with Co.
Percival Y. Rhodes.	Sep. 12, '61	Disch. Dec. 1, '62.
Zach. Swavely.	Sep. 12, '61	Wounded at Antietam and Gettysburg; disch. Sep. 12, '64, exp. of term.
Jacob Shuster.	Oct. 1, '61	Wounded at Hatcher's Run, Mar. 31, '65; disch. June 13, '65.
Aaron Bright, Jr.	Sep. 13, '61	To Co. G., Feb. 16, '64.
Ebenezer Lee.	Sep. 13, '61	Wounded at Gettysburg; died at Annapolis, April 6, '65; buried in Friends' Cem., Amity Township, Berks Co.
Henry Evans.	Sep. 12, '61	Wounded and prisoner at Bull Run; killed at Gettysburg, July 1, '63; buried in Nat. Cem., grave 61.
Wm. D. Clemens.	Sep. 12, '61	Captured on Weldon R. R.; died in Salisbury Prison Pen, Mar. 25, '65.
Corporals.		
Henry Moore.	Sep. 9, '61	M. o. with Co.
John Friesleben.	Nov. 11, '63	To Corp., May 1, '65; m. o. with Co.
Chas. S. Butler.	Sep. 12, '61	From Priv. to Corp.; disch. Sep. 12, '64, in field before Petersburg, exp. of term.
Isaac J. Brown.	Sep. 2, '61	Wounded at Laurel Hill, May 8, '64, disch. Sep. 6, '64, exp. of term.
Aaron Guenther.	Sep. 2, '61	Wounded at Kelly's Ford; disch. Sep. 2, '64, exp. of term.
Jno. R. Laucks.	Sep. 12, '61	Disch. Feb. 14, '63.
Lewis W. Bonnin.	Sep. 11, '61	Wounded in hip, and prisoner at Gettysburg, July 1, '63; transf. to V. R. Corps; disch. Sep. 11, '64, exp. of term.

Rank.	Mustered In.	Record.
Corporals.		
John Eagle.	Sep. 11, '61	Wounded by guerillas, and died at Alexandria, Sep. 16, '62.
Pierson O. Miller.	Oct. 3, '61	Wounded at Bull Run; mortally wounded at Petersburg, June 18; died June 28, '64; buried at City Point.
Reuben Neider.	Sep. 12, '61	Captured on Weldon R. R.; died at Salisbury, Dec. 28, '64.
Chas. V. Yerger.	Sep. 23, '61	Captured on Weldon R. R.; killed on cars bet. Salisbury and Goldsborough, Feb. 25, '65.
Musicians.		
George W. Leader.	Sep. 19, '61	Wounded at Bull Run; prisoner from July 1 to Aug., '63; disch. July 7, '65.
Edwin Ball.	Sep. 12, '61	Prisoner at Gettysburg; disch. Sep. 12, '64, exp. of term.
William Sands.	Sep. 12, '61	Prisoner at Gettysburg; to Principal Musician, Feb. 6, '64.
Privates.		
Burkart, Samuel.	Sep. 2, '61	Wounded at Antietam, Gettysburg, and with loss of left arm, May 25, '64; disch. Nov. 3, '64, exp. of term.
Brakeman, David.	Sep. 16, '61	Disch. July 4, '62.
Browning, George.	Sep. 16, '61	Disch. April 8, '63.
Beidler, Daniel.	Sep. 12, '61	Disch. Sep. 12, '64, exp. of term.
Behm, Jacob.	Sep. 12, '61	Disch. Sep. 12, '64, exp. of term.
Boger, George W.	Sep. 17, '61	Brigade butcher; disch. Sep. 18, '64, exp. of term.
Behm, Jesse K.	Mar. 30, '64	Wounded in Wilderness; disch. Jan. 17, '65.
Blewitt, B. P.	Sep. 9, '61	To V. R. Corps, Mar. 15, '64.
Bowman, Geo.	Oct. 4, '61	Wounded at Fredericksburg; to V. R. Corps, Nov. 15, '63.
Clement, Joseph C.	Sep. 9, '61	Captured at Gettysburg; disch. Oct. 18, '64, exp. of term.
Colton, Chas.	Sep. 11, '61	To V. R. Corps, Mar. 16, '64.
Colton, Michael.	Sep. 11, '61	To V. R. Corps, Mar. 16, '64.
Conway, Francis.	Sep. 18, '61	Died at Alexandria, July 12, '62, of injuries rec'd May 7; grave 83.
Cavender, Jos. M.	Sep. 16, '61	Died in hosp. at Falls Church, Aug. 18, '62.
Drexle, Jacob.	Sep. 12, '61	Prisoner from Aug. 18, '64, to Mar. 13 '65; disch. May 2, '65.
Drexle, Henry.	Sep. 20, '61	Disch. June 4, '62.
Deemer, Tobias.	Sep. 21, '61	Disch. Sep. 21, '64, exp. of term.
Diffenbach, Adam.	Sep. 12, '61	Died at Alexandria, Dec. 23, '62, of wounds rec'd at Fredericksburg; buried in Chas. Evans Cem., Reading.

Rank.	Mustered In.	Record.
Privates.		
Ermentrout, Alfred D.	Sep. 12, '61	Disch. Aug. 20, '62.
Ebling, Edw. G.	Sep. 12, '61	Wounded and prisoner at Bull Run; disch. Feb. 28, '63.
Fry, Henry H.	Sep. 12, '61	Disch. Feb. 9, '62.
Gardiner, Saml. B.	Sep. 4, '61	Transf. to V. R. Corps, Nov. 15, '63; disch. Sep. 4, '64, exp. of term.
Greim, Henry.	Sep. 20, '61	Wounded; disch. Sep. 20, '64, exp. of term.
Hawkins, Josh. B.	Sep. 11, '61	Wounded at Petersburg, June 18, '64; in hosp. at m. o.
Hickle, Jos.	Sep. 12, '61	Wounded at Fredericksburg; disch. Sep. 12, '64, exp. of term.
Hunterson, Henry.	Sep. 2, '61	Prisoner at Gettysburg, July 1, '63; to V. R. Corps, Mar. 16, '64.
Hell, Jacob.	Sep. 12, '61	Wounded and prisoner at Bull Run; to 16th U. S. Inf'y.
High, Wm.	Sep. 12, '61	Deserted.
Jacoby, Geo. W.	Sep. 2, '61	Wounded at Bull Run; disch. May 27, '65.
Kelly, Jno.	Sep. 16, '61	Absent wounded at m. o.
Keller, Adam.	Sep. 12, '61	Absent wounded at m. o.
Kuhn, Henry M.	Sep. 26, '61	Disch. Aug. 19, '62.
Longmire, Saml. D.	Sep. 11, '61	Killed at Bull Run, Aug. 30, '62.
Lindermuth, J.	April 12, '62	To V. R. Corps, Nov. 15, '63.
Lee, G. W.	July 12, '62	Deserted Dec. 12, '62.
Morris, Samuel.	Sep. 11, '61	Wounded Mar. 31, '65; disch. July 15, '65.
McCullough, Jno.	Sep. 2, '61	Prisoner at Bull Run; absent at m. o.
McComb, Wm.	Sep. 2, '61	Disch. Aug. 11, '62.
McNeal, David.	Sep. 20, '61	Wounded at Fredericksburg; disch. June 21, '63.
McNulty, Cornelius.	Sep. 18, '61	Wounded and prisoner at Bull Run; killed at Dabney's Mills, Feb. 7, '65; buried in Poplar Grove Cem., Petersburg, grave 32.
Peterman, Geo.	Sep. 20, '61	Disch. Feb. 27, '63.
Porter, N.	Sep. 16, '61	Deserted May 25, '65. (?)
Reppert, Albert H.	Nov. 14, '61	M. o. with Co., June 30, '65.
Read, Henry.	Sep. 2, '61	Wounded at Gettysburg, July 3, '63; absent in hosp. at m. o.
Reifsnyder, Joel.	Sep. 12, '61	Wounded at Antietam; disch. Sep. 12, '64, exp. of term.
Reif, William.	Sep. 12, '61	Disch. Sep. 12, '64, exp. of term.
Reif, Henry D.	Sep. 12, '61	Wounded and prisoner at Bull Run; disch. Sep. 12, '64, exp. of term.
Ramich, Wm.	Sep. 12, '61	To Co. G, Feb. 6, '64.
Smith, Daniel.	Sep. 20, '61	M. o. with Co., June 30, '65.
Stauffer, Christ.	Sep. 12, '61	Absent in hosp. at m. o.

Rank.	Mustered In.	Record.
Privates.		
Snyder, Jacob.	Feb. 23, '64	Disch. June 5, '65.
Shearer, Peter D.	Sep. 12, '61	Captured at Gettysburg, July 1, '63; disch. in front of Petersburg, Sep. 12, '64, exp. of term.
Shelley, Jesse.	Sep. 12, '61	Disch. Nov. 22, '62.
Seidel, R. W.	Sep. 12, '61	Disch. Feb. 22, '63.
Sterney, Joseph.	Sep. 13, '61	Disch. April 6, '63.
Seyfert, Jas.	Sep. 12, '61	Wounded at Antietam, and loss of left arm at Petersburg, June 18, '64; disch. Dec. 9, '64.
Shonour, John.	Sep. 12, '61	Wounded in arm at Gettysburg; to V. R. Corps, Nov. 30, '64.
Shuster, Samuel.	Sep. 17, '61	Died at Fairfax, Aug. 22, '62; buried at Alexandria, grave 1550.
Seery, Jno.	Sep. 5, '64	Died at Point Lookout, Mar. 18, '64.
Turner, Chas. H.	Sep. 12, '61	Disch. Sep. 12, '64, exp. of term.
Teed, Geo.	Sep. 12, '61	Wounded at Cedar Mountain, Aug. 9, '62; to V. R. Corps, Sep. 30, '63; first member of Reg. wounded.
Vankirk, Samuel.	Sep. 14, '61	Disch. Mar. 2, '63.
Wentzel, Jonathan L.	Sep. 18, '61	Disch. Sep. 18, '64, exp. of term.
Weidener, Wm.	Sep. 12, '61	Wounded at Antietam; disch. Feb. 6, '63.
Wesley, Samuel.	Sep. 18, '61	Disch. Sep. 18, '64, exp. of term.
Whitehead, Edw.	Sep. 14, '61	To V. R. Corps, March 16, '63.
Whitehead, Wm. H.	Sep. 14, '61	Died in hosp.
Warren, Jas. W.	Sep. 2, '61	To Co. D, Feb. 6, '64.
Waterman, Jno.	Sep. 13, '61	Wounded at Gettysburg; prisoner; died at Andersonville, Mar. 23, '65; grave 128.
Waterman, Lewis.	July 30, '63	Prisoner; died at Salisbury, Feb. 7, '65.
Yoder, James.	Mar. 30, '64	Killed at Dabney's Mills, Feb. 7, '65.
Ziegler, Geo.	Feb. 26, '64	Disch. June 13, '65.

Company B, Recruits.

Rank.	Mustered In.	Record.
Corporals.		
J. Nagle.	Aug. 3, '64	Substitute; m. o. with Co.
J. Young.	Oct. 1, '64	Substitute; m. o. with Co.
W. Kenney.	Oct. 5, '64	Substitute; m. o. with Co.
W. Chambers.	Jan. 19, '65	Substitute; m. o. with Co.
George W. Gaylord.	Aug. 30, '64	Substitute; disch. June 10, '65.

Rank.	Mustered In.	Record.
Privates.		
Bush, T.	Sep. 28, '64	Substitute; disch. June 19, '65.
Cravener, D.	Sep. 30, '64	Substitute; disch. June 10, '65.
Fritz, F. E.	Sep. 21, '64	Drafted; disch. June 15, 65.
Fagler, H.	. . . . . .	To 102d P. V.
Gartland, M.	Sep. 27, '64	Substitute; disch. June 10, '65.
Huttenstine, P.	Sep. 22, '64	Drafted; died Dec. 17, '64; grave 8594, Arlington Cem.
King, G.	Sep. 21, '64	Drafted; disch. June 10, '65.
Kentz, C.	Sep. 26, '64	Substitute; m. o. with Co.
Levis, S.	Oct. 4, '64	Substitute; m. o. with Co.
Maynard, E.	Sep. 6, '64	Substitute; disch. July 19, '65.
McGeehan, J.	Sep. 27, '64	Substitute; disch. June 10, '65.
McNelly, W.	Aug. 27, '64	Substitute; disch. June 10, '65.
Magel, A.	Oct. 4, '64	Missing in action, Dec. 10, '64.
Powers, W.	Sep. 28, '64	Substitute; disch. June 10, '65.
Sohns, F.	Sep. 8, '64	Substitute; disch. June 10, '65.
Sowers, A.	Sep. 12, '64	Drafted; disch. June 13, '65.
Waterson, N.	Sep. 21, '64	Drafted; disch. June 10, '65.
Yount, D.	Oct. 5, '64	Drafted; disch. June 23, '65.
Yockey, G. W.	Sep. 30, '64	Drafted; disch. June 10, '65.
Yockey, F.	Sep. 30, '64	Drafted; disch. June 10, '65.
Zacarius, E.	Aug. 24, '64	Substitute; disch. June 15, '65.

Company C, Recruited in Manayunk, Conshohocken, and Vicinity

Rank.	Mustered In.	Record.
Captains.		
John J. Belsterling.	Sep. 13, '61	Killed at Bull Run, Aug. 30, '62.
J. Sarazin Steeple.	Sep. 10, '61	From 1st Lt., Sep. 1, '62; Maj., Feb. 17, '64; wounded through lung at Antietam.
Andrew J. Wamsley.	Sep. 3, '61	To 1st Lt., Sep. 1, '62; Capt., Feb. 16, '64; disch. May 2, '64, for wounds rec'd at Antietam.
Robert Thwait.	Dec. 13, '61	From 1st Sgt. to 1st Lt., Oct. 31, '64; to Capt., Dec. 18, '64; wounded at Bull Run and Laurel Hill; absent at m. o.
John Bemesderfer.	Aug. 24, '61	To 1st Lt., Mar. 7, '64; Capt., May 4, '64; not must.; wounded at Fredericksburg, and disch., Oct. 22, '64, for wounds rec'd at Spottsylvania.
First Lieutenant.		
Robert Herron.	Aug. 24, '61	From 1st Sgt. to 1st Lt., Dec. 18, '64; wounded at Bull Run in right ankle, and at Spottsylvania through both thighs; m. o. with Co.

Rank.	Mustered In.	Record.
Second Lieutenants.		
Harry Hudson.	Sep. 13, '61	Killed on R R. bridge over Cedar Run, Va., Aug. 18, '62.
Jonathan E. Rogers.	Sep. 9, '61	From Corp. to Sgt., May 1, 65; 2d Lt., June 9, '65; not must.; wounded at Bull Run; m. o. with Co.
Nath. L. Jones.	Aug. 24, '61	From Sgt. to 2d Lt.; not must.; wounded at Fredericksburg and Hatcher's Run; disch. June 13, '65.
Sergeants.		
Jno. N. Hanson.	Sep. 3, '61	1st Sgt.; wounded at Fredericksburg; disch. exp. of term.
Geo. H. Fulton.	Aug. 24, '61	1st Sgt.; killed at Fredericksburg; buried in Military Asylum Cem., D. C.
Chalkley Fox.	Nov. 17, '61	From Corp., June 13, '65; wounded at Antietam; captured Aug. 19, '64; prisoner until Mar. 19, '65; m. o. with Co.
Edmund Davis.	Feb. 27, '64	To Corp., May 1, '65; Sgt., June 13, '65; m. o. with Co.
Jno. McFeeters.	Feb. 29, '64	To Corp., May 1, '65; Sgt., June 13, '65; m. o. with Co.
Robt. Timbers.	Sep. 12, '61	Wounded at Gettysburg; absent on furlough at m. o.
Chas. B. Keil.	Sep. 9, '61	Wounded at Gettysburg; disch. exp. of term.
Jno. W. Waters.	Sep. 3, '61	Wounded at Bull Run and Gettysburg; disch. exp. of term.
Geo. W. Vaughn.	Sep. 23, '61	Wounded at Bull Run; disch. June 13, '65.
Jno. B. Donahoe.	Sep. 3, '61	Disch., date unknown.
Jno. T. Williams.	Sep. 9, '61	Captured at Bull Run, but escaped; wounded at Spottsylvania, May 12, '64, ball in right side; m. o. with Co.
Corporals.		
David Trexler.	Sep. 12, '61	Wounded at Gettysburg; to Corp., June 13, '65; m. o. with Co.
Jos. J. Cloud.	Mar. 9, '64	To Corp., May 1, '65; m. o. with Co.
Henry Townsend.	Mar. 3, '64	To Corp., June 13, '65; m. o. with Co.
Ellis P. Aldred.	Sep. 13, '61	To Corp., June 13, '65; m. o. with Co.
Thos. Hurley.	Feb. 29, '64	To Corp., June 13, '65; m. o. with Co.
Henry C. Richardson.	Sep. 3, '61	Wounded at Bull Run; disch. Sep. 6, '64, exp. of term.
Neal Boyd.	Aug. 28, '61	Wounded at Bull Run and Gettysburg; disch. Sep. 8, '64, exp. of term.
Jas. W. Colen.	Aug. 24, '61	Wounded at Bull Run; disch. Aug. 25, '64, exp. of term.
Jno. Pugh.	Sep. 14, '61	Wounded on the Rappahannock; disch. exp. of term.

Rank.	Mustered In.	Record.
Corporals.		
Jas. McCaulley.	Sep. 12, '61	Wounded at Gettysburg, July 3; to V. R. Corps, Nov. 15, '63.
Harry Austin.	Aug. 24, '61	Killed at Bull Run, Aug 30, '62.
Patrick Blaney.	Aug. 24, '61	Died at Philadelphia, Oct. 8, '62, of wounds rec'd at Bull Run.
John Kellum.	Feb. 4, '62	Died of wounds rec'd at Antietam.
Musician.		
Geo. W. Lewis.	Nov. 1, '61	Prisoner at Gettysburg; m. o. with Co.
Privates.		
Albright, Thos.	Sep. 12, '61	Wounded at Bull Run; disch. Sep. 12, '64, exp. of term.
Andrews, Jos.	Feb. 12, '62	Disch., exp. of term.
Bradshaw, David.	Sep. 9, '61	Wounded at Bull Run; disch. Nov. 5, '62.
Binns, Samuel.	Aug. 24, '61	Wounded at Bull Run, Minié-ball in forehead, with loss of right eye; disch. Mar. 11, '63.
Buckings, Wm.	Sep. 14, '61	Wounded at Bull Run; disch. exp. of term.
Boyd, Wm.	Aug. 28, '61	Disch. Jan. 5, '64.
Burke, L.	Aug. 24, '61	Wounded; deserted.
Charles, Francis.	Aug. 28, '61	Wounded at Dabney's Mills, Feb. 5, '65; disch. June 16, '65.
Clinch, Jas.	Mar. 3, '64	Wounded at Petersburg; absent in hosp. at m. o.
Comstock, Clayton.	Sep. 3, '61	Disch., date unknown.
Congle, Jno.	Sep. 14, '61	Wounded at Fredericksburg; disch., date unknown.
Christy, Jas.	Sep. 14, '61	Wounded at Bull Run; disch., date unknown.
Ducy, Geo. W.	Sep. 13, '61	M. o. with Co.
Dixon, Thos. J.	Aug. 24, '61	Died at Manayunk, Oct. 9, '62, of wounds received at Bull Run.
Davis, Geo. W.	Dec. 16, '61	Wounded at Antietam; disch. Sep. 8, '64.
Downey, Jas.	Aug. 14, '61	Killed at Antietam.
Davis, Jno.	Aug. 24, '61	Deserted.
Elmer, William J.	Dec. 19, '61	Disch. Dec. 3, '62.
Errickson, Fred.	Sep. 12, '61	Disch. Nov. 30, '62.
Ferrier, Jas.	Feb. 21, '64	Absent in hosp. at m. o.
Fimple, Jas.	Sep. 12, '61	Died at Alexandria, Jan. 1, '62.
Githens, Joshua.	Sep. 12, '61	Discharged Feb. 13, '63.
Green, Geo. W.	Sep. 13, '61	Captured at Gettysburg; disch. Dec. 3, '64.
Goodex, Edw.	Oct. 4, '61	Wounded at Bull Run, and loss of left arm at Laurel Hill; disch. Nov. 7, '64.

Rank.	Mustered In.	Record.
Privates.		
Hartzell, David K.	Sep. 3, '61	Wounded at Bull Run and left on field; to V. R. Corps, Mar., '64.
Hague, James.	Sep. 9, '61	Captured at Gettysburg, and prisoner to Sep. '63; wounded at Spottsylvania, May 10, '64; disch. in front of Petersburg, Sep. 23, '64, exp. of term.
Hannum, D. N.	Sep. 3, '61	Disch. Aug. 13, '62.
Holden, Peter.	Feb. 14, '62	Disch. Oct. 14, '62, for wounds.
Hinkle, Peter.	Sep. 9, '61	Wounded at Antietam and Gettysburg; disch. Oct. 5, '64, exp. of term.
Hall, Jas.	Aug. 28, '61	Wounded at Bull Run; disch., date unknown.
Hollacher, Michael.	Aug. 24, '61	Killed July 1 at Gettysburg.
Herman, William.	Sep. 3, '61	Wounded at Bull Run; deserted.
Jeandell, William H.	Sep. 12, '61	Disch., date unknown.
Johnston, William.	Jan. 6, '62	Died Oct. 1, '62; buried in Military Asylum Cem., D. C.
Jones, Lewis.	Aug. 24, '61	Killed at Bull Run.
Kyte, Jno. L.	Sep. 12, '61	Transf. to hosp. service.
Levins, David.	Sep. 14, '61	Disch., date unknown.
Levi, J. J.	Sep. 10, '61	To Sgt.-Maj., Sep., '61.
Lewis, Phineas.	Aug. 24, '61	Died at Alexandria, Feb. 12, '64.
Mulholland, Joseph.	Sep. 12, '61	Disch. July, '62.
Murphy, Patrick.	Sep. 14, '61	Disch., date unknown.
Maddis, Wm.	Nov. 20, '61	Mortally wounded at Bull Run; died at Finley Hosp., Oct. 7, '62; buried in Military Asylum Cem., D. C.
McElwee, James.	Sep. 14, '61	Disch. Mar. 21, '63.
McDowell, Jos.	Sep. 10, '61	Wounded at Bull Run and Spottsylvania; disch. exp. of term.
Pierson, Thomas.	Aug. 24, '61	Disch. Jan. 10, '63.
Palmer, Thomas.	Aug. 28, '61	Disch. 1863.
Pinyard, Matt.	Sep. 9, '61	Disch. exp. of term.
Righter, Jno. D.	Aug. 28, '61	M. o. with Co.
Reed, Wm.	July 30, '64	M. o. with Co.
Reaver, Jno. B.	Sep. 9, '61	Wounded at Spottsylvania; absent at m. o.
Rodgers, Geo. M.	Feb. 28, '64	Wounded at Spottsylvania; prisoner from Aug. 19, '64, to Mar. 14, '65; died in hosp.
Ruth, Simpson.	Aug. 24, '61	Wounded at Antietam; disch. Mar. 24, '63.
Rex, Wilson.	Sep. 3, '61	Wounded at Bull Run; disch. Mar. 21, '63.
Rex, D.	July 22, '64	Disch. June 10, '65.
Raider, Henry.	Aug. 24, '61	Died at Emory Hosp., Washington, Sep. 22, '63.
Rodgers, James.	Sep. 9, '61	Killed at Bull Run.

Rank.	Mustered In.	Record.
Privates.		
Still, George.	Mar. 16, '64	M. o. with Co.
Stemple, Henry.	Mar. 3, '64	Wounded at Laurel Hill, May 8, '64; m. o. with Co.
Smith, Benj.	Mar. 3, '64	Wounded and prisoner, May 8, '64; paroled Sep., '64; absent in hosp. at m. o.
Southwick, Jno. H.	Sep. 12, '61	Wounded at Antietam; disch. Sep. 29, '64, exp. of term.
Snyder, Amos.	Sep. 12, '61	Wounded at Gettysburg; disch., date unknown.
Scantling, Peter.	Sep. 14, '61	Disch., date unknown.
Speer, Jas.	Sep. 9, '61	Wounded at Gettysburg; died of wounds rec'd at Spottsylvania, May 10, '64.
Toland, Geo. H.	Sep. 14, '61	Wounded at Fredericksburg and Gettysburg, ball in eye and out of mouth; to V. R. Corps, Nov. 15, '63.
Williams, Jas.	Aug. 28, '61	Prisoner from May 7 to Nov. 17, '64; disch. June 13, '65.
Webster, Curtis.	Sep. 3, '61	Disch., date unknown.
Winn, Thos.	Mar. 1, '64	Wounded; disch. Mar. 18, '65.
Ward, Jos.	Sep. 14, '61	Wounded on Weldon R. R.; disch., date unknown.
Wortz, Chas.	Sep. 10, '61	To Co. B, 12th Reg. V. R. Corps, '63.
Wier, And. J.	Aug. 28, '61	Wounded; disch. Feb. 21, '63.
Wilfong, Peter.	Nov. 24, '61	Wounded at Bull Run; disch. exp. of term.
Williams, Wm.	Sep. 12, '61	To V. R. Corps, April 28, '64.
White, Robt.	Aug. 28, '61	Died at Philadelphia.
Williams, And.	Sep. 14, '61	Died at Philadelphia, July 18, '64.
Zazier, Chas. A.	Sep. 12, '61	Killed at Gettysburg, July 1, '63.

Company C, Recruits.

Rank.	Mustered In.	Record.
Corporal.		
J. A. Buch.	Oct. 5, '64	Substitute; m. o. with Co.
Privates.		
Denuth, P.	Aug. 20, '64	Drafted; disch. June 10, '65.
Euhler, H.	Aug. 20, '64	Drafted; disch. June 10, '65.
Gondy, G.	Aug. 20, '64	Substitute; disch. June 10, '65.
Grande, H.	Aug. 29, '64	Substitute; m. o. with Co.
Henry, D.	Jan. 31, '65	Substitute; wounded Mar. 31, '65.
McCullough, W.	Aug. 24, '64	Substitute; disch. May 16, '65.

Rank.	Mustered In.	Record.
Privates.		
Reynolds, J. D.	Sep. 24, '64	Drafted; disch. June 5, '65.
Reynolds, C. T.	Sep. 24, '64	Drafted; disch. June 5, '65.
Seybold, F.	Aug. 20, '64	Drafted; disch. June 10, '65.
Tippit, J. A.	Sep. 28, '64	Substitute; disch. June 10, '65.
Wagner, P.	Aug. 20, '64	Drafted; disch. June 13, '65.
Wise, J. G.	Aug. 25, '64	Drafted; disch. June 10, '65.

Company D, Recruited in Philadelphia.

Rank.	Mustered In.	Record.
Captains.		
Geo. W. Fairlamb.	Sep. 13, '61	Resigned April 30, '62.
Louis Wagner.	Aug. 11, '61	From 1st Lt., April 30, '62, to Lt.-Col., Feb. 24, '63. (See Field and Staff.)
Wm. H. Fairlamb.	Sep. 13, '61	From 2d to 1st Lt., April 30, '62; Capt., Dec. 1, '62; wounded at Bull Run; dis. Oct. 21, '63.
Robt. E. Cuskaden.	Aug. 30, '61	From 2d Lt. Co. F, Feb. 17, '64; disch. Nov. 11, '64.
Jas. P. Meade.	Jan. 3, '65	To Brevet Maj., Mar. 13, and Brevet Lt.-Col., April 1, '65; m. o. with Co. June 30, '65.
First Lieutenants.		
George E. Wagner.	Aug. 31, '61	From 1st Sgt. to 2d Lt., April 30, '62; 1st Lt., Dec. 1, '62; Capt. 8th U. S. C. Troops, Oct. 14, '63; to Brevet-Col., '65.
George M. Donnelly.	Sep. 24, '61	From Sgt.-Maj., Mar. 7, '64; disch. Aug. 12, '64, for wounds rec'd at Laurel Hill.
Charles Hunter.	Aug. 31, '61	From Sgt. to 1st Lt., Jan. 16, '65; wounded at Laurel Hill; resigned June 12, '65.
Jno. Ewing.	Sep. 11, '61	From Sgt. to 2d Lt., June 9, '65; 1st Lt., June 14, '65; not must.; wounded at Petersburg; m. o. with Co.
Second Lieutenants.		
Robert B. Beath.	Sep. 5, '61	From Sgt. to 2d Lt., Dec. 1, '62; to Capt. 6th Reg. U. S. C. Troops, Aug. 29, '63; wounded at Bull Run, Aug. 30, '62; to Brevet Col., '65.
Mortimer Wisham.	Sep. 12, '61	From Sgt. to 2d Lt., June 14, '65; not must.; wounded at Dabney's Mills, Feb. 6, '65; m. o. with Co.

Rank.	Mustered In.	Record.
Sergeants.		
Wm. Chambers.	Aug. 31, '61	From Priv. to 1st Sgt.; killed at Fredericksburg.
Wm. M. Richards.	Sep. 21, '61	To Sgt., Feb. 1, '65; wounded at Petersburg, June 18, '64; m. o. with Co.
Jos. Trainer.	Sep. 12, '61	To Sgt., April 1, '65; m. o. with Co.
Henry M. Burker.	Sep. 9, '61	To Sgt., April 1, '65; m. o. with Co.
Aug. M. Ruth.	Sep. 9, '61	Wounded at Antietam; disch. Feb. 23, '63.
Jno. M. Taylor.	Aug. 31, '61	Disch. April 10, '63.
Wm. Coppes.	Aug. 28, '61	Disch. Aug. 28, '64, exp. of term.
Wm. B. Rodgers.	Sep. 2, '61	Died Oct. 17, '62, of wounds rec'd at Antietam.
Charles H. Kartsher.	Aug. 31, '61	To Adj., Nov. 24, '62; not must.; killed at Fredericksburg.
Jas. A. Devlin.	Mar. 25, '62	Captured at Gettysburg; died June 17, '64, of wounds rec'd at Spottsylvania.
Corporals.		
Harvey Myers.	Sep. 1, '61	From Priv. to Corp.; m. o. with Co.
Geo. Stitchenbox.	Aug. 29, '61	From Priv. to Corp.; wounded and prisoner at Bull Run; wounded at Five Forks; m. o. with Co.
Edw. Murray.	Sep. 6, '61	Wounded and prisoner at Bull Run; wounded at Gettysburg; from Priv. to Corp.; m. o. with Co.
Jos. Murphy.	Feb. 27, '64	To Corp., April 1, '65; m. o. with Co.
Wm. Frederick.	Feb. 27, '64	To Corp., April 1, '65; m. o. with Co.
Henry B. Boyer.	Aug. 31, '61	To Corp., May 1, '65; m. o. with Co.
Robt. Anderson.	Feb. 26, '64	To Corp., May 1, '65; wounded at Cold Harbor; absent in hosp. at m. o.
Henry M. West.	Sep. 9, '61	Disch. Sep. 1, '62.
Theodore McIlheney.	Sep. 12, '61	Disch. Feb. 11, '63.
Albert Williams.	Sep. 9, '61	Disch. Feb. 23, '63, for wounds rec'd at Rappahannock, Aug. 22, and at Bull Run, Aug. 30, '62.
C. S. Stuart.	Sep. 5, '61	Disch. May 17, '63.
George W. Armstrong.	Sep. 20, '61	To Corp., July 1, '63; disch. Sep. 20, '64, exp. of term.
Jno. S. Walton.	Sep. 3, '61	Wounded; to V. R. Corps, Dec. 9, '63.
Musicians.		
Albert F. Hardy.	Aug. 31, '61	To Principal Musician, May 30, '65.
George C. Cuskaden.	Feb. 26, '64	Disch. June 12, '65.
Privates.		
Allen, Wm.	Sep. 10, '61	Disch. on writ of *habeas corpus*, Oct. 8, '61.
Armitage, C. W.	Aug. 31, '61	Disch. Sep. 26, '63.
Burke, Wm.	Sep. 9, '61	Disch. April 25, '62.

Rank.	Mustered In.	Record.
Privates.		
Boyer, Wm.	Aug. 31, '61	Disch. July 27, '62.
Burris, Edw.	Aug. 30, '61	Wounded at Antietam; disch. Feb. 13, '63.
Bozarth, Rich. F.	Aug. 31, '61	Died at Washington, Sep. 20, '62; buried in Military Asylum Cem., D. C.
Bratton, G.	Sep. 6, '61	Deserted Mar. 21, '63.
Caldwell, Samuel.	Sep. 28, '61	Died of wounds rec'd at Antietam.
Carson, Wesley.	Feb. 25, '64	Captured Dec. 12, '64; died in prison, Jan. 29, '65.
Collins, Wm.	Oct. 3, '61	Captured; died in captivity.
Carter, J.	Feb. 11, '64	Disch. June 12, '65.
Cornish, B. F.	Aug. 31, '61	Disch. Feb. 9, '63.
Cullen, D.	Aug. 26, '61	Disch. Nov. 16, '62.
Coffin, L. B.	Sep. 12, '61	Wounded and prisoner at Bull Run; captured at Gettysburg; deserted April 1, '64.
Dickhart, George W.	Sep. 11, '61	Captured at Gettysburg; to V. R. Corps May 15, '64.
Davidson, Thos.	Sep. 10, '61	Killed at Bull Run.
Egner, Conrad.	Sep. 2, '61	Disch. Sep. 2, '64, exp. of term.
Early, Jno.	Sep. 9, '61	Wounded and prisoner at Bull Run; disch. Nov. 10, '63, and died at Philadelphia.
Fling, Howell.	Sep. 13, '61	Disch. April 25, '62.
Follin, Michael.	Sep. 2, '61	Died at Washington, Mar. 17, '64; buried in Military Asylum Cem., D. C.
Friel, Jno.	Aug. 31, '61	Died, date unknown.
Fisher, Thomas.	Sep. 28, '61	Deserted July 22, '63.
Gray, Henry B.	Mar. 18, '64	M. o. with Co.
Griffin, Patrick.	Sep. 14, '61	Disch. Mar. 20, '63.
Gannon, Michael.	Oct. 4, '61	Died Oct. 10, '62, of wounds rec'd at Bull Run.
Grace, Jas. Y.	Sep. 5, '61	Died at Alexandria, Oct. 21, '61, of typhoid fever. First member of the Reg. to die.
Hunt, Elwood.	Aug. 31, '61	Disch. Aug. 31, '62.
Heintzleman, J. C.	Sep. 9, '61	Disch. Feb. 20, '63.
Heddinger, Wm.	Aug. 28, '61	Killed at Bull Run.
Hirst, David.	Sep. 5, '61	Died at Alexandria, Feb. 28, '62; buried in Nat. Cem., grave 1075.
Harmon, L.	Sep. 3, '61	Deserted July 22, '63.
Hooper, P.	Aug. 3, '61	Deserted April 1, '64.
Irwin, Jno.	Dec. 2, '61	Died May 31, '64, of wounds rec'd at Laurel Hill.
Kirby, W.	Dec. 9, '61	Deserted June 9, '62.
Kernan, Jas. A.	Mar. 22, '62	Deserted Mar. 21, '63.
Larrison, William.	Sep. 14, '61	Disch. Oct, 17, '63.
Loudenstine, Chas.	Aug. 30, '61	Disch. July 17, '62.

Rank.	Mustered In.	Record.
Privates.		
Lauer, Wm.	Aug 31, '61	Died Sep. 22, '62, of wounds rec'd at Bull Run; buried in Military Asylum Cem., D. C.
Little, Wm.	Aug. 31, '61	Wounded at Gettysburg; to V. R. Corps.
Lappin, J.	Aug. 31, '61	Deserted Ju'y 20, '62.
Linus, Jno.	Sep. 28, '61	Absent sick at m. o.
Meeks, Oliver P.	Sep. 6, '61	Disch. Nov. 18, '63.
Monroe, George.	Sep. 2, '61	Disch. April 25, '62.
Morgan, J.	Sep. 16, '61	Deserted Jan. 22, '62.
McConnel, Thos.	Sep. 10, '61	Died at Alexandria, Sep. 9, '62, of wounds rec'd at Bull Run; buried in Nat. Cem., Alexandria, grave 269.
McClintock, W.	Sep. 13, '61	Killed at Bull Run.
McVey, Jas.	Mar. 12, '64	Prisoner; died at Lynchburg, June 23, '64; buried in Poplar Grove Cem., grave 131.
Nugent, Jno.	Sep. 14, '61	M. o. with Co.
Norris, Thos.	Feb. 25, '64	Absent at m. o.
Neter, Joseph.	Aug. 31, '61	Disch. Feb. 7, '63.
Onimus, R. S.	Sep. 13, '61	Disch. Sep. 20, '64.
Penair, Geo.	Sep. 3, '61	Wounded at Gettysburg; to V. R. Corps, Mar. 7, '65; disch. July 10, '65.
Ruth, Michael.	Sep. 10, '61	Wounded at Gettysburg; disch. Dec. 8, '64, exp. of term.
Russel, Wes.	Sep. 2, '61	Disch. Feb. 6, '63.
Rodgers, Wm.	Sep. 2, '61	Disch. Aug. 31, '62.
Simms, Jno.	Feb. 6, '64	Wounded at Bull Run; killed at Spottsylvania.
Sanders, Jno.	Aug. 26, '61	Disch. Sep. 5, '64, exp. of term.
Sutton, Jno.	Aug. 30, '61	Disch. Dec. 3, '62.
Searles, Edward.	Sep. 6, '61	Disch. Oct 6, '62.
Thompson, H. H.	Sep. 16, '61	To V. R. Corps; disch. Dec. 6, '64.
Thomas, Jos. S.	Sep. 3, '61	Disch. April 25, '62.
Thomas, John D.	Sep. 5, '61	Disch. Feb. 20, '63.
Tapper, Chas.	Mar. 20, '62	Deserted Mar. 21, '63.
Vanderkerchen, S.	Mar. 15, '64	Disch. May 29, '65.
Warren, Jas. W.	Sep. 2, '61	From Co. B, Feb. 6, '64; m. o. with Co.
Winn, Fras.	Sep. 5, '61	Wounded at Gettysburg; real name Mark Grigg; m. o. with Co.
Wilday, Chas.	Sep. 26, '61	Disch. Sep. 26, '64, exp. of term.
Wood, Elijah.	Sep. 3, '61	Disch. Nov. 12, '63.
Walton, Albert.	Sep. 11, '61	Disch. Dec. 31, '61.
Wagner, Adam.	Aug. 29, '61	Killed at Bull Run.
Williams, John B.	Sep. 5, '61	Deserted June 23, '62.

Company D, Recruits.

Rank.	Mustered In.	Record.
Corporal.		
M. Malone.	Jan. 19, '65	Substitute; m. o. with Co.
Privates.		
Clark, W.	Nov. 26, '64	Drafted; m. o. with Co.
Cline, Daniel.	Jan. 18, '65	Missing in battle, Dabney's Mills, Feb. 7, '65.
Crownover, G.	Sep. 21, '64	Drafted; disch. June 2, '65.
Coyle, J.	Sep. 21, '64	Substitute; disch. June 20, '65.
Eberhart, J.	June 22, '64	Drafted; m. o. with Co.
Farster, F.	Sep. 21, '64	Disch. on Surg. certif.
Garrison, G.	Jan. 17, '65	Disch. May 9, '65.
Houser, David.	Sep. 4, '64	Drafted; died Sep. 21, '64; grave 9065, Arlington Cem.
Jones, W.	Dec. 16, '64	Drafted; m. o. with Co.
Johnson, J. W.	Sep. 24, '64	Substitute; disch. June 10, '65.
Jaques, Hartley.	Oct. 6, '64	Substitute; killed at Dabney's Mills, Feb. 7, '65.
Knapp, C.	Oct. 4, '64	Substitute; m. o. with Co.
Kerr, D.	Sep. 19, '64	Drafted; disch. June 10, '65.
Lemmon, T.	Sep. 21, '64	Drafted; disch. June 10, '65.
Miller, D.	Sep. 21, '64	Drafted; disch. June 30, '65.
Morrison, Edw.	Mar. 15, '65	Drafted; died Aug. 30, '65. The last member of the 88th to die while in the service.
Musselman, H.	July 29, '64	Substitute; disch. June 10, '65.
Myer, C.	Sep. 29, '64	Substitute; disch. June 10, '65.
Rosenberger, G.	Sep. 21, '64	Drafted; disch. June 10, '65.
Sexton, W.	Aug. 26, '64	Drafted; wounded at Five Forks, April 1, '65.
Stuart, A.	Sep. 21, '64	Drafted; disch. June 10, '65.
Schrecongost, S. S.	Sep. 21, '64	Drafted; disch. June 10, '65.
Shofstall, W.	Aug. 30, '64	Substitute; disch. June 10, '65.
Smith, J.	Aug. 31, '64	Substitute; disch. June 17, '65.
Stoss, C.	Sep. 26, '64	Substitute; disch. June 10, '65.
Steiner, M. C.	Sep. 29, '64	Substitute; missing on Weldon R. R., Dec. 12, '64.
Wert, Jonas.	Mar. 16, '65	Drafted; died June 22, '65; grave 3259, Alexandria Cem.
Wilson, Jas. F.	Mar. 15, '65	Drafted; died May 1, '65; grave 758, Poplar Grove Cem.
Wentz, J.	Sep. 28, '64	Substitute; disch. June 10, '65.
Whidden, M.	Sep. 30, '64	Substitute; disch. June 10, '65.

Company E, Recruited in Philadelphia and Vicinity.

Rank.	Mustered In.	Record.
Captains.		
Christian S. Carmack.	Nov. 5, '61	Disch. Dec. 31, '62, for wounds rec'd at Antietam.
Jas. H. Johnston.	Nov. 5, '61	To 1st Lt., June 17, '62; Capt., Dec. 31, '62; captured at Bull Run; resigned Mar. 17, '63.
Jos. H. Richards.	Sep. 9, '61	To Capt., May 1, '63; disch. April 26, '64.
Edward L. Gilligan.	Oct. 22, '61	To 1st Lt., Oct. 31, '64; Capt., Dec. 18, '64; wounded Mar. 31, '65; m. o. with Co. Awarded a Medal of Honor by War Dept. for bravery at Gettysburg.
First Lieutenants.		
Wm. H. Shearman.	Oct. 22, '61	Resigned June 18, '62.
Jas. A. Napier.	Oct. 24, '61	To 1st Lt., Dec. 31, '62; disch. Mar. 23, '63, for wounds—with loss of arm —rec'd at Fredericksburg.
Gerrit S. Nichols.	Sep. 9, '61	To 1st Lt., May 18, '63; wounded at Antietam; disch. Oct. 3, '64, for wounds rec'd in Wilderness.
Daniel J. Lehman.	Sep. 20, '61	To 1st Lt., Dec. 19, '64; captured at Gettysburg; died at Washington, May 20, '65, of wounds rec'd at Five Forks; buried in Arlington Cem.
Jno. S. Campbell.	Oct. 4, '61	Wounded at Bull Run; captured at Gettysburg; to 1st Lt., June 17, '65; not must.; m. o. with Co.
Second Lieutenants.		
Albert Booz.	Oct. 15, '61	From Sgt. to 2d Lt., May 27, '63; disch. for disability, June 20, '63.
Joseph Burris.	Sep. 23, '61	From Sgt. to 2d Lt., June 14, '65; not must.; wounded at Spottsylvania, May 10, '64; m. o. with Co.
Sergeants.		
Chas. Barber.	Aug. 30, '61	From Priv. to 1st Sgt.; wounded at Gettysburg; disch. Sep. 17, '64, exp. of term.
Saml. K. English.	Oct. 14, '61	From Priv. to Sgt.; prisoner at Gettysburg; also captured on skirmish line, May 12, '64; m. o. with Co.
Laf. Hickman.	Dec. 9, '61	Absent on furlough at m. o.
Henry Ford.	Oct. 17, '61	From Corp. to Sgt., June 14, '65; wounded at Antietam and Gettysburg; on furlough at m. o.
And. Hill.	Dec. 10, '61	From Corp., June 14, '65; wounded at Antietam; m. o. with Co.

Rank.	Mustered In.	Record.
Sergeants.		
Wm. Montgomery.	Oct. 15, '61	Disch. exp. of term.
Henry P. Force.	Sep. 16, '61	From Corp; disch. June 13, '65.
Jno. R. Jones.	Oct. 24, '61	Disch. Nov. 6, '64, exp. of term.
Jno. Monyer, Jr.	Sep. 9, '61	Disch. July 12, '62.
Jacob D. Ninesteel.	Aug. 23, '61	To Co. A, Dec. 22, '62.
Charles A. Sines.	Oct. 4, '61	Died of wounds rec'd at Spottsylvania, May 10, '64.
Corporals.		
Saml. T. Fox.	Dec. 9, '61	Captured at Gettysburg; wounded at Spottsylvania; to Corp., May 1, '65; m. o. with Co.
Wm. P. Reynolds.	. . . . '61	Disch. Nov. 19, '63, for wounds rec'd at Gettysburg, with loss of arm.
Benj. B. Lee.	Aug. 26, '61	Killed at Antietam.
Musicians.		
Henry Brown.	Dec. 10, '61	M. o. with Co.
Jacob Hannabery.	Oct. 4, '61	Disch., date unknown.
Privates.		
Andrews, Jacob.	. . . . '61	Captured at Bull Run; killed at Gettysburg.
Brainerd, Josiah.	Sep. 19, '61	Had leg accidentally broken; disch. exp. of term.
Britton, Wm.	Oct. 30, '61	Captured at Gettysburg; absent in hosp. at m. o.
Borgard, John A.	Mar. 18, '64	Absent in hosp. at m. o.
Booz, Henry S.	Oct. 15, '61	Wounded and prisoner at Bull Run; disch. in field before Petersburg, Oct. 15, '64, exp. of term.
Barclay, James W.	Oct. 11, '61	Disch. Jan. 6, '63, for wounds rec'd at Thoroughfare Gap.
Bowker, Jos.	. . . . '61	Disch. Feb. 9, '63.
Boas, Wm., Sr.	Dec. 9, '61	Killed at Antietam; buried in City Cem., Reading.
Boas, Wm., Jr.	Dec. 9, '61	Wounded at Fredericksburg.
Bruner, Jos. S.	Oct. 14, '61	Killed at Gettysburg.
Campbell, Wm. S.	Apr. 4, '62	Captured May 12, '64; disch. Feb. 3, '65.
Clark, Henry.	Oct. 17, '61	Wounded at Antietam; died at Alexandria, June 6, '64; buried in Alexandria Nat. Cem., grave 1270.
Colbridge, Wm.	Oct. 4, '61	Disch. Aug., 1862.
Conkey, Joseph.	Oct. 17, '61	Disch., date unknown.
Davidson, Jno.	Oct. 24, '61	Killed at Bull Run; buried in Alexandria Nat. Cem., grave 346.
Eppeheimer, C. W.	Oct. 14, '61	To V. R. Corps, April 18, '63.
Ferrier, Jesse.	'61	Disch. Jan. 28, '63.
Fetters, David.	Sep. 25, '61	No record.

Rank.	Mustered In.	Record.
Privates.		
Gray, Thos.	Oct. 4, '61	Disch., date unknown.
Griffith, Thos.	Sep. 17, '61	No record.
Hicken, Jesse.	Oct. 15, '61	Disch. April 24, '62.
Halfman, Herbert W.	Oct. 15, '61	Disch. Oct. —, '62.
Hallowell, Alex.	Oct. 15, '61	Disch. July 18, '62.
Hallowell, George W.	Oct. 15, '61	No record.
Horner, G. N.	Dec. 9, '61	No record.
Jones, Wm. H.	Oct. 3, '61	Disch. Jan. 31, 63.
Jackson, Wm.	Sep. 16, '61	Wounded at Antietam; to V. R. Corps, Nov. 15, '63.
Keville, Patrick.	. . . . '61	Wounded at Gettysburg; disch. Sep. 12, '63.
Kram, J. S.	Aug. 23, '61	To Com. Sgt., Oct. 4, '61.
Lloyd, Henry.	Oct. 15, '61	Wounded at Gettysburg; disch. exp. of term.
Lukens, Garret.	Oct. 30, '61	Wounded at Gettysburg; to V. R. Corps, April 28, '65.
Lewis, Jno. E.	Nov. 2, '61	No record.
Myers, Jno.	Oct. 3, '61	M. o. with Co.
Markley, Benj.	Mar. 6, '62	Wounded at Gettysburg; disch. Mar. 6, '65, exp of term.
Murphy, John S.	Oct. 15, '61	Disch. Dec. 6, '61.
Mallison, Joseph.	Sep. 19, '61	Disch. Aug. 8, '62.
Murphy, Frank K.	Oct. 21, '61	To Hosp. Steward.
McDonald, Joseph.	Oct. 29, '61	Disch. Oct. 28, '62.
McIntire, I.	Feb. 23, '64	To Sgt.-Maj.
O'Donnell, Cornelius.	. . . . . .	Wounded at Fredericksburg; disch. April 16, '63.
Ochs, Josiah.	Jan. 18, '62	Deserted April 21, '62.
Peacock, Eber.	Mar. 24, '62	Disch. April 22, '62.
Rittenhouse, Miles.	Oct. 24, '61	Disch., date unknown.
Riley, Christian.	Sep. 17, '61	Died at Windmill Point, June 23, '63.
Spohn, William.	Mar. —, '62	Disch. Dec. 18, '62.
Snyder, Jacob.	Dec. 9, '61	Prisoner of war; disch. Feb., '63.
Stamm, Wm.	Dec. 9, '61	M. o. with Co.
Shinn, Elias.	Nov. 2, '61	No record.
Thomas, Stephen.	Sep. 25, '61	Disch., date unknown.
Troxle, C. A.	Dec. 9, '61	Deserted May 6, '62.
Wheeler, Jno.	Oct. 4, '61	Deserted April 24, '62.
White, Alex. H.	Oct. 14, '61	Captured at Bull Run; to 27th P. V., Mar. 24, '63.

Company E, Recruits.

Rank.	Mustered In.	Record.
Corporals.		
B. Simpson.	June 4, '64	Drafted; m. o. with Co.
J. Dougherty.	Jan. 25, '65	Drafted, m. o. with Co.
E. O'Neill.	Oct. 4, '64	Substitute; m. o. with Co.
J. Daly.	Oct. 8, '64	Substitute; m. o. with Co.
J. Young.	Jan. 17, '65	Substitute; m. o. with Co.
Privates.		
Andrews, G. C.	Sep. 30, '64	Substitute; died May 29, '65; grave 9701, Arlington Cem.
Bryner, Jos.	Sep. 30, '64	Died Feb. 13, '65, of wounds rec'd at Dabney's Mills; buried in Louden Park Cem., Baltimore.
Bennett, W.	Oct. 5, '64	Substitute; m. o. with Co.
Burns, P.	Oct. 7, '64	Substitute; m. o. with Co.
Blanchard, A. S.	Sep. 21, '64	Drafted; disch. April 25, '65.
Bearington, T.	Sep. 20, '64	Substitute; disch. Oct. 29, '64.
Davis, H. A.	Sep. 30, '64	Substitute; disch. May 17, '65.
Fillinger, E.	Aug. 30, '64	Substitute; wounded at Dabney's Mills, Feb. 7, '65.
Hess, E.	Sep. 30, '64	Substitute; disch. June 10, '65.
Johnson, W.	Feb. 13, '65	Substitute; disch. July 10, '65.
Lundy, D.	Feb. 26, '65	Drafted; disch. May 15, '65.
Lewis, D.	Feb. 30, '64	Substitute; disch. June 10, '65.
McDonough, J.	Feb. 27, '64	Substitute; disch. Mar. 22, '65.
McGinnis, M.	Oct. 1, '64	Substitute; disch. June 3, '65.
Phillips, Edw.	Oct. 5, '64	Substitute; killed at Dabney's Mills, Feb. 7, '65.
Price, W. H.	Mar. 22, '65	Substitute; died May 31, '65; grave 2989, Alexandria Cem.
Silberman, J.	Aug. 2, '64	Substitute; disch. June 2, '65, for wounds.
Vogle, S.	Aug. 20, '64	Substitute; disch. June 10, '65.
Whitlow, J.	Oct. 4, '64	Substitute; m. o. with Co.
Winters, M. R.	Sep. 3, '64	Substitute; wounded at Dabney's Mills, Feb. 7, '65.
Wahls, J. S.	Sep. 5, '64	Substitute; disch. June 10, '65.

Company F, Recruited in Philadelphia.

Rank.	Mustered In.	Record.
Captains.		
Theo. W. Dunham.	Sep. 16, '61	Disch. Oct. 9, '62.
J. Parker Martin.	Sep. 16, '61	From 1st Lt., Oct. 9, '62; resigned Feb. 8, '63.

Rank.	Mustered In.	Record.
Captains.		
Geo. B. Rhoads.	Sep. 18, '61	From 1st Lt. Co. B, April 10, '63; killed by a cannon-ball at White Oak Swamp, June 13, '63; buried in Chas. Evans Cem., Reading.
Richard B. Clevinger.	Aug. 30, '61	From Sgt. to 1st Lt., Oct. 17, '64; Capt., Dec. 28, '64; m. o. with Co.
Wm. L. Street.	Sep. 16, '61	From 2d Lt., Oct. 9, '62; Brevet Capt., Maj., and Col., Mar. 13, '65; wounded and prisoner at Bull Run, Aug. 30, '62; resigned Feb. 1, '63.
First Lieutenants.		
Henry M. Middleton.	Sep. 5, '61	From Sgt. to 1st Lt., Feb. 1, '63; resigned Aug. 14, '63.
Matthew Myers.	Jan. 2, '62	From Corp. to 1st Lt., Mar. 18, '65; wounded at Gettysburg; m. o. with Co.
Atwood G. Sinn.	Aug. 27, '61	From Sgt. to 1st Lt., Aug. 15, '63; not must.; killed at Petersburg, June 18, '64.
Second Lieutenants.		
Wm. H. Forbes.	Sep. 5, '61	To 2d Lt., Oct. 9, '62; resigned Jan. 18, '63.
Robert E. Cuskaden.	Aug. 30, '61	To 2d Lt., Jan. 18, '63; to Capt. Co. D, Feb. 17, '64; wounded at Gettysburg.
Henry S. Wade.	Sep. 16, '61	From Sgt. to 2d Lt., June 16, '65; wounded at Five Forks, April 1, '65; m. o. with Co.
Sergeants.		
Michael Bright.	Feb. 29, '64	1st Sgt.; m. o. with Co.
Jas. Cox.	Sep. 5, '61	1st Sgt.; wounded at Antietam; disch. Mar. 5, '63.
Jno. M. Allen.	Sep. 5, '61	1st Sgt.; disch. Jan. 1, '62.
Wm. H. Fenlin.	Sep. 5, '61	1st Sgt.; wounded, with loss of leg, at Fredericksburg; disch. Sep. 12, '64, exp. of term.
Jos. Jones.	Sep. 27, '61	M. o. with Co.
Albert H. Goodenough.	Feb. 29, '64	To Sgt., May 1, '65; m. o. with Co.
Chas. M. Clark.	Sep. 14, '61	To Sgt., May 1, '65; m. o. with Co.
Henry B. Wortz.	Sep. 19, '61	To Sgt., June 6, '65; prisoner at Gettysburg; m. o. with Co.
Corporals.		
A. Fenstermacher.	Sep. 16, '61	To Corp., May 1, '65; m. o. with Co.
Samuel Warner.	Feb. 25, '64	To Corp., May 1, '65; on furlough at m. o.
Abraham Barker.	Sep. 24, '61	Wounded at Antietam; m. o. with Co.
Jno. Bechtel.	Sep. 17, '61	Disch. Feb., '63; re-enlisted Feb. 5, '64; m. o. with Co.
Geo. W. Achuff.	Aug. 29, '61	Disch. Nov. 18, '61.
Isaac L. Street.	Sep. 2, '61	Disch. May 1, '62.

Rank.	Mustered In.	Record.
Corporals.		
Geo. W. Fortner.	Sep. 13, '61	Disch. Nov. 25, '62.
Alf. Wood.	Aug. 30, '61	Disch. Jan. 1, '63.
Jno. A. Lackey.	Sep. 5, '61	Wounded at Antietam; disch. exp. of term.
William H. Hallman.	Sep. 16, '61	Wounded at Gettysburg; disch. June 10, '65.
Aug. Kissinger.	Feb. 29, '64	Wounded at Hatcher's Run; disch. May 15, '65.
Harry B. Grey.	Aug. 30, '61	Wounded at Fredericksburg; to V. R. Corps, Nov. 15, '63.
Geo. Schaffer.	Sep. 16, '61	Killed at Bull Run.
John II. Russell.	Aug. 27, '61	Deserted Aug. 30, '62.
Musicians.		
Joel R. Krick.	Aug. 30, '61	Disch. June 12, '65.
Francis M. Brooks.	Oct. 2, '61	Disch. July 14, '62.
Privates.		
Anderson, I. P.	Sep. 16, '61	Deserted Aug. 24, '62.
Betzold, Jno.	Sep. 14, '61	Killed at Bull Run.
Clark, Jas. G.	Sep. 14, '61	Wounded at Bull Run, Gettysburg, and Petersburg; disch. Sep. 27, '64, exp. of term. Awarded Medal of Honor by War Dept. for bravery at Petersburg, June 18, '64.
Cutler, John S.	Sep. 14, '61	Wounded at Fredericksburg; disch. July 13, '63.
Dehart, Henry M.	Sep. 1, '62	Wounded at Gettysburg; absent sick at m. o.
De Haven, Jno.	Sep. 16, '61	Wounded and prisoner at Bull Run; disch. Dec. 31, '62.
Dinkle, Fred.	Mar. 30, '64	Wounded at Hatcher's Run; disch. June 14, '65.
Davis, David C.	Sep. 16, '61	Wounded at Fredericksburg; killed at Spottsylvania, May 10, '64; buried in Nat. Cem., Fredericksburg, grave 53.
Eshman, H.	Feb. 29, '64	Deserted Jan. 22, '65.
Force, II. P.	Sep. 16, '61	To Co. E, Jan. 28, '64.
Flickinger, B.	Feb. 27, '64	Died at Washington, June 5, '64.
Fry, C. M.	Sep. 16, '61	Deserted Sep. 14, '62.
Foster, George W.	Aug. 27, '61	Disch. April 1, '63.
Good, Samuel.	Sep. 23, '61	Disch. July 5, '62.
Glenroy, Jno.	Aug. 29, '61	Captured at Gettysburg; to V. R. Corps, Nov. 19, '63.
Goodhart, Jno. F.	Mar. 1, '64	Died at Philadelphia, June 5, '64, of wounds rec'd at Spottsylvania; buried at Reading.
Goodheart, Benj.	Feb. 27, '64	Captured; died at Salisbury, Feb. 1, '65.

Rank.	Mustered In.	Record.
Privates.		
Griffith, C.	Sep. 16, '61	Deserted May 5, '64.
Hays, J. B.	Sep. 30, '61	Disch. Aug. 14, '62.
Hersh, Adam.	Sep. 19, '61	Disch. Sep. 23, '64, exp. of term.
Hampton, D. P.	Sep. 16, '61	Deserted June 13, '62.
Johnston, James.	Sep. 14, '61	Wounded and prisoner at Bull Run; to V. R. Corps, July 1, '63.
Krewson, Isaac S.	Sep. 16, '61	Prisoner at Gettysburg; absent sick at m. o.
Kram, Henry	Sep. 16, '61	Disch. July 15, '62.
Keys, Alex.	Sep. 30, '61	Disch. April 14, '65, to date Dec. 6, '64.
Livingstone, Samuel.	Oct. 2, '61	Wounded at Gettysburg; to V. R. Corps, Nov. 28, '63.
Loudenslager, R. H.	Sep. 13, '61	Killed at Antietam.
Landell, Benjamin F.	Aug. 27, '61	Killed at Antietam.
Lister, A.	Aug. 30, '61	No record.
Marquardt, J.	Sep. 17, '61	Disch. Oct. 9, '62.
Mervine, Geo.	Sep. 26, '61	Disch., date unknown.
Miller, Jas.	Sep. 2, '61	Died at Philadelphia, July 10, '64, of wounds rec'd at Spottsylvania.
Marion, J.	Sep. 5, '61	Deserted April 4, '62.
McCabe, John.	Sep. 27, '61	Disch. July 14, '62.
Naher, Chas.	. . . . '61	Killed at Bull Run.
Nugent, J.	Sep. 14, '61	To Co. D, Jan. 28, '64.
Newton, Charles O.	Sep. 14, '61	Disch. Feb. 25, '63.
Otto, Wm. W.	Sep. 16, '61	Disch. Aug. 12, '62.
Poole, Thomas.	Sep. 14, '61	Wounded and prisoner at Bull Run; disch. Dec. 24, '62.
Perry, Jno.	Sep. 14, '61	To Quartermaster Sgt., May 5, '62.
Read, Peter.	Aug. 30, '61	M. o. with Co.
Rimbe, Joseph E.	Sep. 16, '61	Absent sick at m. o.
Remshaird, F.	Sep. 14, '61	Disch. June 18, '62.
Roland, Lewis.	Sep. 23, '61	Disch. Aug. 14, '62.
Robbins, Elisha.	Aug. 29, '61	Disch. Aug. 6, '62.
Ristine, Fred.	Sep. 16, '61	Wounded and prisoner at Bull Run; wounded at White Oak Swamp, June 13, '64; disch. Feb. 14, '65.
Reitz, D. L.	Mar, 24, '64	Captured at Dabney's Mills, Mar. 30, '65; disch. May 29, '65.
Russel, J. H.	. . . . '61	Deserted Aug. 30, '61.
Smallwood, John T.	Sep. 16, '61	Disch. April 14, '62.
Shuster, Charles W.	Sep. 14, '61	Disch. Nov. 28, '63.
Simms, Jno.	Aug. 29, '61	Wounded at Bull Run, with loss of arm; disch. Oct. 10, '62.
Scott, Wm. H.	Sep. 7, '61	Disch. Sep. 7, '64, exp. of term.
Street, Richard L.	Sep. 5, '61	Disch. Mar. 4, '65.
Sundag, F.	May 1, '64	Disch. June 15, '65.
Smith, Charles W.	Aug. 30, '61	Accidentally wounded; to V. R. Corps, Dec. 9, '63.

Rank.	Mustered In.	Record.
Privates.		
Schriner, Phil.	Aug. 29, '61	Wounded and captured at Gettysburg; to V. R. Corps, Mar. 6, '64.
Simmons, William H.	. . . . '61	Died at Alexandria, Dec. 24, '64; grave 2969.
Thibault, E.	Aug. 29, '61	Disch. Dec. 18, '61.
Umback, A.	Sep. 19, '61	Deserted Aug. 31, '62.
Williams, Jno.	Sep. 16, '61	Wounded and prisoner at Bull Run; wounded at Spottsylvania; absent sick at m. o.
Wallace, S. G.	Sep. 5, '61	Disch. May 29, '62.
Weber, J. W.	Sep. 16, '61	Disch. June 18, '62.
Winn, Francis.	Sep. 5, '61	Correct name Mark Grigg; to Co. D, Feb. 4, '64.
Wise, Albert G.	Sep. 16, '61	To Co. A., Feb. 1, '64.
Wester, A. C.	Sep. 2, '61	To Quartermaster Sgt., Oct. 1, '61.
Wickline, Enos.	Feb. 27, '64	Died at Washington, July 5, '64; buried in Nat. Cem., Arlington, grave 6433.
White, W.	Feb. 22, '62	Deserted April 16, '62.
Young, E. C.	Feb. 27, '64	Deserted June 17, '64.

Company F, Recruits.

Rank.	Mustered In.	Record.
Corporals.		
H. O'Neil.	Oct. 3, '64	Substitute; m. o. with Co.
J. Smith.	Oct. 4, '64	Substitute; disch. June 15, '65.
J. Carothers.	Sep. 21, '64	Drafted; disch. May 1, '65.
Privates.		
Buckland, T. J.	Sep. 26, '64	Drafted; disch. June 10, '65.
Beardslee, A.	Sep. 24, '64	Substitute; disch. June 3, '65.
Campman, F.	Oct. 3, '64	Drafted; m. o. with Co.
Conway, N.	Feb. 16, '65	Absent sick at m. o.
Connery, J.	Oct. 7, '64	Substitute; disch. June 9, '65.
Dobson, J.	Sep. 26, '64	Drafted; disch. June 10, '65.
Hinchberger, N.	Sep. 19, '64	Drafted; disch. June 10, '65.
Manion, M.	Sep. 26, '64	Drafted; disch. June 10, '65.
Maxwell, R. B.	Sep. 20, '64	Drafted; disch. June 10, '65.
Portmaman, J.	Sep. 21, '64	Drafted; deserted June 10, '65.
Schoonover, G. W.	Sep. 24, '64	Drafted; disch. June 10, '65.
Schumela, J.	Oct. 7, '64	Substitute; sick at m. o.
Williams, W. X.	Sep. 26, '64	Drafted; disch. June 10, '65.
Warfield, J. S.	Sep. 24, '64	Drafted; disch. June 10, '65.

Company G, Recruited in Philadelphia.

Rank.	Mustered In.	Record.
Captains.		
Jno. S. Dull.	Apr. 14, '62	Disch. Nov. 21, '63.
Henry Korn, Jr.	Feb. 26, '62	To Capt., Feb. 17, '64; disch. Aug. 20, '64.
Aaron Bright, Jr.	Sep. 13, '61	From Co. B, '64; to Capt., Dec. 14, '64; to Field and Staff.
Alex. S. Gardiner.	Oct. 30, '62	To Capt., Aug. 21, '64; not must.; wounded at Bull Run; disch. Dec. 4, '64, exp. of term.
Wm. Huber.	Jan. 14, '62	To Capt., June 14, '65; not must.; m. o. with Co.
First Lieutenant.		
Cyrus R. Soder.	Nov. 9, '61	To 1st Lt., June 14, '65; not must.; Wounded at Bull Run; m. o. with Co.
Second Lieutenants.		
Walter S. Wingate.	Apr. 14, '62	Wounded at Antietam; resigned Nov. 7, '62.
Wm. Truett.	Sep. 17, '61	From Co. I, '64; 2d Lt., June 14, '65; not must.; m. o. with Co.
Sergeants.		
Wm. Sands.	Sep. 12, '61	From Principal Musician to 1st Sgt., Jan. 31, '65; wounded at Amelia C. H.; disch. May 31, '65; awarded Medal of Honor by War Dept. for bravery at Dabney's Mills.
John M. Wallace.	Aug. 23, '61	From Co. A, Feb. 6, '64, to Sgt., June 1, '65; prisoner from Aug. 19, '64, to Mar. 9, '65; disch. June 9, '65.
Wm. Ramich.	Sep. 12, '61	To Sgt., April 1, '65; m. o. with Co.
Henry C. Betz.	July 17, '63	To Sgt., June 1, '65; m. o. with Co.
Reub. Beldon.	Mar. 11, '64	To Sgt., June 17, '65; m. o. with Co.
Lewis Gale.	Jan. 30, '62	Disch., date unknown.
Henry Hutt.	Sep. 17, '61	Disch. Nov. 17, '63.
C. A. J. Polson.	Dec. 12, '61	Disch. Dec. 16, '63.
Wm. S. Eagle.	Sep. 11, '61	Killed at Laurel Hill, May 8, '64.
Corporals.		
Charles H. Mossman.	Mar. 31, '62	To Hosp. Steward U. S. A., May 25, '63.
A. W. Reigert.	Mar. 15, '62	Deserted Sep. 13, '62.
Musicians.		
Julius A. Hawk.	Feb. 19, '64	M. o. with Co.
Howard H. Betz.	Feb. 18, '62	Disch. Sep , '62.
Fred. Perry.	Jan. 22, '62	To V. R. Corps.
Jas. T. Reilley.	Apr. 4, '62	Disch., date unknown.
Daniel J. McLean.	May 1, '62	Disch. Aug. 9, '62.

Rank.	Mustered In.	Record.
Privates.		
Blackford, H.	Apr. 22, '62	Deserted June 14, '62.
Cornish, H.	Nov. 20, '61	Disch. Oct. 29, '62.
Carter, Andrew J.	Aug. 23, '61	Disch. Feb. 27, '63.
Caryell, T. R.	Nov. 20, '61	Disch., date unknown.
Canovan, Chas.	Sep. 14, '61	Died at Alexandria, Nov. 4, of wounds received at Bull Run.
Davis, G. W.	Dec. 16, '61	Disch., date unknown.
Erven, P. T.	Apr. 4, '62	Disch. Sep. 23, '62.
Ely, M.	Mar. 29, '62	Deserted July 1, 62.
Elmer, W. J.	Dec. 19, '61	No record.
Ferguson, J.	Jan. 30, '62	Deserted.
Ferguson, Alex.	Mar. 17, '62	Wounded at Laurel Hill; absent at m. o.
Ferguson, D. A.	Mar. 11, '62	Disch. Aug. 14, '62.
Ferkler, F. H.	Apr. 12, '62	Disch. Jan. 14, '63, for wounds.
Frazier, D.	Apr. 9, '62	Disch. Nov. 21, '62.
Gardiner, George W.	Mar. 19, '64	Captured at North Anna, May 23, '64, but recaptured; on furlough at m. o.
Gordon, James L.	Mar. 28, '62	Disch. Mar. 23, '63.
Hill, Jno.	Dec. 5, '61	Disch. Mar. 27, '63.
Hill, Lewis.	Dec. 3, '61	Died in camp near Sharpsburg, Oct. 18, '62.
Kite, Mahlon M.	Mar. 14, '62	Wounded at Gettysburg; absent at m. o.
Kurtz, G. W.	Mar. 28, '62	Disch Dec. 11, '62.
Krose, Lewis.	Jan. 22, '62	To V. R. Corps, Sep. 30, '63.
Land, Chas.	Jan. 18, '62	Disch. Aug. 11, '62.
Marks, C. S.	Apr. 11, '62	Disch. Oct. 25, '62.
Morris, H. C.	Feb. 10, '62	Deserted Aug. 30, '62.
Mundell, D.	Apr. 14, '62	Deserted June 15, '63.
Mulholland, G. W.	Dec. 16, '61	No record.
Meader, E. S.	Mar. 17, '62	Disch. Aug. 4, '62.
Nice, John.	Apr. 12, '62	Wounded at Gettysburg; disch. April 17, '65.
Preston, Jos. H.	Mar. 8, '62	Disch. April, '64, for wounds rec'd at Bull Run.
Rodenbush, P.	Jan. 28, '62	Disch. July 31, '62.
Reagan, James.	Mar. 24, '62	Disch. Feb. 7, '63.
Storch, Israel.	Dec. 9, '61	Disch. Dec. 12, '62.
Stokes, Jos. F.	Nov. 26, '61	Disch. Feb. 19, '63.
Scholl, Griffith F.	Apr. 9, '62	To Hosp. Steward, U.S.A., Feb. 19, '63.
Strickland, H. T.	Feb. 5, '62	Wounded at Fredericksburg; disch. June 13, '65.
Sullivan, Michael.	Apr. 15, '62	Disch., date unknown.
Saulsbury, T.	Mar. 28, '62	Deserted July 1, '62.
Tyler, George W.	Apr. 4, '62	Disch. Jan. 16, '63.
Tomlinson, J.	Dec. 21, '61	Deserted Mar. 1, '62.
Wright, J.	Jan. 14, '62	Deserted April 16, '62.
Wiant, Charles.	Apr. 2, '62	No record.
Yerger, Evan S.	Aug. 23, '61	From Co. A; on detached service at m. o.

Company G, Recruits.

Rank.	Mustered In.	Record.
Sergeant.		
Jos. F. Campbell.	Sep. 20, '64	Drafted; disch. May 17, '65.
Corporals.		
J. W. Hancock.	Sep. 10, '64	Substitute; m. o. with Co.
A. Korn.	Sep. 28, '64	Substitute; disch. June 10, '65.
J. A. Patterson.	Sep. 27, '64	Substitute; disch. June 10, '65.
D. Ritter.	Sep. 30, '64	Substitute; disch. June 10, '65.
S. Meals.	Sep. 21, '64	Drafted; disch. June 10, '65.
Privates.		
Agin, P.	Sep. 30, '64	Substitute; disch. June 20, '65.
Alabaugh, W.	Sep. 27, '64	Substitute; disch. June 10, '65.
Bowman, C.	Mar. 11, '65	Drafted; died June 3, '65.
Brogan, P.	Feb. 21, '65	Substitute; m. o. with Co.
Clouse, C. H.	Sep. 26, '64	Drafted; disch. May 11, '65.
Englehart, N.	Sep. 19, '64	Drafted; disch. June 10, '65.
Hitchcock, J. A.	Oct. 4, '64	Substitute; disch. July 17, '65.
Hannewell, N.	Sep. 6, '64	Substitute; disch. June 10, '65.
Hiles, Jonathan.	Sep. 27, '64	Substitute; died May 25, '65.
Kissler, J.	Sep. 26, '64	Drafted; disch. June 10, '65.
Kepple, J.	Sep. 27, '64	Drafted; disch. May 19, '65.
Martin, R.	Sep. 27, '64	Substitute; disch. June 10, '65.
Morgle, H.	Sep. 28, '64	Substitute; disch. June 21, '65.
Nankan, A.	Sep. 26, '64	Substitute; disch. May 23, '65.
Painter, L.	Sep. 17, '64	Substitute; absent at m. o.
Roland, J. A.	Sep. 24, '64	Drafted; m. o. with Co.
Rymer, T.	Sep. 26, '64	Drafted; disch. June 10, '65.
Sickler, W.	Aug. 18, '64	Substitute; disch. June 10, '65.
Stricklin, J. A.	Sep. 20, '64	Substitute; disch. June 10, '65.
Shackley, A. B.	Sep. 27, '64	Substitute; disch. June 10, '65.
Smith, J. R.	Sep. 26, '64	Drafted; disch. May 31, '65, for wounds.
Snooks, L.	Sep. 26, '64	Drafted; disch. June 10, '65.
Taylor, J.	Jan. 4, '65	Drafted; m. o. with Co.
Thompson, J.	Sep. 20, '64	Drafted; disch. June 10, '65.
Weber, L.	Sep. 20, '64	Drafted; disch. June 10, '65.
Warren, A.	Sep. 20, '64	Drafted; disch. June 10, '65.

Company H, Recruited in Reading.

Rank.	Mustered In.	Record.
Captains.		
David A. Griffith.	Sep. 14, '61	To Maj., Sep. 1, '62.
Frank B. Shalters, Jr.	Sep. 14, '61	From 2d to 1st Lt., May 7, '62; Capt., Sep. 1, '62; wounded at Antietam and Fredericksburg; resigned April 10, '63.
Jacob Houder.	Aug. 30, '61	To 2d Lt., Dec. 31, '62; Capt., Feb. 17, '64; killed Aug. 19, '64, on Weldon R. R.
Jos. H. Lawrence.	Sep. 11, '61	To 1st Lt., April 9, '64; Capt., Oct. 17, '64; absent at m. o.
First Lieutenants.		
Geo. W. Rapp.	Sep. 14, '61	Resigned May 7, '62.
Henry E. Quimby.	Aug. 30, '61	To 1st Lt., Sep. 1, '62; wounded at Antietam; resigned Oct. 20, '63.
Jas. McChaliker.	Sep. 10, '61	From Sgt. to 1st Lt., Jan. 1, '65; prisoner at Gettysburg; wounded at Petersburg, June 18, '64; disch. May 15, '65.
Jeff. Good.	Sep. 10, '61	From Sgt. to 2d Lt.; to 1st Lt., May 16, '65; not must.; m. o. with Co.
Second Lieutenants.		
Jas. C. Pettit.	Aug. 30, '61	To 2d Lt., May 7, '62; resigned Dec. 31, '62.
John Witmoyer.	Sep. 6, '61	To 2d Lt., May 16, '65; not must.; wounded at Bull Run and Antietam; m. o. with Co.
Sergeants.		
Geo. W. Hain.	Aug. 30, '61	To Sgt., May 1, '65; wounded in Wilderness; m. o. with Co.
Jno. K. Wesner.	Aug. 30, '61	To Sgt., May 1, '65; wounded; m. o. with Co.
Reuben Drexle.	Aug. 23, '61	To Sgt, June 15, '65; wounded in Wilderness; m. o. with Co.
Henry J. Rutz.	Aug. 24, '61	Wounded at Laurel Hill; absent in hosp. at m. o.
Benner Humma.	Sep. 13, '61	Wounded at Antietam; disch., date unknown.
Samuel Husk.	Aug. 20, '61	Disch. Oct. '62.
Wm. M. Krick.	Sep. 12, '61	Wounded at Antietam; disch., date unknown.
Johnston Flack.	Sep. 27, '61	Wounded at Gettysburg; to. V. R. Corps, Nov. 15, '63.
Thos. R. Hartman.	Aug. 30, '61	Died of wounds, June 6, '65; buried at Arlington Nat. Cem.
Jas. M. Thompson.	Sep. 11, '61	Died Nov. 16, '62, of wounds rec'd at Antietam.

Rank.	Mustered In.	Record.
Corporals.		
Isaac Fields.	Aug. 30, '61	To Corp., May 1, '65; m. o. with Co.
Jos. R. Smith.	Aug. 30, '61	To Corp., May 1, '65; wounded at Rappahannock, Aug. 22, '62; m. o. with Co.
E. D. Kerst.	Aug. 30, '61	To Quartermaster-Sgt., Feb. 28, '65.
Joel R. Krick.	Aug. 30, '61	To Co. F.
Musicians.		
Mayberry Dautrich.	Aug. 30, '61	Prisoner at Gettysburg; m. o. with Co.
Danl. Kissinger.	Aug. 30, '61	Wounded at Antietam; prisoner at Gettysburg; m. o. with Co.
L. J. Spohn.	. . . . . .	No record.
Jno. Bell.	Oct. 2, '61	Disch. May 8, '63.
Privates.		
Abel, Emanuel.	Sep. 17, '61	Disch. Sep. 17, '64, exp. of term.
Albright, Jno.	Sep. 19, '61	Disch. Sep. 19, '64, exp. of term.
Bechtel, Jno. A.	Aug. 30, '61	Wounded at Antietam; absent at m. o.
Bord, J. C.	Aug. 31, '61	Disch., date unknown.
Boardy, G. A.	Aug. 27, '61	Deserted Sep. 6, '62.
Bland, R.	Sep. 11, '61	Disch. Jan. 20, '62.
Breidegam, Daniel.	Aug. 30, '61	Wounded at Gettysburg; disch. May 14, '65, for wounds.
Bixenstine, Wm.	Sep. 10, '61	Wounded at Gettysburg; disch. Sep. 10, '64, exp. of term.
Boyer, Aaron S.	Aug. 30, '61	Disch. Mar. 4, '63.
Bosler, Geo.	Feb. 26, '64	Wounded at Spottsylvania; disch June 14, '65.
Bosler, Henry.	Aug. 30, '61	Disch. Aug. 30, '64, exp. of term.
Burkhart, Cyrus.	Aug. 30, '61	Transf., date unknown.
Brittain, Jno. H.	Oct. 3, '61	Killed at Antietam; buried in Chas. Evans Cem., Reading.
Becker, Jos.	Mar. 1, '64	Died June 15, '64, of wounds; buried in Wilderness Cem.
Carey, Wm.	Sep. 10, '61	Prisoner from Aug. 19, '64, to Feb. 24, '65; disch. May 15, '65.
Call, Henry W.	Sep. 13, '61	Disch. Aug. 30, '62.
Diehm, Charles F.	Aug. 30, '61	Disch. Feb. 27, '63.
Dorsey, D.	Apr. 23, '64	M. o. with Co.
Dautrich, Alfred.	Aug. 23, '61	Captured at Bull Run; disch. for wounds, May 14, '65.
Debord, J.	Aug. 30, '61	Deserted Aug. 23, '62.
Eckert, Daniel.	Sep. 13, '61	M. o. with Co.
Eddinger, Harrison.	Sep. 4, '61	Disch. Sep. 14, '64, exp. of term.
Ely, D. E.	Sep. 13, '61	Disch. Feb. 12, '63.
Fabian, J.	Aug. 30, '61	Disch., date unknown.
Frill, Henry.	Sep. 4, '61	Disch., date unknown.

Rank.	Mustered In.	Record.
Privates.		
Ferner, Fred.	Sep. 11, '61	Killed at Bull Run.
Green, Wm.	. . . . . .	Disch. May 4, '63.
Goodheart, Joel R.	Sep. 26, '61	Disch. Sep. 29, '62.
Gorman, Israel K.	Sep. 13, '61	Disch. Sep. 13, '64, exp. of term.
Good, Celestine.	Sep. 4, '61	Captured at Gettysburg; disch. Sep. 4, '64, exp. of term.
Hutchinson, Wm.	Sep. 10, '61	Wounded and prisoner at Bull Run; prisoner from Aug. 19, '64, to Feb. 23, '65; disch. Mar. 31, '65, exp. of term.
Hafer, Wm.	Sep. 4, '61	Died of wounds rec'd in battle.
Hefner, Jno.	Mar. 22, '64	Died June 17, '64.
Hawk, Chas.	Aug. 30, '61	Died Feb. 27, '62; buried in Alexandria Cem., grave 26.
Hinnershitz, James H.	Sep. 5, '61	Killed at Antietam; buried in Alsace Cem., Reading.
Humma, Lewis.	Sep. 12, '61	Died Jan. 20, '63, of wounds rec'd at Bull Run; buried in Alexandria Cem., grave 696.
Holt, Edward.	Sep. 4, '61	Disch. May 16, '62.
Heller, Franklin.	Sep. 11, '61	Captured at Fredericksburg; disch. Sep. 10, '64, exp. of term.
High, Jas. A.	Sep. 11, '61	Transf. to U. S. A.
Harbold, H. A.	Aug. 30, '61	Wounded at Fredericksburg; to V. R. Corps, Nov., '63.
Herman, Jno. F.	Sep. 12, '61	Wounded in Wilderness; to V. R. Corps.
Hepp, H. R.	Nov. 23, '61	Deserted April 26, '62.
Hoffman, J.	Dec. 7, '61	Deserted April 22, '62.
Hoffman, J. W.	Sep. 11, '61	To Co. A.
Koch, Orlando.	Sep. 10, '61	To V. R. Corps, Sep. 17, '63.
Krebs, Jno.	Sep. 3, '61	Killed at Bull Run.
Lawrence, Wm.	Sep. 11, '61	Disch. May 19, '62.
Myers, Joseph.	Sep. 3, '61	Wounded at Antietam; killed at Spottsylvania; buried in Fredericksburg Cem., grave 187.
Miller, David.	Sep. 10, '61	Disch. Mar. 2, '63.
McCombs, Thos.	Sep. 4, '61	Disch. May 16, '62.
McClellan, Alex.	Sep. 4, '61	Disch. June 14, '65.
McChaliker, David.	Dec. 9, '61	Disch. Nov. 19, '62.
McClellan, Jas.	Mar. 1, '64	To V. R. Corps.
Parker, Erastus.	Aug. 30, '61	M. o. with Co.
Peoples, Jas.	Aug. 30, '61	Wounded at Gettysburg; disch. Sep. 21, '64.
Reigel, Lewis.	Aug. 30, '61	Disch. May 20, '63, for wounds.
Ruhl, Jno.	Sep. 12, '61	Wounded at Gettysburg; to V. R. Corps, March 16, '64.
Ringler, Mark.	Sep. 12, '61	Killed at Bull Run.

Rank.	Mustered In.	Record.
Privates.		
Reigel, Jonathan.	Aug. 30, '61	Wounded Aug. 22, '62; died June 26, '64, of wounds; buried at Arlington Cem.
Roth, Henry.	Aug. 24, '61	Wounded at Gettysburg; killed June 18, '64, at Petersburg.
Rhoads, Henry.	Aug. 30, '61	Wounded at Gettysburg; killed June 18, '64, at Petersburg.
Rightmeyer, W.	Sep. 4, '61	Deserted Aug. 31, '62.
Swavely, Matt.	Feb. 25, '64	Wounded; disch. July 3, '65.
Swavely, Frank.	Sep. 13, '61	Captured at Gettysburg and exchanged; captured; killed at Salisbury, Jan. 12, '65.
Simons, Robert.	Aug. 30, '61	Killed at Gettysburg.
Shaw, Enoch.	Sep. 10, '61	Captured and died at Salisbury, Feb. 8, '65.
Shule, And.	Aug. 30, '61	Disch. May 6, '62.
Staunton, Jno.	Sep. 4, '61	Disch. May 16, '62.
Sailor, Jos.	Sep. 4, '61	Disch. Dec. 2, '62.
Seiders, W. W.	Sep. 4, '61	Disch. Jan. 20, '63.
Stine, Jno.	Aug. 30, '61	Disch. Jan. 20, '63.
Spicker, Wm.	Sep. 4, '61	Disch. Sep. 4, '64, exp. of term.
Springer, Jos.	Oct. 1, '61	To V. R. Corps, Sep. 29, '63.
Tinney, Wm.	Oct. 1, '61	Disch. Oct. 14, '62.
Wise, William A.	Mar 16, '64	To V. R. Corps, Oct. 17, '64.
Whitman, Adam B.	Sep. 10, '61	Died Dec. 18, '62, of wounds rec'd at Fredericksburg.
Weiser, Jonathan.	Aug. 27, '61	Died May 12, '64, of wounds rec'd at Spottsylvania; buried in Fredericksburg Cem., grave 56.
Wolf, Peter.	Aug. 27, '61	Died June 20, '64, of wounds rec'd at Petersburg.
Youse, G. D.	Aug. 30, '61	Deserted Aug. 31, '62.

Company H, Recruits.

Rank.	Mustered In.	Record.
Corporals.		
J. P. Clury.	Aug. 12, '64	Substitute; m. o. with Co.
G. Lape.	Sep. 24, '64	Substitute; m. o. with Co.
J. F. Sprang.	Oct. 5, '64	Substitute; m. o. with Co.
Privates.		
Flanders, A. H.	Oct. 5, '64	Drafted; prisoner, Mar. 31, '65; disch. May 27, '65.
Gloak, G.	Aug. 15, '64	Substitute; m. o. with Co.

Rank.	Mustered In.	Record.
Privates.		
Hockrine, J.	Sep. 27, '64	Substitute; disch. June 10, '65.
Heinrich, C.	Sep. 27, '64	Substitute; disch. June 10, '65.
Hartman, W.	Sep. 26, '64	Substitute; disch. June 7, '65.
Kuhn, C.	Oct. 25, '64	Substitute; m. o. with Co.
Maloney, J.	Oct. 6, '64	Substitute; m. o. with Co.
Oney, C. B.	Sep. 22, '64	Substitute; disch. June 10, '65.
Piper, J.	July 11, '64	Drafted; absent at m. o.
Rudy, J.	Oct. 3, '64	Substitute; disch. May 26, '65.
Roberts, W.	Oct. 6, '64	Drafted; disch. May 12, '65.
Steinbach, H.	Oct. 5, '64	Substitute; m. o. with Co.
Scharff, J.	Aug. 30, '64	Substitute; disch. June 10, '65.
Umbacher, B.	Sep. 25, '64	Substitute; disch. June 10, '65.
Volkir, Michael.	Sep. 9, '64	Substitute; died Feb. 6, '65, of wounds.
Wonderlick, C.	Sep. 30, '64	Substitute; disch. June 10, '65.
Wise, G.	Sep. 30, '64	Substitute; disch. June 10, '65.

Company I, Recruited in Philadelphia.

Rank.	Mustered In.	Record.
Captains.		
J. Reeside White.	Sep. 23, '61	Resigned June 17, '62.
Jacob S. Stretch.	Sep. 23, '61	From 1st Lt., June 17, '62; wounded at Bull Run; resigned Nov. 11, '62.
Wm. J. Harkisheimer.	Sep. 23, '61	From 2d to 1st Lt., June 17, '62; Capt., Nov. 11, '62; injured in groin at battle of Fredericksburg; resigned Jan. 1, '63; Brevet Maj., July, '65.
Geo. L. Schell.	Sep. 24, '61	To 2d Lt., June 17, '62; 1st Lt., Nov. 11, '62; Capt., Jan. 1, '63; captured at Gettysburg, and prisoner until Mar., '65; disch. April 28, '65.
Henry T. Copestick.	Oct. 4, '61	From 1st Sgt. to Capt., June 14, '65; not must.; captured at Spottsylvania; m. o. with Co.
First Lieutenants.		
Chas. W. Nunneville.	Sep. 19, '61	To 1st Lt., Jan. 1, '63; disch., Oct. 20, '64, exp. of term.
Harry O'Niel.	Aug. 29, '61	From Quartermaster Sgt., Jan. 2, '65; disch. for wounds, June 14, '65.
Henry D. Evans.	Sep. 17, '61	To 1st Lt., June 13, '65; not must.; wounded at Laurel Hill; m. o. with Co.

Rank.	Mustered In.	Record.
Second Lieutenants.		
Chas. Murtha.	Sep. 21, '61	To 2d Lt., Nov. 11, '62; disch. Feb. 18, '63.
Eldridge E. Levan.	Sep. 13, '61	To 2d Lt., April 10, '64; dis. Jan. 31, '65.
Jas. K. Shelcup.	Sep. 21, '61	To 2d Lt., June 13, '65; not must.; captured at Gettysburg; wounded at Spottsylvania; m. o. with Co.
Sergeants.		
Morris Robbins.	Sep. 21, '61	Captured on Weldon R. R., Aug. 19, '64, and prisoner until Feb. 28, '65; disch. June 14, '65.
Saml. C. Fusman.	Sep. 18, '61	Wounded at Spottsylvania; m. o. with Co.
Reuben B. Sanders.	Sep. 21, '61	To Sgt., June 14, '65; wounded at Bull Run; captured at Gettysburg; m. o. with Co.
Jno. Nuskey.	Aug. 28, '61	To V. R. Corps, Mar. 7, '64.
Corporals.		
Wm. W. Perkenpine.	Sep. 20, '61	To Corp., June 1, '65; m. o. with Co.
Wm. A. Boyd.	Sep. 19, '61	Wounded at Antietam and Hatcher's Run; captured at Gettysburg; in hosp. at m. o.
Geo. W. Mulfray.	Sep. 19, '61	Disch. Sep. 1, '62.
David Gillmore.	Sep. 24, '61	Regimental Mail Carrier; disch. Mar. 7, '64.
Thos. H. Anderson.	Sep. 23, '61	Wounded at Laurel Hill and Boydton plank road; disch. June 16, '65.
Hugh Rutherford.	Sep. 19, '61	Disch. Oct. 15, '64, exp. of term.
Nathan S. Auble.	Jan. 1, '62	Captured at Gettysburg; wounded at Spottsylvania; disch. June 13, '65.
Robert Jones.	Dec. 13, '61	Killed at Bull Run.
William Rose.	Sep. 17, '61	Killed at Fredericksburg.
Musicians.		
Jno. F. Keller.	Jan. 1, '62	To Principal Musician, Feb. 28, '65.
Wm. P. Hand.	Sep. 23, '61	Captured at Gettysburg; m. o. with Co.
Jno. H. Snyder.	Sep. 12, '61	Deserted Aug. 30, '62.
Privates.		
Armstrong, Thos.	Sep. 12, '61	Disch. Dec. 4, '62.
Arnot, David Gail.	Sep. 17, '61	Killed at Spottsylvania.
Boyer, Joseph.	Sep. 17, '61	Killed at Fredericksburg.
Baurmaster, H.	Sep. 21, '61	Disch. Oct. 3, '62.
Beiderman, Wm. B.	Oct. 4, '61	Disch. Nov. 30, '62.
Bagley, Wm. H.	Sep. 19, '61	Disch. Feb. 11, '63.
Barrett, Wm. P.	Feb. 15, '64	Disch. June 15, '65.
Conlogue, Patrick.	Oct. 4, '61	Killed at Antietam.

Rank.	Mustered In.	Record.
Privates.		
Campbell, Jno.	Sep. 23, '61	Disch. Nov. 1, '62.
Carter, Jno.	Sep. 18, '61	Disch. June 12, '63.
Cowan, Gilbert.	Sep. 19, '61	Wounded at Bull Run; disch. Feb. 11, '63.
Dunbar, Jno.	Sep. 18, '61	Disch. Dec. 25, '62.
Durfer, H. C.	Sep. 19, '61	To Co. K, Feb. 6, '64.
Drexler, David.	Sep. 10, '61	Captured at Bull Run; died at Philadelphia, Sep. 5, '64.
Danfield, Wm. A.	Sep. 18, '61	Disch. June 27, '67, to date June 30, '65.
Foley, Jno.	Sep. 18, '61	Soldier in War of 1812-15; disch. Mar. 13, '63.
Garwood, Thos.	Sep. 19, '61	Disch. Mar. 13, '63.
Harland, David.	Aug. 28, '61	Killed at Gettysburg, July 3, '63.
Hilson, Chas.	Sep. 23, '61	Died at Alexandria, Dec. 3, '62; buried in Alexandria Nat. Cem., grave 558.
Hand, Jos. H.	Aug. 28, '61	To V. R. Corps, Feb. 11, '64.
Hart, Jno.	Sep. 19, '61	Captured at Gettysburg; to V. R. Corps, Mar. 9, '64.
Jefferies, Samuel J.	Oct. 1, '61	Disch. Dec. 12, '62.
Johnston, Wm.	Sep. 19, '61	Deserted June 24, '62.
Keyser, Jno.	Mar. 18, '62	Died at Washington, June 23, '62.
Link, Jno.	Aug. 28, '61	Wounded at Antietam; killed at Gettysburg, July 3, '63.
Levan, Edw. F.	Sep. 14, '61	Disch. Nov. 18, '61.
Lehman, Daniel J.	Sep. 20, '61	Disch. June 18, '62.
Lewis, Geo. Connor.	Sep. 22, '61	Died at Alexandria, Jan. 23, '63; buried in Lafayette Cem., Philadelphia.
Learmont, And.	Sep. 24, '61	Wounded at Antietam; disch. April 20, '63.
Miller, Jas. S.	Sep. 19, '61	Captured on Weldon R. R.; absent at m. o.
Miller, Chas. R.	Sep. 19, '61	Wounded at Bull Run; disch. Feb. 16, '63.
Moore, Geo. W.	Sep. 23, '61	Disch. Nov. 16, '61.
Manypenny, Lewis R.	Sep. 17, '61	Disch. Nov. 29, '62, for wounds rec'd at Antietam.
Moran, Barnet.	Sep. 21, '61	Leg accidentally broken; disch. May 21, '62.
MacNichol, Summerfield J.	Sep. 20, '61	Killed at Antietam.
McGinley, Joseph E.	Sep. 14, '61	Absent in hosp. at m. o.
McCleary, George R. C.	Sep. 18, '61	Wounded at Antietam; disch. Feb. 28, '63.
McCoy, Chas. J.	Sep. 19, '61	Wounded at Bull Run; disch. Mar. 14, '63.
McLearn, Wm.	Sep. 18, '61	To V. R. Corps, April 28, '64.
McCrudden, Thos.	Feb. 22, '64	Wounded at Spottsylvania; in hosp. at m. o.

Rank.	Mustered In.	Record.
Privates.		
McCormick, John.	Sep. 21, '61	Captured on Weldon R. R.; disch. Aug. 14, '65.
Nette, Chas.	Sep. 24, '61	Killed at Spottsylvania, May 10, '64; buried in Nat. Cem., Fredericksburg, grave 48.
Nunneville, Edward D.	Sep. 19, '61	Regimental Armorer; disch. Sep. 19, '64, exp. of term.
Nunneville, George W.	Sep. 19, '61	Disch. June 12, '62.
Newell, Daniel.	Oct. 4, '61	Disch. Feb. 11, '63.
Neill, Thos. B.	Sep. —, '61	Wounded at Laurel Hill; disch. June 15, '65.
Perara, Jas.	Aug. 28, '61	Disch. Aug. 28, '64, in field before Petersburg, exp. of term.
Rutherford, Jos.	Sep. 18, '61	Killed at Bull Run.
Rutherford, Jno. C.	Sep. 18, '61	Wounded at Antietam; disch. Feb. 20, '63.
Riley, Clem. S.	Sep. 10, '61	Disch. Nov. 3, '62.
Richardson, Jas. H.	Sep. 19, '61	Wounded at Spottsylvania; disch. June 13, '65.
Renz, Dietrich.	Sep. 27, '64	Died Nov. 30, '64; buried in Poplar Grove Cem., grave 22.
Sturges, Edw.	Sep. 28, '61	Died at Frederick, July 24, '63.
Stretch, G. O.	Sep. 7, '61	Wounded at Laurel Hill; in hosp. at m. o.
Stretch, Wm. W.	Apr. 1, '62	Wounded at Fredericksburg; disch. April 22, '65, exp. of term.
Shaw, Frank.	Sep. 17, '61	Disch. June 10, '63.
Truett, Wm.	Sep. 17, '61	Captured at Gettysburg; to Co. G., Feb. 6, '64.
Tyson, Jesse.	Sep. 19, '61	Killed at Antietam; buried in Nat. Cem., grave 75.
Thomas, Samuel.	Sep. 20, '61	Died at Alexandria, July 27, '64; buried in Alexandria Nat. Cem., grave 2463.
Vautier, Jno. D.	Sep. 18, '61	Wounded at Cold Harbor, June 3, '64; disch. Sep. 19, '64, in field before Petersburg, exp. of term.
Vansant, Jas.	Aug. 1, '62	Captured at Gettysburg; deserted Sep. 18, '63.
Wright, Jas. M.	Sep. 23, '61	Disch. Aug. 4, '62.
White, Nathan S.	Sep. 18, '61	Wounded at Antietam; killed at Fredericksburg.

Company I, Recruits.

Rank.	Mustered In.	Record.
Privates.		
Baker, Wm.	Sep. 20, '64	Substitute; disch. June 10, '65.
Boyer, J.	Sep. 21, '64	Drafted; disch. June 23. '65.
Baush, J.	Aug. 11, '64	Substitute; disch. July 5, '65.
Dougherty, J.	Jan. 26, '65	Wounded at Five Forks; disch. June 10, '65.
Devlin, L.	Sep. 5, '64	Substitute; disch. June 10, '65.
Foil, J.	Mar. 27, '65	Drafted; died May 30, '65.
Fox, J.	Aug. 29, '64	Substitute; disch. June 10, '65.
Gleeson, W.	Sep. 20, '64	Substitute; disch. June 10, '65.
Henderson, B.	Sep. 21, '64	Drafted; disch. June 10, '65.
Hamil, J	Sep. 5, '64	Substitute; disch. June 10, '65.
Herald, T.	Aug. 22, '64	Substitute; disch. June 15, '65.
Irwin, W.	Sep. 21, '64	Drafted; disch. June 10, '65.
Jordan, J.	Sep. 22, '64	Drafted; disch. Feb. 6, '65.
Kerin, T.	Sep. 22, '64	Drafted; wounded Feb. 6, '65; disch. June 30, '65.
Laddons, W.	Aug. 20, '64	Substitute; m. o. with Co.
Monroe, Francis.	Oct. 4, '64	Substitute; killed Feb. 7, '65.
Monroe, F.	Oct. 4, '64	Substitute; m. o. with Co.
Miller, J.	Sep. 27, '64	Drafted; disch. June 10, '65.
McEntyre, E.	Oct. 4, '64	Substitute; sick at m. o.
McNamara, J.	Sep. 21, '64	Drafted; disch. June 10, '65.
Nelson, J.	Sep. 24, '64	Drafted; disch. June 10, '65.
Roberts, R.	Aug. 30, '64	Substitute; m. o. with Co.
Vallaly, J.	Oct. 5, '64	Substitute; m. o. with Co.
Wilcox, B.	Aug. 21, '64	Substitute; prisoner from Dec. 11, '64, to Feb. 5, 65; disch. June 15, '65.

Company K, Recruited in Philadelphia.

Rank.	Mustered In.	Record.
Captains.		
Wm. F. Powell.	Oct. 6, '61	Resigned June 16, '62.
Syl. S. Bookhammer.	Oct. 5, '61	To Capt., June 17, '62; wounded at Bull Run; disch. Nov. 11, '62.
Edmund Y. Patterson.	Oct. 5, '61	To Capt., Nov. 11, '62; wounded at Bull Run; disch. Feb. 13, '65.
Sylvester H. Martin.	Sep. 14, '61	To 2d Lt., Nov. 11, '62; 1st Lt., Feb. 25, '63; Capt., Jan. 30, '65; not must.; wounded at Antietam; disch. June 9, '65, for wounds rec'd at Hatcher's Run; awarded a Medal of Honor by War Dept. for bravery on Weldon R. R., Aug., '64.

Rank.	Mustered In.	Record.
Captains.		
Chas. McKnight.	Sep. 30, '61	To 1st Lt., June 9, '65; Capt., June 14, '65; not must.; wounded at Bull Run; m. o. with Co.
First Lieutenants.		
Robert L. Carns.	Aug. 28, '61	To 2d Lt., June 17, '62; 1st Lt., Nov. 11, '62; resigned Feb. 2, '63.
Daniel Linsenbigler.	Sep. 30, '61	To 1st Lt., June 14, '65; not must.; m. o. with Co.
Second Lieutenants.		
Jno. O. Hanlon.	Aug. 23, '61	To 2d Lt., May 1, '63; dis. July 22, '64.
Chas. C. Lambert.	Oct. 1, '61	To 2d Lt., June 14, '65; not must.; m. o. with Co.
Sergeants.		
Cyrus S. Detre.	Oct. 1, '61	To Adj., Dec. 14, '62. (See Field and Staff.)
Harry O'Niel.	Aug. 29, '61	Captured at Gettysburg; to Quartermaster Sgt. Nov. 1, '64.
Jas. Peoples.	Sep. 3, '61	To Sgt., June 9, '65; m. o. with Co.
Chas. H. Marple.	Sep. 20, '61	To Sgt., June 9, '65; captured at Gettysburg; m. o. with Co.
Jos. Sergeant.	Sep. 18, '61	Wounded at Antietam, ball remaining in left breast, and at Spottsylvania; m. o. June 30, '65.
Theo. W. Griffin.	Sep. 14, '61	Disch. Sep. 9, '62.
Uriah Fraley.	Sep. 23, '61	Wounded at Gettysburg, ball through left lung; disch. Nov. 21, '63.
Daniel Devine.	Sep. 18, '61	Disch. June 10, '65.
Benj. B. Pugh.	Sep. 14, '61	Died at Philadelphia, Sep. 28, '63.
Albert Van Dyke.	Aug. 27, '61	Killed at Bull Run.
Corporals.		
Daniel Kinsley.	Aug. 29, '61	Wounded May 3, '63; m. o. with Co.
Hugh McMullin.	Sep. 11, '61	Wounded June 3, '64; m. o. with Co.
David Miller.	Sep. 14, '61	Wounded at Gettysburg; m. o. with Co.
Robt. Wallace.	Sep. 2, '61	Wounded at Gettysburg; m. o. with Co.
John McKee.	Sep. 28, '61	Wounded at Spottsylvania; disch. June 1, '65.
Gideon Moyer.	Oct. 2, '61	Disch. Oct. 2, '64, exp. of term.
Arch. Campbell.	Sep. 23, '61	Disch. June 28, '63.
Alex. Peoples.	Sep. 27, '61	Died at Annapolis, Oct. 21, '64.
G. W. Chatham.	Sep. 14, '61	Deserted Dec. 13, '62.
Jno. Valentine.	Feb. 24, '64	Wounded at Cold Harbor, June 3, '64; m. o. with Co.
W. Boocock Threapleton.	Mar. 14, '64	Wounded at Spottsylvania; m. o. with Co.
Lorenzo F. Wilson.	Aug. 29, '61	Color Corp.; wounded at Antietam, with loss of left leg; disch. Jan. 16, '63.

Rank.	Mustered In.	Record.
Corporals.		
Davison Young.	Mar. 15, '64	To Corp., June 9, '65; m. o. with Co.
Samuel Sherlock.	Dec. 12, '61	Wounded at Fredericksburg; disch., date unknown.
Musicians.		
E. A. Winnemore.	Sep. 2, '61	Captured at Gettysburg; disch. Jan. 12, '65.
Wilson Bell.	Oct. 2, '61	Disch. Jan. 19, '63.
Geo. W. Gilligan.	Feb. 6, '65	M. o. with Co.
Samuel Martin.	Feb. 20, '64	Absent on furlough at m. o.
Privates.		
Ayers, Robert B.	Sep. 14, '61	Disch. May 28, '62.
Boocock, Jas. L.	Mar. 10, '64	M. o. with Co.
Burbridge, Chas.	Oct. 1, '61	Wounded at Spottsylvania; disch., date unknown.
Burroughs, Thos. L.	Oct. 3, '61	Disch. Jan. 23, '65.
Clickett, Patrick.	Aug. 23, '61	Wounded in Wilderness and injured by falling tree on Weldon R. R.; m. o. with Co.
Campbell, Jas. S.	Feb. 26, '64	Wounded Mar. 31, '65; disch. June 3, '65.
Cahall, John.	Sep. 14, '61	Wounded at Antietam; disch. Mar. 12, '63.
Callahan, D. F.	Aug. 23, '61	Disch. Feb. 19, '63, captured at Bull Run.
Clark, Wm. P.	Sep. 30, '61	Wounded at Antietam; disch. Sep. 30, '64, exp. of term.
Cooper, Jno.	Oct. 20, '61	Disch. Dec. 9, '62.
Conover, Michael.	Sep. 28, '61	Wounded at Antietam and Gettysburg; disch. Dec. 4, '64, exp. of term.
Corn, John.	Nov. 30, '61	Died Aug. 9, '63, of wounds rec'd at Gettysburg; buried at Mount Moriah, Philadelphia.
Devine, Edw.	Oct. 9, '61	Disch. Nov. 11, '62.
Durfer, Henry C.	Sep. 19, '61	From Co. I, Feb. 6, '64; prisoner from Aug. 19, '64, to April, '65; disch. June 15, '65.
Dougherty, William.	Sep. 30, '61	Disch. Nov. 21, '62.
Devine, Neal.	Sep. 13, '62	Captured at Gettysburg; wounded in Wilderness; disch. June 10, '65.
Duswald, J. J.	Oct. 4, '61	Wounded at Antietam; disch. Mar. 6, '63.
Doyle, Jas.	Sep. 27, '61	Missing in action, Aug. 19, '64.
Flemming, Jno.	Sep. 18, '62	Wounded at Fredericksburg; disch. Mar. 7, '64.
Finn, Patrick.	Sep. 12, '61	Disch. June 8, '62.
Finley, Wm. Jno.	Sep. 18, '61	Wounded June 18, '64; Disch. June 10, '65.

Rank.	Mustered In.	Record.
Privates.		
Gracey, Thomas.	Oct. 1, '61	Disch. June 8, '62.
Grow, William B.	Sep. 25, '61	Disch. July 17, '62.
Gallagher, William.	Oct. 14, '61	Disch. on writ of *habeas corpus*, Jan. 4, '63.
Gallagher, James.	Sep. 17, '61	Wounded at Gettysburg; transf. to V. R. Corps, Feb. 24, '64.
Groom, E. A.	Sep. 14, '61	Deserted Aug. 29, '62.
Heist, Geo. W.	Sep. 26, '61	Wounded at Antietam; absent sick at m. o.
Hutchinson, Isaac.	Sep. 28, '61	Disch. May 30, '65, exp. of term.
Hoagland, Jos.	Oct. 2, '61	Disch. July 30, '62.
Hicken, Wash.	Oct. 1, '61	Disch. Oct. 29, '62.
Hackett, Wm. W.	Sep. 28, '61	Wounded at Antietam; disch. Feb. 16, '63.
Hanaman, Jos. W.	Sep. 30, '61	Disch. Dec. 7, '64, exp. of term.
Hallman, Thos.	Sep. 27, '61	Died at Washington, Sep., '62.
Hardinger, Simon.	Oct. 2, '61	Died at Alexandria, Sep. 2, '62, of wounds rec'd at Bull Run.
Kombs, E.	Sep. 25, '61	Deserted Aug. 1, '62.
Kibler, Jno.	Sep. 12, '61	Deserted Sep. 14, '62.
Miller, Jno.	Sep. 18, '62	Disch. June 10, '65.
Miller, Adolph.	Oct. 3, '61	Disch. Dec. 20, '62.
Miller, Robt.	Sep. 27, '61	Disch. Feb. 4, '63.
Mills, Saml.	Aug. 23, '61	Disch. June 14, '63.
McKee, Patrick.	Sep. 12, '61	Disch. June 8, '62.
McElwee, Jno.	Sep. 14, '61	Disch. Dec. 24, '62.
McGlinchey, T.	Sep. 25, '61	Deserted Sep. 14, '62.
Newcomb, Isaac.	Sep. 20, '61	Disch. July 30, '62.
Pope, John.	Aug. 23, '61	Disch. Oct. 8, '62; re-enlisted Feb. 20, '64; to V. R. Corps, Jan. 9, '65; disch. Oct. 2, '65.
Patterson, W. H.	Sep. 14, '61	Disch. Dec. 10, '62.
Risley, Thomas.	Oct. 1, '61	Disch. July 3, '62.
Raider, Wm.	Oct. 2, '61	Killed at Spottsylvania.
Stork, Fred.	Sep. 14, '61	M. o. with Co.
Small, Chas.	Mar. 1, '64	Wounded at Five Forks; m. o. with Co.
Sickles, Jno. W.	Sep. 24, '61	Disch. Aug. 6, '62.
Sinkinson, R.	Sep. 25, '61	Disch. Sep., '62.
Seads, Jacob M.	Sep. 29, '61	Disch. Oct. 25, '62.
Stauffer, Henry K.	Oct. 3, '61	Disch. Dec. 9, '62.
Winnemore, Wm.	Sep. 2, '61	Disch. July 2, '62; re-enlisted, and m. o. with Co.
Walton, Jesse.	Oct. 1, '61	Deserted June 19, '63.
Whitehouse, Charles.	Sep. 23, '61	Wounded at Bethesda Church; m. o. with Co.

Company K, Recruits.

Rank.	Mustered In.	Record.
Privates.		
Anderson, J.	Sep. 1, '64	Substitute; disch. June 10, '65.
Crispin, W.	Sep. 8, '64	Substitute; wounded at Five Forks; in hosp. at m. o.
Egner, P.	Jan. 20, '65	Substitute; m. o. with Co.
Fowler, D. S.	Aug. 5, '64	Substitute; disch. June 10, '65.
Hill, J. H.	Aug. 29, '64	Substitute; disch. June 10, '65.
Hopps, J.	Sep. 7, '64	Substitute; wounded Mar. 31, '65; disch. June 2, '65.
Patterson, H.	Aug. 2, '64	Substitute; disch. June 10, '65.
Pease, C. A.	Sep. 29, '64	Substitute; disch. June 10, '65.
Rohn, A. S.	Sep. 30, '64	Substitute; disch. June 10, '65.
Sweeney, P.	Sep. 14, '64	Substitute; disch. June 19, '65.
Simons, E.	Sep. 22, '64	Substitute; disch. June 10, '65.
Shively, G. W.	Sep. 27, '64	Substitute; disch. June 10, '65.
Wheeler, B.	Aug. 13, '64	Substitute; m. o. with Co.

Roll of Drafted Men and Substitutes assigned to the Regiment after the Surrender.

COMPANY A.—All mustered in after February 25, 1865, some after April 1. *Corporals,* C. Davis, S. Griffith, F. Esties, W. Clark. *Privates,* J. H. Albright, C. Ackerman, J. Berkleypile, W. E. Beatty, J. L. Berkley, A. B. Barnet, P. Coleman, S. Dempsey, G. Eshelman, A. Fredline, J. Frech, H. Gardiner, P. Johnson, W. Kline, C. Kaylor, J. Lohr, W. L. Livingstone, A. Lantz, J. Lake, Z. T. Lohr, D. B. Miller, J. Mangus, P. Olmstead, S. T. Riffle, J. Riffle, G. Raymond, J. J. Rhoades, J. Roddy, I. Rock, B. Stuff, W. H. Swank, P. Spicher, J. Stahl, E. Seece, S. Swoyer, W. F. Shaum, P. K. Thomas, Samuel Varner, J. Walters, J. Witt, C. Wagner, P. H. Walters, W. Wringle, F. Young.

COMPANY B.—All mustered in after March 8, 1865. *Sergeant,* Wm. Gillmore. *Corporals,* J. E. Applebaugh, J. H. Harris, B. Holland. *Privates,* J. Anderson, T. J. Albright, P. Belzer, F. Boquiel, W. Bruebaker, A. Burger, W. B. Coder, W. Carney, A. Dever, J. Esterline, W. Gates, T. German, G. Gonflow, H. Gross, G. Hoffman, S. Hickle, T. Higgins, W. Kamer, E. Kerzer, L. Leibecke, G. Mingle, C. Miller, A. J. Miller, N. Miller, J. Mair, N. Morris, W. Maffitt, H. Owen, H. Pretlove, R. Roseburgh, C. Risestetler, L. Ross, P. Roach, B. Roger, S. Sharoskey, J. Storks, W. H. Smith, A. Sohns, A. Smith, F. Walter, G. Wartz, J. Wagenhaght, G. Zeller.

COMPANY C.—All mustered in after February 24, 1865, except W. McFeeters (February 7). *Corporal*, J. Regan. *Privates*, O. Altman, J. Adams, B. F. Atkinson, J. Baldwin, B. B. Banford, J. Bryner, J. Brett, J. Corwin, J. Cook, W. Conelley, T. Conelley, W. Carey, A. Eddinger, R. Eisman, J. Evans, J. Freeling, W. H. Fuhr, V. D. Gibson, M. Golden, H. Greenway, E. M. Holt, M. Hope, F. Hall, E. Hardoin, W. Hood, M. Haley, H. Hines, J. Hines, J. Johnston, O. Jeffries, J. Keating, J. Lehman, I. Linn, P. Luce, E. Leonard, M. Lavin, P. Lenheady, P. Mooney, W. J. Major, R. McAdams, W. McFeeters, A. McAllister, J. Mez, M. W. Oles, J. Reilley, P. A. Sherry, J. Scanlon, J. Sullivan, W. Sutton, G. Underwood, D. L. Wonsetler, T. Watson, J. West, J. Woodfield.

COMPANY D.—All mustered in after March 1, 1865. *Privates*, T. Brought. G. W. Burns, C. Baker, G. Buckley, G. Bath, W. Binger, J. Brown, M. Brown, N. Brice, G. Campbell, R. Ebach, F. Fisher, G. W. Fulton, J. F. Greasmyer, S. Gass, G. Garrison, J. Gibboney, L. Houser, G. Hollabaugh, P. Hammon, H. Hooper, C. Hummel, W. Hoffman, C. B. Himmelwright, E. Havercanne, J. Hoffman, J. A. Jones, A. Kelley, H. Lentz, M. Michamer, A. Maben, S. Mohney, E. McBride, J. L. Parson, M. Powell, W. Rowley, G. Reed, F. Sacarmen, J. Sproate, M. Shoape, W. Stimeley, S. Shearer, G. Sailor, C. P. Trapp, W. Warley, G. W. Wise, P. Whitezell, W. G. Wagner, J. White, P. Wagner.

COMPANY E.—All mustered in after February 28, 1865. *Corporals*, J. H. Horton, D. Gilbert. *Privates*, J. Abrams, T. Abrams, A. Alexander, J. Arthurs, H. Brailey, O. Brannen, W. J. Briggs, W. Baker, L. Betz, R. Cook, N. Callen, T. Caney, A. French, C. Falty, J. Good, A. Gready, W. Heckendon, L. Hart, J. Kavin, J. Kernan, W. King, G. Lind, J. Lyons, W. Lyons, S. Logan, M. Myers, D. W. Myers, J. Menzies, P. Madden, J. Mack, D. Murphy, G. W. Miller, A. G. Mallory, J. McCord, J. McGrail, E. McCarthy, G. Nixon, L. Olsen, J. O'Brien, G. A. Pierce, J. Rork, L. Reyer, I. L. L. Rickert, J. A. Schofield, G. Stomm, B. Spencer, B. Stake, F. Schlund, J. Schanks, G. Staples, J. Sullivan, C. H. Tubbs, F. Thomas, C. H. Wilson, R. W. Waltz, A. W. Worrell, G. Yocum.

COMPANY F.—All mustered in after March 3, 1865. *Corporals*, M. Howard, J. Barry. *Privates*, J. Anderson, J. Aregger, M. Allen, D. Bemisderfer, W. Boyer, J. Bones, P. J. Boland, W. J. Castater, R. C. Cooper, C. Cole, H. Donohue, E. Frantz, I. Grant, G. H. Gunn, F. Gross, H. Holla, P. Hinchberger, J. Haughey, J. A. Hoovan, H. F. Inch, M. Johnson, G. James, J. Jones, T. Johnson, G. Knoblock, C. Keiffe, A. Lutz, R. Lee, J. Lannigan, R. D. Laten, D. F. Lowry, J. Miller, M. Miller, C. Merkle, F. Murray, P. G. Nason, C. Ohlweiler, A. Oberg, C. Owens, S. Plank, W. Parrat, J. Phillips, M. K. Reese, F. Rhoades, W. O. Rich, T. Riddle, E. F. Sergeant, P. Schuster, J. H. Smith, W. Scheetz, E. Vanluven, P. Varmbrodt, F. Warnith, C. E. Whitney, A. Wood.

COMPANY G.—All mustered in after March 9, 1865. *Corporals*, D. Wagner, G. W. Sloan, G. Jenkins, T. Cargill, S. Serr, L. C. Washburn, A. F. Jones, A. Curtz. *Privates*, Jno. Allfather, Jos. Allfather, J. Arnold, P. Brogan, J. H. Boyd, D. Bowman, W. H. Burch, W. H. Barnhart, G. Barnickle, D. M. Beghley, S. Beltz, J. Cuchall, H. Dively, B. Drapp, W. H. Earhart, B. A. Fichtner, M. Hyatt, J. Hilkey, J. Havaline, J. Jackson, C. Kennell, J. Lape, J. Landis, S. W. Lewis, H. Loechel, D. Marstellar, J. Miller, M. Miller, G. Mull, Jno. Miller, J. Pugh, H. J. Phillips, A. W. Ringler, P. Rhoades, S. Robison, P. Spangler, W. Spangler, H. Snyder, J. Shank, H. Woy, C. Weckfus, P. Wagner, J. Wagner, H. Yon, J. Zeigler.

COMPANY H.—All mustered in after February 24, 1865. *Corporals*, J. H. Thompson, P. Heck, L. H. Ingram, J. R. Lord. *Privates*, J. Adams, B. Angstadt, G. Arnold, D. Bellman, H. Bridgeham, J. Brightbill, H. S. Burger, D. G. Brouse, A. Corzell, A. Clouser, J. Carl, D. Christman, A. Cox, J. Foust, E. Fisher, G. Flemming, D. Good, S. Houck, W. Hoyer, J. H. Hoffman, S. Hoffman, O. Hoffman, J. R. Hottenstine, D. D. Hunter, T. B. Heiser, D. K. Irey, W. Keller, H. Kerper, J. L. Kupp, H. Lingg, F. Master, J. Miller, A. Moore, E. Moore, B. Nemond, F. E. Potter, A. Peter, J. Rankins, M. Rose, N. Reimert, J. D. Richter, W. H. Schlipp, S. Stanley, G. W. Schull, A. Spencer, F. Soulliard, J. Stern, T. Searfoss, J. Ulrich (1st), J. Ulrich (2d), G. W. Wireman, A. Weikel, B. Youse.

COMPANY I.—L. Benary and L. Beecher were mustered in on February 7, all the remainder in March and April, 1865. *Corporals*, D. E. Baldwin, G. Rubright, J. Griffith, E. Shade, F. Ankeney, S. Ulch. *Privates*, A. Adams, L. Benary, P. Baker, A. Baldwin, C. K. Bittner, W. H. Bowman, L. Beecher, A. Consolar, J. Fredline, J. Filson, E. Finnegan, J. Gross, J. H. Huston, A. Harbst, J. Hoover, Jas. Hoover, J. Haltzhower, J. Hartman, J. Hurtz, C. Jurom, G. P. King, G. Kavis, F. Kuntz, H. C. Keicester, T. King, J. Keneddy, J. Middlestrader, P. Miller, A. Ohler, W. Ohler, J. A. Philipi, C. Queer, F. Sumstine, J. Simmerman, Jos. Schrocks, J. Shrock, H. Saylor, W. Stableford, G. Snyder, F. Sturn, J. Trimble, H. Williams, J. G. Williamson, C. Wymer.

COMPANY K.—All mustered in the last of February and during March and April, 1865. *Privates*, L. B. Adams, E. H. Butz, H. D. Brady, L. V. Corson, M. S. Cowles, H. Crownover, J. De Lair, P. Egner, D. W. Fogelman, H. A. Fogelman, J. Figgles, J. W. Foust, A. Fish, Jos. Firestone (died May 2, 1865), P. B. Gardiner, J. L. Gardiner, G. W. Gerhart, P. Gilbert, A. Gerhart, W. Hall, W. Henze, T. Henry, W. H. Jones, W. Kyper, J. W. King, N. S. Kregger, E. Lape, F. Lampman, T. La Hays, W. C. Miller, F. May, C. May, M. Montgomery, W. Meredith, L. Myers, A. Mare, J. McGrigger, W. S. Nail, W. O. Nelson, U. J. Pollard, W. Roth, A. Stair, J. M. Smith, F. H. Shenwood, S. S. Snyder, P. C. Vanhorn, J. Vanatten, L. Walker, H. W. Wheaton, A. Weyand, H. J. Whipkey, R. Williamson, J. Wall.

Tabular List of Casualties.

The number of deaths given in the accompanying table is believed to be correct, but the record of wounded is very imperfect ; many of the latter are not so marked, because of failure to obtain necessary data. However, the total is as near right as is possible under the circumstances. The "Official, but no data given" line and the "Captured" are included in the totals, but it is impossible to accurately apportion them among the companies. The total loss is 707.

The number of names on the rolls, including the recruits received while the regiment was on veteran furlough, is 965, and from these came nearly all the loss, indicating a percentage of about fifty-five in dead and wounded, with a total of about seventy per cent. from all causes, the remaining casualties being placed to the credit of the recruits who fell in for the last act. The band numbered twenty-one, and in the fall and winter of 1864, 227 recruits (making a total of 1213) were assigned to the regiment, but these sustained no great loss. After the last ditch was found, and "Johnny was marching home," 530 conscripts joined ; they, however, are not reckoned with our fighting men. Their names are given for reference only.

The writer regrets that the records of many respected comrades who were wounded are not noted here, and, consequently, will not have justice done them in this Roster.

	F. & S.		A.		B.		C.		D.		E.		F.		G.		H.		I.		K.		TOTAL.	
	K.	W.	K.	W.	K.	W.	K.	W.	K.	W.	K.	W.	K.	W.	K.	W.	K.	W.	K.	W.	K.	W.	Killed.	Wounded.
Cedar Mountain	2																						1	1
Rappahannock		2																						4
Thoroughfare Gap																								
Bull Run				22		41		20		37		21		63		27		27		13		25		65
Antietam			1		1					8			20			3		8		3	3		29	57
Fredericksburg		1		3	1	6	1	8		3	2	7	1	7	1	9	1	3	1	4	2	9	16	23
Chancellorsville						6	1	3		3	1	2		5			2	4		2		2	9	
Gettysburg	1	1		3		5		3	7		1		11		3		6	7	2	8	1	5	10	56
Kelly's Ford									3											2	1			2
Wilderness			1			5			1		2		4	2		1	4			1				7
Laurel Hill						2		1		1		1	7					1						7
Spotsylvania						2		8	1	20	7			8	2	4	1	8		3	2	5	14	25
North Anna								1			2		4							1			3	7
Bethesda Church						1				7									2		1		3	4
Cold Harbor				2	1	6		7	4		2		7				3			3	4		14	25
White Oak Swamp																		1						3
Petersburg, June 18				2	2			4		2			1	1	3		1				2	2	7	11
Weldon Railroad					1					1				3						7		4	7	11
Boydton Plank Road						1		1													1			4
Hatcher's Run									3															2
Dabney's Mills						1						2										2	6	6
Gravelly Run							2						3											6
White Oak Road												1												2
Five Forks										1														9
Amelia Court-House																								3
Accidentally killed					1			4		2		4		3		4						4	3	1
Unknown				1						9				1		1		1						14
Missing in action				3			3			3			4						4					
Died in hospital				7					7							3				8			54	
Died in captivity			3				5			3			2		3				8		1	4	14	
Killed by guerillas				1			1								2		2				4		4	
Died of wounds				2		1		1		2		1			1							1	3	1
Official, but no data given														1		1								
TOTAL	2	2	22	41	20	37	21	63	27	27	13	25	15	29	5	9	24	29	21	28	9	35	179	363

Total enrolment, 1213. Aggregate loss

Killed and died . . .	179
Wounded . . .	363
Captured, etc. . . .	165
Total . . .	707

From the Official Records.

The following detailed account of losses is taken from the Official Records, but does not include the later campaigns.   These reports were made immediately after the battles, but subsequent information has shown the existence of many errors, especially under the head of "Missing," many of those so classed having been either killed or wounded.

	Killed.	Wounded.	Missing.	Total.
Pope's Campaign, to September 1, 1862	12	101	48	161
Antietam	10	62	5	77
Fredericksburg	6	33	5	44
Chancellorsville	. .	. .	. .	. .
Meade's Mine Run Campaign, etc.	. .	. .	. .	. .
Gettysburg	4	55	51	110
Wilderness, May 5-7, 1864	. .	1	. .	1
Spottsylvania, May 8-21	14	65	2	81
North Anna, etc., May 22 to June 1	. .	6	5	11
Cold Harbor, etc., June 2-15 . . .	1	4	. .	5
Petersburg, June 15-30	3	19	. .	22
Weldon Railroad, August 18-21 . .	1	3	28	32
Poplar Grove, Hatcher's Run, etc., September 30 to November 1 . .				
Dabney's Mills, etc., February 1 to March 1, 1865	. .	. .	. .	. .
The last campaign	. .	. .	. .	. .
	51	349	144	544

TAPS. J.McK.

BUGLE.